Handbook
of Family Life
Education

Handbook of Family Life Education

Foundations of Family Life Education

Volume 1

edited by

Margaret E. Arcus
Jay D. Schvaneveldt
J. Joel Moss

 SAGE Publications
International Educational and Professional Publisher
Newbury Park   London   New Delhi

For information address:

SAGE Publications, Inc.
2455 Teller Road
Newbury Park, California 91320

SAGE Publications Ltd.
6 Bonhill Street
London EC2A 4PU
United Kingdom

SAGE Publications India Pvt. Ltd.
M-32 Market
Greater Kailash I
New Delhi 110 048 India

Printed in the United States of America

Library of Congress Cataloging-in-Publication Data

Handbook of family life education.
    p. cm.
    Includes bibliographical references and index.
    Contents: v. 1. Foundations of family life education / edited by
Margaret E. Arcus, Jay D. Schvaneveldt, J. Joel Moss.
    ISBN 0-8039-4294-X (v. 1) — ISBN 0-8039-4295-8 (v. 2)
    1. Family life education—United States—Handbooks, manuals, etc.
I. Arcus, Margaret E. II. Schvaneveldt, Jay D. III. Moss, J. Joel.
HQ10.5 .U6H36 1993
306.85′07—dc20
                                        93-26637
                                           CIP

93 94 95 96 10 9 8 7 6 5 4 3 2 1

Sage Production Editor: Rebecca Holland

Contents

Preface

The *Handbook of Family Life Education* had its genesis in the invitational Symposium on Family Life Education held at Brigham Young University in February 1986. This symposium brought together 20 family life educators from across the United States and from Canada and Spain to discuss selected developmental issues in the field of family life education. The symposium was modeled on the National Council on Family Relations Theory Workshop. Several major papers were prepared by selected individuals and were precirculated to all symposium participants, two discussants were invited to make brief presentations on each paper, and all participants were involved in intensive and extensive discussions of each paper. These formal experiences were further enhanced by small group discussions during luncheons and by the summary discussions that concluded each day.

During these discussions, several developmental issues in family life education were identified that were in need of attention if the field was to grow and prosper. These developmental issues included the need to examine more systematically the definition, the basic assumptions, and the parameters of family life education; the need to address more seriously the theme of values in family life education; the need to link the special and/or unique aspects of educating for family living more adequately to existing theories of education; and the need to ensure that family life education programs were based on a solid, scholarly foundation. The development of a handbook of family life education was identified as one of the ways to address these needs.

There were at least two reasons that this *Handbook on Family Life Education* seemed timely. Although the 1964 *Handbook of Marriage and the*

Family edited by Christensen had given some attention to family life education, only a single chapter had been devoted to this topic. This chapter, written by Richard Kerckhoff, was a valuable contribution to the literature, but much has happened in family life education since that time. (The 1987 *Handbook of Marriage and the Family,* edited by Sussman and Steinmetz, was published shortly after the BYU symposium and also gave attention to family life education. But, again, only a single chapter was devoted to this topic.) During the symposium, it became apparent that the themes of family life education (both the developmental issues identified above and the other important topics that had not been addressed in the invited papers) were in need of greater attention than could possibly be provided in a single chapter. Thus symposium participants believed that there was a need for a handbook devoted specifically to the issues and concerns of family life education.

A second reason for such a handbook was that, although there was a burgeoning literature dealing with a variety of family life education topics, there had been no attempt to pull this literature together in any sort of critical or integrative way. It was therefore difficult to determine what kind of progress (if any) was being made on the various issues and concerns of family life education or to decide where the priorities and the energies of the field should be directed. The time seemed right for family life education to synthesize the literature of the field and to do some serious stock-taking.

Because this *Handbook of Family Life Education* is the first handbook to focus specifically on the themes and issues of family life education, it is a benchmark publication documenting the current status of the field. Its primary purpose is to provide an introduction to and a critical perspective on the broad field of family life education, both its major themes and its areas of practice. It is intended to help clarify many of the issues and questions in the field and to serve as a major resource for those who teach, practice, and do research in family life education.

The handbook has been written for use by several different audiences. It would be appropriate for use as a text or as a major reference for graduate and upper-level undergraduate courses in family life education and thus would help to fill a major gap in the family life education literature. It would also be appropriate for use in various in-service education courses and workshops for practicing family life educators. As well, the two volumes of the handbook would be important references for individual practitioners or practitioner units (e.g., community agencies, churches, schools, extension offices) as they enhance their existing areas of service or develop new ones. Finally, because the various chapters in the handbook give attention to needs and new directions in family life education, the handbook would be an important resource for family scholars as they conduct research and develop theory relevant to family life education.

The *Handbook of Family Life Education* is published in two volumes. Volume 1 is subtitled *Foundations of Family Life Education,* and chapters address such topics as the nature of family life education, its evolution as a field of practice, and its process of professionalization. The central theme of values in family life education and the central tasks of planning, implementation, and evaluation of family life programs are examined, as are the important "audience characteristics" that have particular relevance for family life education: gender, ethnicity and diversity, and religion. These topics were selected for inclusion in this volume of the handbook not only because they were central themes in family life education but also because there appeared to be a reasonable amount of literature available on which to base the chapter. Other important topics, such as the politics of family life education, were not included in this volume because there did not appear to be sufficient relevant family life education literature on the topic.

Volume 2 focuses on the practice of family life education. Most of the chapters deal with the content or the subspecialty areas of family life education, with some attention also given to issues relevant to the delivery of family life programs. This volume could have been organized in several different ways, that is, according to topic areas (such as parenting), to settings (such as parent education in community settings, parent education in schools, parent education in churches), or to specific audiences (such as single parents, remarried parents, adolescent parents). A decision was made to focus on topic areas rather than on settings or on audiences for two reasons. First, it would avoid the redundancy that would be likely to occur if several chapters had been written on different aspects of the same topic area. Second, although chapters were not organized according to setting or audience, authors were asked to address these aspects in the development of their chapters. Thus there was the potential for highlighting the similarities and differences that might be a function of either setting or audience. In the view of the editors, this integration across settings/audiences could provide a valuable perspective for practitioners that might be missed if each setting or audience had been addressed individually.

Authors in both volumes were asked to write chapters that were both scholarly and readable. The content of each chapter was to be based on a review of the literature relevant to that chapter and was to take a critical and integrative look at that literature. Because it was not possible within the limitations of the handbook to be exhaustive on each topic, authors were asked to be selective in their use of the literature as they addressed the topic in the context of family life education and to cite what they saw as the best and/or the most important sources so that interested readers could pursue topics in greater depth on their own. Thus an important part of each chapter is its reference list. It should be noted that nearly all authors indicated that their topics could have become an entire book in its own right, and we would agree. The task here was to prepare a chapter for a handbook volume, however, and the development of these ideas into a more extensive publication is a task for the future.

In addition to these general guidelines, authors in Volume 2 who prepared chapters on the topic areas of family life education were asked to address three common purposes as they developed their chapters: (a) to provide a critical and succinct introduction to the relevant content area, (b) to provide a critical review of current educational practice in the content area, and (c) to provide a brief discussion of issues, needs, and new directions in their particular area of family life education. They were also requested to give particular attention to outcome research in the content area, because one of the key questions raised by both family life educators and family life participants has to do with "what works." Each chapter was also to incorporate or address age, gender, and ethnicity issues as these were relevant to the topic area.

The task set for these authors was a tall one and was complicated by at least two limitations. First, there were limits placed by the editors on chapter length. A major criticism of recent handbooks has been that they are too long, too costly, and (sometimes) difficult to use. Thus a conscious decision was made, in consultation with the publisher, both to limit the number of chapters in each volume and to limit the number of pages in each chapter. Authors were asked to write as succinctly as possible so that this limitation would not compromise the quality of the handbook. It was intended that this handbook be user friendly, in size, in cost, and in content.

The second limitation had to do with the available literature. Authors were necessarily limited by the amount and kind of literature that has been published. Some important information simply is not available, but, in our view, it is essential for family life education to compile the information that is available and to identify those areas where further work needs to be done. In many ways, the lack of information is as important as its presence in documenting the current status of the field. Special comment needs to be made about the potential international audience for this handbook. It was not possible for authors to do justice to the relevant literature that has been published in many different countries around the world. Many of the chapters provide specific data on U.S. families, but these were intended to serve as examples only and to indicate to readers in other countries the kinds of family patterns and trends that are relevant to family life education. Both editors and authors have assumed that many of the broad themes and issues of family life education as discussed in the handbook have significance outside the boundaries of the United States.

An important part of the process of the development of this handbook has been the use of one or more external reviewers for each of the chapters. These individuals made many important contributions to the shaping of each chapter and helped to ensure the quality of the overall publication. The editors are indebted to these reviewers for their interest in the handbook, their serious and thoughtful critique of each draft, and their generous sharing of insights and resources with the authors. The editors wish to acknowledge and thank the following individuals who served as external reviewers for one or more of the chapters in this handbook:

Dr. Ruth Brasher—Brigham Young University, Provo, Utah
Dr. Wesley Burr—Brigham Young University, Provo, Utah
Dr. Mary Dellman-Jenkins—Kent State University, Kent, Ohio
Dr. Peggye Dilworth-Anderson—University of North Carolina-Greensboro, Greensboro, North Carolina
Ms. Rosanne Farnden—British Columbia Council for the Family, Vancouver, British Columbia
Dr. Dottie Goss—Oklahoma State University, Stillwater, Oklahoma
Dr. Maxine Lewis-Rowley—Brigham Young University, Provo, Utah
Dr. Nelwyn Moore—Southwest Texas State University, San Marcos, Texas
Dr. Gerry Neubeck—University of Minnesota, St. Paul, Minnesota
Dr. Vicki Schmall—Oregon State University, Corvallis, Oregon
Dr. Barbara Settles—University of Delaware, Newark, Delaware
Dr. Rebecca Smith—University of North Carolina-Greensboro, Greensboro, North Carolina
Dr. Jane Thomas—Vancouver School Board, Vancouver, British Columbia
Dr. James Walters—University of Georgia, Athens, Georgia
Ms. Margaret Young—Utah State University, Logan, Utah

Contributions from several other individuals also need to be acknowledged. First, there are those individuals who provided anonymous reviews of the original proposal for the handbook submitted to Sage Publications. These individuals provided valuable input and insights and helped to shape the thinking of the editors and thus the direction of the publication. As well, colleagues in each of our institutions and communities provided substantial assistance and support to the editors at various stages of the project. These colleagues include Jane Thomas, Vancouver School Board, and Rosanne Farnden, British Columbia Council for the Family, both in Vancouver, Canada; Margaret Young, Utah State University; and Ruth Brasher and Maxine Lewis-Rowley, Brigham Young University.

The editors also wish to thank Mitch Allen of Sage for his support and encouragement throughout the development and writing of this handbook. He has helped to keep it all on track, and we hope that the response to the publication meets his expectations and justifies his support. Our appreciation is also extended to the production staff at Sage and especially to Rebecca Holland, whose exceptional organizational skills and attention to detail have helped ensure that this *Handbook* is a quality publication.

Finally, no project of this kind succeeds without the support and encouragement of family members. Our heartfelt thanks go to Peter, Karen, and Audra.

1

The Nature of Family Life Education

Margaret E. Arcus
Jay D. Schvaneveldt
J. Joel Moss

PREPARING INDIVIDUALS AND families for the roles and responsibilities of family living is nothing new (Gaylin, 1981; Kirkendall, 1973). Humans have no built-in knowledge about human development and family living, and therefore they must learn it from somewhere (Laycock, 1967). All societies have thus developed ways through which they transmit the wisdom and the experience of family living from one generation to succeeding ones. Although some of this transmission occurs through formal events such as puberty or initiation rites, much is learned in the family setting itself, as family members observe and participate in family activities and interactions (Hill & Aldous, 1969).

It is, however, only in relatively simple societies where little social change occurs that families can "go it alone" in meeting the needs of their family members for learning about family living (Somerville, 1971). In more complex and changing societies, the development of new knowledge, advances in technology, and changes in social conditions all create circumstances in which the teachings of previous generations may not be appropriate or sufficient. In such circumstances, families must be supported in their educational efforts by the activities of other institutions and agencies and by the actions of individuals on their own behalf.

Furthermore, changes occurring in the broader society may create strains or tensions in individuals and families that may disrupt family living. Kirkendall (1973) suggested that certain family difficulties (e.g., an increased divorce rate, increased parent-child strife, shifts in marital and familial roles) commonly occur in societies as they become industrialized and urbanized and that these give rise to attempts to strengthen the family through the efforts of outside agencies. Over time, these efforts have become increasingly formalized and have led to the establishment of the movement called "family life education" (Kerckhoff, 1964; Kirkendall, 1973). These efforts have been seen as one way to assist families with their educational tasks, to improve family living, and to reduce family-related social problems.

Although the preceding provides a brief rationale for the emergence of family life education, it says little about the nature of this activity. The purpose of this chapter is to clarify the nature of family life education, based on a critical examination and discussion of the literature. This discussion focuses first on the issue of definition in family life education and then turns to an examination of selected features of the concept of family life education (rationale, purpose, content, and operational principles). A historical perspective is taken in this chapter, but this does not constitute a history of the events and activities that have taken place within the family life education movement. Such a chronology remains to be written. The evolution of efforts to educate for family life since the mid-1700s is, however, discussed in Chapter 2.

DEFINING FAMILY LIFE EDUCATION

Although family life education is now fairly well established and many activities take place under this name, defining the term *family life education* has been problematic. In the early 1960s, Lee (1963) noted that the term meant different things to different family life educators, and, according to Kerckhoff (1964), the otherwise growing field of family life education was being retarded by confusion regarding definition. Similar concerns were reiterated in the 1970s (e.g., Somerville, 1971) and again in the 1980s (e.g., Darling, 1987; Fisher & Kerckhoff, 1981). In general, the various definitions proposed for family life education over time have been criticized for being too vague, ambiguous, and idealistic (e.g., Hill, in Avery & Lee, 1964; The Vanier Institute of the Family, 1971) and because consensus on a definition is lacking (e.g., Arcus, 1986; Gaylin, 1981).

Agreement on a definition of family life education is important for several reasons. Definitions help to clarify thinking about appropriate goals and purposes; they provide a perspective or an orientation to educational practice; they help to delineate the scope of educational activity; and they assist in communicating effectively with others. Moreover, agreement on meaning is seen as an essential step in developing theory (B. L. Fisher, 1986), training teachers (Gaylin, 1981), and surveying and evaluating relevant research (Somerville, 1971). When the term *family life education* is not defined consistently, it is difficult to compare studies, to accumulate knowledge, and to develop the field both conceptually and empirically.

An attempt was made in the 1960s to gain consensus on a definition of family life education (Avery & Lee, 1964). Ninety eminent family life educators (30 each in higher education, community or national agencies, and public schools) were invited to evaluate and comment on the following working definition:

> Family life education involves any and all school experiences deliberately and consciously used by teachers in helping to develop the personalities of students to their fullest capacities as present and future family members—those capacities which equip the individual to solve most constructively the problems unique to his family role. (Avery & Lee, 1964, p. 27)

The general reaction to this definition was positive (nearly 75% accepted it as a working definition), but of particular interest here are the additional comments and suggestions provided by those responding to the survey.

First, although many accepted the breadth and comprehensiveness of the working definition, they also questioned whether it was in fact *too* broad, encompassing everything from "flower arrangements to sex, to finances, to driver education, to cooking, to making a living" (Avery & Lee, 1964, pp. 28-29). Respondents were concerned that family life education might include so much that it would wind up doing nothing very specific at all.

Second, respondents generally agreed that family life education was purposive rather than incidental (as indicated by the words *deliberately* and *consciously*). Although some were concerned that this might rule out family life education that was, in part, the product of interrelationships among those in the educational setting (e.g., teacher-student interaction), others questioned whether it was legitimate to classify such interactions as "education."

Third, respondents were evenly divided on whether the phrase *personality development* adequately represented the major focus of family life education as well as on whether family life education should have an "individual" or a "family unit" focus.

Finally, the emphasis on school settings was of some concern. Although Avery and Lee had not intended to imply that other settings were unimportant, this had not been clear in the survey, and it became an issue, particularly for those who represented community or national agencies.

Other issues raised by the respondents included (a) the need to distinguish family life education from other educational areas such as sex education or mental health, (b) the need to clarify "education" as distinct from "instruction," (c) a concern that the definition emphasized only functional family living and left out any academic approach to the study of families, and (d) a concern that family life education not be limited to a problem focus (i.e., preparing people to solve problems) but also include helping individuals to acquire the insights, knowledge, and skills needed to help develop family potentials.

In spite of the general agreement among these early family life educators on a working definition, little real consensus was apparently achieved, as family life educators continued their efforts to refine and redefine the term. The definitions listed in Table 1.1 provide a historical perspective on the different definitions developed for family life education since the Avery and Lee working definition. Although some of these appear to be based on or related to the Avery and Lee (1964) definition, others have little apparent connection to this early work.

A review of these definitions indicates that, although there are some similarities among them (e.g., most state or imply a focus on interpersonal relationships), many of the issues raised in the above discussion apparently have not been resolved. As yet, family life educators do not appear to agree on whether family life education is to take an individual focus (e.g., Gross, 1985; Sheek, 1984) or a family unit focus (e.g., National Commission on Family Life Education, 1968; Somerville, 1967), nor are they clear about whether it should be primarily a functional family living course (e.g., Cromwell & Thomas, 1976; Smith, 1968) or an area for academic study (e.g., Darling, 1987; Herold, Kopf, & deCarlo, 1974). Some continue to maintain a problem focus (e.g., Stern, 1969), while others address the development of potentials (e.g., Barozzi & Engel, 1985; National Commission on Family Life Education, 1968). Definitions also differ in whether family life education is primarily cognitive (e.g., Stern, 1969; The Vanier Institute of the Family, 1971) or whether it also includes attention to attitudes and skills (e.g., Kerckhoff, 1964). After 30 years of effort, it appears that the definition of family life education is still "an omnibus of unclarity" (Dager, Harper, & Whitehurst, 1962, p. 370)!

TABLE 1.1. Definitions of Family Life Education

Date	Definition and Author
1962, 1963, and 1964	"Family life education involves any and all school experiences deliberately and consciously used by teachers in helping to develop the personalities of students to their fullest capacities as present and future family members—those capacities which equip the individual to solve most constructively the problems unique to his family role" (Avery, 1962, p. 28; Avery & Lee, 1964, p. 27; Lee, 1963, p. 106).
1964	"Family life education included facts, attitudes, and skills related to dating, marriage, and parenthood. . . . Throughout the concept of family life education is woven the idea of relationships—parent-child, husband-wife, boy-girl, and so on" (Kerckhoff, 1964, p. 883).
1967	"Family life education is the study of the behavior of people as family members . . . to broaden the student's understanding of the alternatives from which he can choose in his functioning as a family member in a changing society which brings new responsibilities and opportunities in spousal, parental, filial, sibling, and grandparental roles" (Somerville, 1967, p. 375).
1968	"It is a program of learning experiences planned and guided to develop the potentials of individuals in their present and future roles as family members. Its central concept is that of relationships through which personality develops, about which individuals make decisions, to which they are committed, and in which they gain convictions of self worth" (Smith, 1968, p. 55).
1968	"To help individuals and families learn what is known about human growth, development, and behavior throughout the life cycle is the main purpose of family life education. Learning experiences are provided to develop the potentials of individuals in their present and future family roles. The central concept is that of relationships through which personality develops, about which individuals make decisions, to which they are committed, and in which they develop self-esteem" (National Commission on Family Life Education, 1968, p. 211).
1969	"Family life education . . . deals with people in groups primarily on a cognitive and information exchange level, around issues and problems of family life . . . [and] the cognitive components of behavioral and emotional functioning. Its techniques involve discussions and didactic teaching around ideas, values, and behavioral patterns of the family as a social system and the consequences of these on individual functioning, as well as more behavioristic material concerning interpersonal functioning within the family unit" (Stern, 1969, p. 40).
1971	". . . any activity by any group aimed at imparting information concerning family relationships and providing the opportunity for people to approach their present and future family relationships with greater understanding" (The Vanier Institute of the Family, 1971, p. i).

continued

TABLE 1.1 *(continued)*

Date	Definition and Author
1973	"Programs of family-life education that will help individuals to prove [sic] their understanding of and capacity for forming and maintaining effective human interrelationships . . . [it] has come to center about the many interactions between individuals and within the family, and the characteristics in individuals that influence the quality of interpersonal relationships" (Kirkendall, 1973, p. 696).
1973	". . . human education in the broadest sense, the essence being human relations . . . concerned with one's total being: physical, mental, and emotional" (Whatley, 1973, p. 193).
1974	"Family life education is the study of individual roles and interpersonal relationships, family patterns and alternative life styles, emotional needs of individuals at all ages, and the physiological, psychological and sociological aspects of sexuality" (Herold, Kopf, & deCarlo, 1974, p. 365).
1975	". . . an educational program geared to enrich family life and help the individual better understand himself in relation to others" (Levin, 1975, p. 344).
1976	"Family life education promotes the development, coordination and integration of family development resources to individual family units in order to improve family life" (Cromwell & Thomas, 1976, p. 15).
1984	". . . instruction to develop an understanding of physical, mental, emotional, social, economic, and psychological aspects of interpersonal relationships . . . between persons of varying ages" (Sheek, 1984, p. 1).
1985	"Family life education . . . builds on the strengths of individuals to extend their knowledge of personality development, interpersonal relations, and the influence of environmental factors on behaviors" (Barozzi & Engel, 1985, p. 6).
1985	". . . as the professional process by which information is offered to individuals of all ages, about various life issues, through the use of the small group setting" (Gross, 1985, p. 6).
1987	". . . concerned with preserving and improving the quality of human life by the study of individuals and families as they interact with the resources in their multi-faceted environments" (Darling, 1987, p. 818).
1989	"Family life education . . . is devoted to enabling adults to increase the effectiveness of their skills in daily living, that is, in relating to others, in coping with life events, and in realizing personal potential" (Tennant, 1989, p. 127).

BEYOND DEFINITIONS

Why is it that family life education has had such difficulty with its definition? One problem may be that the definitions listed in Table 1.1 are what Scheffler (1960) calls "stipulative" or invented definitions, that is, a definition is provided by an author who stipulates that he or she is using the term in a particular way, regardless of how others might use the same term. Although this idiosyncratic use may make sense in the context of an individual author's work and does not "legislate out" other uses of the term, it does appear to contribute to the confusion and lack of clarity that currently exists within the field (Thomas & Arcus, 1992). It also may exacerbate political problems in family life education, because individuals may be operating with different expectations, assumptions, or parameters. Only a few family life educators refer directly to their definitions as stipulative, for example, "I define family life education as . . ." (Gross, 1985, p. 6) and "family life education is conceptualized herein as . . ." (Darling, 1987, p. 818). From the disparate nature of the definitions listed in Table 1.1, however, it can be inferred that the majority of definitions in family life education are indeed stipulative definitions.

A second difficulty may lie in the fact that, while definitions may be *necessary* in family life education, they may not be *sufficient* either to clarify the nature of the field or to provide the kinds of guidance sought by family life educators. These educators have expected a great deal from their definitions (Arcus, 1987). Avery and Lee, for example, intended their definition to explain family life education in "terms acceptable to the professionals, meaningful to lay persons, and capable of being used in measuring or evaluating existing or projected programs" (1964, p. 31). Hill suggested that a definition should refer to "the knowledge about, appreciation of, and skills and abilities required . . . over the life span of the family" (Avery & Lee, 1964, p. 37), while Frasier believed that defining family life education was difficult unless one specified "for whom, at what stage of development, and in what context" such education was to occur (1967, p. 381). Avery and Lee highlighted the difficulty of meeting these kinds of criteria or providing this kind of detail in a typical definition when they concluded at the end of their survey that their redefinition "cannot possibly be as succinct as the 'working definition' " (1964, p. 32). Indeed, their redefinition consisted of four paragraphs and over 400 words!

One further point regarding definitions may be helpful. In *The Language of Education*, Scheffler (1960) distinguished between descriptive and programmatic definitions. According to Scheffler, descriptive (or dictionary-type) definitions purport to adequately describe whatever is being defined. While descriptive definitions might have multiple meanings, these multiple meanings are intended to indicate how the term is to be used in different contexts and do not permit users to make arbitrary choices among these meanings. Programmatic definitions, however, are ones that indicate, either implicitly or explicitly, how things should be; that is, they prescribe certain norms, values, and ends.

Soltis (1977) has suggested that most definitions in education are mixtures of the descriptive (what is) and the prescriptive (what ought to be). To paraphrase his view, the search for a definition of family life education is "most probably a quest for a statement of the right or the best program for certain valued means or ends to be sought in educating" (Soltis, 1977, p. 11). A review of the definitions listed in Table 1.1 supports his view, as many of these definitions include certain valued means and ends in family life education (e.g., "solve problems constructively," "choose wisely from alternatives," "develop potentials," "achieve greater understanding," "improve family living"). Soltis believed that, because any decisions involving values and norms are crucial decisions, they require critical and careful judgment rather than simple resolution by some definitional fiat.

THE CONCEPT OF FAMILY LIFE EDUCATION

This view is echoed by Thomas and Arcus (1992), who suggested that what is needed at the current time in family life education is *not* further efforts at definition but a systematic analysis of the concept of family life education using methods of analytical inquiry. According to Coombs and Daniels (in press), such analytical methods are designed to investigate questions of meaning and are intended to increase both one's understanding and one's use of concepts.

Thomas and Arcus (1992) used methods of analytical inquiry to investigate the question: "What features must something have in order to be called family life education?" Their investigation was based on the premise that one needs to be clear about what counts as family life education before essential questions in the field (e.g., "Should family life education be required?" and "Does family life education make a difference?") can be adequately answered. They identified several features of the concept of family life education that they believed required analytical attention (i.e., general purposes or intended outcomes, subject matter or content, assumptions and normative beliefs, intended audiences, methods of practice), but their own analysis examined only two of these features, namely, general purposes or intended outcomes and subject matter or content.

The Rationale for Family Life Education

Before discussing the results of the Thomas and Arcus analysis, it is useful to elaborate more fully on the rationale for family life education, as this rationale has been of considerable importance in establishing the purposes and the content for family life education.

According to Kerckhoff (1964), family life education originally developed out of a concern for the social problems of the times and for the perceived inadequacies of families in dealing with social change. This "dealing with problems focus" has continued throughout the development of family life education (e.g., Kirkendall, 1973; National Commission on Family Life Education, 1968; Sheek, 1984). In fact, Smith pointed to the "staggering list of social ills which impinge on families" as the primary "facts of life" that seemed to call for family life education in this part of the century (1968, p. 55).

The early focus in family life education was not just on dealing with problems, however. There was also a "preventing problems focus," based on the relatively unchallenged assumption that, if people could only be convinced to "do the right things" in their family life, then "the divorce rate would drop, children would be reared properly, and the institution of the family would be saved" (Kerckhoff, 1964, p. 898). Programs in family life education were seen as one way to attack and reduce problems such as unwanted pregnancies, promiscuity, and marital discord. This view has been challenged by Stern (1969), who proposed that *amelioration* was a more appropriate term than *prevention*. In his view, problems such as unwanted pregnancies and marital discord cannot be prevented, although their extent and intensity might be lessened. In spite of Stern's challenge, many family life educators continue to identify problem prevention as a major rationale and focus for the field: "family life education is perceived . . . as the foremost preventive measure for the avoidance of family problems" (Darling, 1987, p. 816).

Although it has been a pervasive focus, problems have not been the only rationale for family life education. In the Avery and Lee survey (1964), several respondents noted the importance of developing family potentials as well as addressing family problems. This "developing potentials" orientation has also continued throughout the development of family life education (e.g., National Commission on Family Life Education, 1968) and has been described variously as "developing healthy and responsible relationships" (Sheek, 1984), "developing a constructive and fulfilling personal and family life" (National Council on Family Relations, 1970), "building on strengths" (Barozzi & Engel, 1985), "enriching family life" (Levin, 1975), and "promoting the quality of family life" (Darling, 1987; C. D. Fisher, 1982). Regardless of the particular language used, family life education programs based on a developing potentials rationale are intended to build upon positive aspects of family life and to evoke those human capacities that will enhance and enrich individual and family living.

Thus the development of family life education appears to have been influenced by three different though related rationales: dealing with problems, preventing problems, and developing potentials. Little is known about the specific priorities assigned to these rationales by individual family life educators as they develop their own programs, although many educators are quick to claim that family life education is more than problems.

The Purposes of Family Life Education

From these rationales, many different goals and objectives have been identified for family life education. In an early survey of 475 school and college family life teachers, Christiansen (1958) reported that the most frequently selected objectives for family life education were to assist students in understanding relationships in modern marriage and to assist them in understanding self in relation to other family members. Avery and Lee identified four "subgoals" (understanding self and others; understanding and adjusting to sexuality; understanding marriage and the family; mastering skills essential to family living) that they believed led to the ultimate goal of family life education—"the development of stable families contributing constructively to the society in which they live" (Avery & Lee, 1964, p. 32).

According to the National Commission on Family Life Education, the main purpose of family life education is to build strengths in families, to help individuals and families "learn what is known about human growth, development, and behavior in the family setting throughout the life cycle" (1968, p. 211), and to develop the potentials of individuals in their current and future family roles. The commission also listed five major learning objectives: to learn about families, to learn about individual and family development, to learn about coping processes, to develop the ability to perceive and to evaluate actions, and to explore new ways of behaving. A position paper issued by the National Council on

Family Relations (1970) stated that the purposes of family life education were to aid individuals in developing a constructive and fulfilling personal and family life, to guide individuals and families in improving their interpersonal relationships and furthering their maximum development, and to improve their quality of life. Among other goals that have been identified for family life education are gaining insight into self, others, and the environment (Whatley, 1973); enhancing self-image and promoting one's comfort level within one's family system (Levin, 1975); and enabling individuals and families to make their own rational decisions (Rodman, 1970).

Not surprisingly, important questions have been raised about the number and the breadth of these goals in family life education. In particular, Fisher and Kerckhoff observed that one agency listed 42 objectives for family life education and queried whether it was possible for one profession to have such diverse goals as "to understand the personality of self and others," "to learn to manage the household," as well as "to promote physical health, mental health, democratic family life, and the standard of living" (Fisher & Kerckhoff, 1981, p. 505). Their concern that the goals and objectives of family life education are potentially overwhelming is an important one, but, as Thomas and Arcus (1992) have indicated, it is possible to bring some kind of analytical order to these goals.

Based on the work of Litke (1976), Thomas and Arcus recommended that family life educators first distinguish between those goals that are ultimate goals or ends (the higher objectives) and those that are subgoals or means to these ends (the lower objectives). These goals should then be arranged into a "means-to-ends" relationship so that it becomes apparent how the lower objectives are a means to the higher objectives. Thomas and Arcus illustrated this process using the above Fisher and Kerckhoff statement, noting that "understanding personality" is a means of "promoting mental health" and that "managing the household" is a means of "promoting the standard of living." To take this point one step further, both promoting mental health and promoting the standard of living may be means of strengthening families.

As the above discussion indicates, not all of the espoused goals of family life education are necessarily diverse or distinct goals but may be more interrelated than first appears. Thus any particular family life education program may indeed be able to address several goals simultaneously. This does not mean, however, that serious and critical attention should not be given to the issue of diversity of goals and to determining which goals are in fact most central or most appropriate for family life education.

In their analysis of the concept of family life education, Thomas and Arcus (1992) systematically reviewed the scholarly literature in family life education published since 1960 to determine whether there was reasonable conceptual agreement among family life educators concerning the general purposes or ultimate ends of family life education (the higher objectives). Interestingly, most of this literature did not specifically address the question of ultimate ends, although a few notable exceptions were found. The National Commission on Family Life Education, for example, identified "strengthening families" as the underlying goal of family life education (1968), while Sheek (1984) and Rodman (1970) referred to "individual and family well-being." An additional purpose, to "enrich" or "enhance" family living, was also apparent in some of the literature (e.g., National Commission on Family Life Education, 1968). Based on this analysis, Thomas and Arcus concluded that, at the current time, there appears to be reasonable conceptual agreement in the field that the ultimate goal of family life education is "to strengthen and enrich individual and family well-being."

Although "improving the quality of life" was identified in a number of writings as the goal of family life education (e.g., Darling, 1987; National Council on Family Relations, 1970), Thomas and Arcus rejected this as the appropriate general purpose of the field. This rejection was based on the lack of precision with which the term is often used (Arcus, 1984) and on the considerable body of literature that has analyzed the concept of "quality of life" (e.g., Baier, 1974; Bedau, 1979; McCall, 1975; Wilcox, 1981). According to these analyses, quality of life does *not* refer to increasing personal and familial satisfaction or well-being but to ensuring that the basic human needs are met for all who live within a given region (a village, a city, a country). In general, the greater the percentage of those in a given region for whom basic needs are satisfied, the higher the quality of life in that region (e.g., Bedau, 1979). Thomas and Arcus concluded that, because "ensuring basic human needs are met" does not seem to describe what is typically done in the practice of family life education, it seemed inappropriate to claim "quality of life" as the intended outcome of family life education.

The Content of Family Life Education

The literature reviewed by Thomas and Arcus in their analysis of the concept of family life education indicated that, at the current time, there is considerable agreement among family life educators concerning the content or subject matter of family life education (Thomas & Arcus, 1992). As with definitions, however, many descriptions of the content of family life education appeared to be stipulations, or indications of the choices about content made by a particular individual, agency, or school district. Indeed, some definitions of family life education were primarily specifications of its content (e.g., Herold et al., 1974; Sheek, 1984). In its 1968 report, the National Commission on Family Life Education listed the following as content areas within family life education: interpersonal relationships; self-understanding; human growth and development; preparation for marriage and parenthood; child rearing; socialization of youth for adult roles; decision making; sexuality; management of human and material resources; personal, family, and community health; family-community interaction; and the effects of change on cultural patterns.

More recently, the National Council on Family Relations Committee on Standards and Criteria for the Certification of Family Life Educators has developed a Framework for Life-Span Family Life Education, which further clarifies the content and thus the nature of family life education (National Council on Family Relations, 1984). This framework identified seven topic areas (each with key supporting concepts) and three processes that together specify the content of the field. Because of its significance in understanding the nature of family life education, the framework is reproduced in its entirety in this book's Appendix.

Several criteria guided the development of the framework (National Council on Family Relations, 1984). First, it was to reflect a broad conception of family life education, consistent with other writings about family life education. At the same time, the number of topic areas was to be limited so as to make the framework manageable without losing important ideas or concepts. This was accomplished by combining related topic areas (e.g., friendships, dating, marriage) that are sometimes listed individually in other documents. Second, the framework was to include all dimensions of learning (knowledge, attitudes, and skills) under each of the content areas. To illustrate these criteria, key concepts under "Interpersonal Relationships" included knowledge such as factors influencing mate selection, attitudes such as respecting self and others, and skills such as initiating, maintaining, and ending relationships. Finally, the framework was intended to reflect the assumption that individuals of all ages need to learn about family life and to demonstrate that "each topic area may be addressed at each age level by varying the focus and the complexity of the key concepts" (Arcus, 1987, p. 8).

The strength of this framework is that it is not a stipulative framework but one that was based on previous literature in the field and that was developed over a period of time with the considered input of many family life education scholars and practitioners, both those who developed the framework and those who served as expert reviewers (National Council on Family Relations, 1984). The framework is thus the culmination of thought about the content of family life education, and it can be presumed to reflect reasonable agreement among family life educators about this feature of the concept of family life education.

As Coombs and Daniels (in press) indicated, however, it is important in the analysis of concepts to examine even well-accepted ideas in some systematic way because agreement may be based on habit or honest but mistaken beliefs rather than on critical reflection. Soltis (1977) has recommended the use of two tests in the analysis of educational concepts: a test for necessity to ensure that a feature is indeed essential for a concept and a test for sufficiency to ensure that the concept can be distinguished from related ones with which it may be confused. Thomas and Arcus (1992) modified these two tests for use in their analysis of the concept of family life education and found that indeed the seven content areas and three processes specified in the Framework for Life-Span Family Life Education are both necessary for the concept of family life education and sufficient to distinguish family life education from other related areas such as sexuality education or family sociology. These same tests have also been used to distinguish family life education from home economics and from health education (Thomas & Arcus, 1991).

The Operational Principles of Family Life Education

Several other features of the concept of family life education have been termed by the authors of this chapter the *operational principles* of family life education; that is, they are features that are generally accepted (or at least professed) by those in family life education and are usually intended to serve as bases for or guides to professional actions and obligations. Some of these are descriptive principles, purporting to describe how family life education *is* carried out, while others are more prescriptive, indicating what family life educators *should do* as they educate for family living. The presence of both "kinds" of operational principles supports the notion (discussed earlier with regard to definition) that the concept of family life education is a programmatic one, including elements of both what is and what ought to be (Soltis, 1977). It is important to point out here that these operational principles have not received the same systematic scholarly treatment as have the features of purpose and content. Nevertheless, a review of the family life education literature relevant to these principles may help to further clarify the nature of the concept of family life education. The principles identified here are discussed in no particular order.

1. Family life education is relevant to individuals and families throughout the life span. According to Kerckhoff (1964), early efforts in family life education were concerned primarily with parent education—or, more technically, with the education of women for parenthood—and were thus directed toward mothers. Over time, however, this focus has expanded to include individuals and families over the entire life span (e.g., Hennon & Arcus, 1993). This expansion reflects the assumption that people of all ages need to learn about the many aspects of family life and a belief that there are opportunities for family life education at each developmental phase (e.g., Gaylin, 1981; National Council on Family Relations, 1970). Some family programs are related to what might be termed *normative developments* for most individuals and families (e.g., getting married, becoming parents, facing loss of family members), while others are based on the special needs and transitions of some individuals and families (e.g., parenting children with special needs, getting divorced, coping with unemployment) (Arcus, 1990).

The Framework for Life-Span Family Life Education (see the Appendix) illustrates how the content of the field varies according to broad age categories or developmental phases. In this framework, broad rather than narrow age categories were used because the developers of the framework believed that readiness to learn was not tied closely to any specific age (National Council on Family Relations, 1984). Specific variations in family life education based on age categories are reflected in the numerous programs in the field. Kerckhoff (1964), for example, identified recognizable differences in the content of family life education at different grade levels in schools and universities, and both Levin (1975) and C. D. Fisher (1982) have reported different kinds of community programs for different age groups or family stages.

2. Family life education should be based on the needs of individuals and families. According to Avery and Lee (1964), family life education should be geared to the immediate needs of individuals and families and should be sensitive to the social and cultural changes that influence these needs. The National Commission on Family Life Education (1968) agreed with this prescription and claimed further that family life programs make their "maximum contribution to the enrichment of family life when they are directly related to immediate personal, family, and community needs" (p. 211). The importance of meeting needs is apparent in other family life education literature as well (e.g., Darling, 1987; Hennon & Arcus, 1993; Hey & Neubeck, 1990).

How are these needs to be determined? There is at least some belief that participants themselves should become involved in and help to determine the nature of a particular program (e.g., National Commission on Family Life Education, 1968). Such participant involvement is included in at least some programs, but in others the programs have been predetermined by specialists, leaving little room for participant input. Thus programs in family life education may vary in whether they are based on felt needs (those expressed by potential learners) or on ascribed needs (those identified by someone other than the learner). Regardless of the source, however, "meeting needs" appears to be a key operational principle in family life education.

In addition to meeting the immediate needs of individuals and families, practice in family life education also appears to include future needs as well. This is reflected in several of the definitions (see Table 1.1) that refer to both "present and future roles." In particular, some aspects of school-based family life education programs emphasize future needs rather than immediate ones (e.g., units on education for the parenting role).

The emphasis in family life education on meeting needs raises some important issues and challenges for family life educators regarding the timing of family life education efforts. Duvall (in Avery & Lee, 1964, p. 34) noted that some programs may "come so late it is ludicrous, or too soon to be effective." Examples of family life education that may come too late include some efforts in premarital education and in sexuality education, while those that may come too soon include education for parenthood in the secondary schools. For example, de Lissovoy (1978) suggested that it is premature to focus on the specific tasks of parenthood during adolescence and that, instead, attention should be directed toward the precursors of parenthood—"the issues of self, interpersonal relationships and skills, and values within a democratic milieu" (p. 331).

Meeting needs also raises important ethical issues. Sork (1988) has suggested that the act of conducting a needs assessment may be interpreted by some to mean that all of the needs identified in this way will be met. But what if (for any reason) all of these needs cannot be met? If some needs warrant a response and others do not, how is the difference between the two to be justified? What values are reflected by the educator who makes such decisions, and whose ideology will prevail when there are disagreements regarding the allocation of resources to meet needs? As Sork has pointed out, any efforts by educators to pass judgment on the appropriateness of identified needs would be unethical because it infringes upon the autonomy of the learner. Thus it is incumbent upon family life educators to review their own practices to identify decisions and actions that might be considered unethical and to ensure that any judgments regarding needs are "made consciously, with full recognition of their philosophical basis and moral consequences" (Sork, 1988, p. 35).

3. Family life education is a multidisciplinary area of study and multiprofessional in its practice. Many authors have stated that family life education is either an interdisciplinary (e.g., Gaylin, 1981) or a multiprofessional area of study and practice (e.g., National Commission of Family Life Education, 1968). These statements have recognized that the important concepts, principles, and perspectives used in family life education come from diverse disciplines and fields of study that focus on individuals and families in particular ways. Among those identified most often are (in alphabetical order) anthropology, biology, economics, home economics, law, medicine, philosophy, physiology, psychology, social work, and sociology (e.g., National Commission on Family Life Education, 1968). Although all of these areas may have some relevance, Fisher and Kerckhoff (1981) suggested that family life education is not really as multidisciplinary as is often claimed. In their view, family life education at the current time is best characterized as "sociology and psychology as it applies to the family," and they urged that family life education "be expanded from the narrow data base from which it now operates" (1981, p. 508).

With respect to this point, it is interesting to note that emphasis in family life education has typically been placed on those areas that focus on the study of individuals and families, with limited acknowledgment of important concepts and principles from the discipline of education (e.g., Fisher & Kerckhoff, 1981). Given that family life education is an educational venture, this apparent omission is noteworthy as the knowledge and use of educational concepts and principles would likely help to ensure that family life education attains its educational goals. (See Chapter 5 in this volume for a discussion of relevant educational literature and for a critique of the use of this literature in family life education.)

One further point should be made. The use of the term *interdisciplinary* implies that there is some collaboration among disciplines. While such collaboration may be both desired and desirable, there is at least some suggestion that competition and rivalry among disciplines has been more characteristic in family life education than has cooperation. Indeed, Somerville (1971) noted that competition among disciplines was one of the obstacles facing family life education in the 1960s. There is some suggestion that this competition still exists (see Chapters 2 and 3 in this volume).

4. Family life education programs are offered in many different settings. Some of the definitions in Table 1.1 appear to specify a particular setting, but it is generally accepted that family life education may be offered by many different institutions and agencies (i.e., schools, churches, business and industry, and community, governmental, and private agencies). This diversity of settings has typically been seen by most family life educators as appropriate in order to provide services across the life span and to provide for a variety of perspectives in meeting the needs of as many individuals and families as possible. Some settings such as schools, churches, and community agencies are well established as providers of family life education, but more recently programs have also been offered in the workplace (e.g., C. D. Fisher, 1982).

Some (e.g., National Commission on Family Life Education, 1968) have recommended that the family, the church, schools, and all family-serving agencies become partners in providing family life education. Such partnership would presumably encourage a community to assess its needs and to avoid duplication or overlap in using its resources to meet these needs. Because the roles of home, school, and church in educating children and youth for family life have not been clearly delineated (e.g., Somerville, 1971), however, concerns have also been expressed about the potential of family life education to usurp parental prerogatives (e.g., Arcus, 1986). These concerns may generate political problems that make it difficult to implement some family life programs. Rivalry among institutions and agencies and concerns about infringing on "territory" may also make it difficult for family life education to become a cooperative community effort.

5. Family life education takes an educational rather than a therapeutic approach. Although the conceptual distinctions between education and therapy are not clear, many family life educators claim that the purpose of action and activity in family life education is to educate or equip rather than to repair. At the same time, however, many have been confused or troubled by the use of the word *education* (e.g., Avery & Lee, 1964). At least some family life educators have appeared to equate the term *education* with a narrow view of cognition. Wright and L'Abate (1977), for example, claimed that family life education takes a relatively passive approach to education and functions on a purely cognitive level. Others, however, have suggested that this view is too narrow, as family life education does more than imparting knowledge (e.g., Gaylin, 1981; Guerney & Guerney, 1981).

Various analyses of the concept of education have revealed that the purpose of education is to empower the learner to use knowledge in making informed, responsible choices and in acting on the basis of reason (e.g., Peters, 1967). According to Thomas and Arcus (1992), this conception of education indicates that it is inappropriate to equate family life education only with information delivery, with the passive acquisition of facts, or with training in skill development. Further, they suggested that, if family life education is to count as *education*, then it must be centrally concerned with the development of justified beliefs and the capacities required to arrive at these beliefs. This implies attention to particular educational goals and practices in family life education and will influence the selection, organization, and presentation of program content.

Most explanations of family life education have referred to several different dimensions of learning, that is, such education is intended to help individuals and families "1) gain *knowledge* about concepts and principles relevant to family living, 2) explore personal *attitudes and values* and understand and accept the attitudes and values of others, and 3) develop interpersonal *skills* which contribute to family well-being" (Arcus, 1990, p. 1). The Framework for Life-Span Family Life Education has included key concepts related to each of these dimensions (National Council on Family Relations, 1984). (See the Appendix.)

Many writers in family life education have differentiated between cognitive (intellectual) development and affective (feelings and attitudes) development (e.g., Moss & Elbert, 1987), and there has been some disagreement about which of these should be emphasized (B. L. Fisher, 1986). According to Peters (1967), however, affective development occurs concurrently with cognitive development and the two cannot be separated. Attitudes and emotions necessarily have a cognitive core; that is, one cannot have feelings or attitudes without having them directed toward something that one knows about (e.g., Coombs, 1989). The recognition that these two dimensions of education occur concurrently may help to reduce some of the conflict and confusion that have arisen in family life education regarding educational aims.

6. Family life education should present and respect differing family values. There has been considerable controversy regarding the role of values in family life education (e.g., Arcus, 1987; Kerckhoff, 1964). Some have claimed that values are the prerogative of families and therefore that values should not be included in family life education programs. Others have suggested that attention to values cannot be avoided, given the purpose and content of family life education, and thus the focus must be on how best to handle values within family life education programs. Those who support the principle of respect for differing values tend to hold the latter view concerning values education. The concept of values, its role in family life education, and approaches to values education are addressed in Chapter 4 of this volume and will not be further elaborated upon here. Attention to religious values and family life education is discussed in Chapter 8 of this volume.

7. Qualified educators are crucial to the successful realization of the goals of family life education. According to the National Commission on Family Life Education, "competently prepared family life educators are crucial to the successful realization of the goals" of family life education (1968, p. 212). Although this principle is generally well accepted (e.g., Fohlin, 1971; Whatley, 1973), some believe that there has been inadequate attention to the preparation of family life educators and thus some justifiable concerns about the qualifications of these educators (e.g., Somerville, 1971). In addition, Fisher and Kerckhoff (1981) have suggested that the role of the family life educator is potentially overwhelming. The preparation of family life educators is the focus of Chapter 3 in this volume.

The above operational principles have been identified through a review of the family life education literature. As noted earlier, however, they have not received the same scholarly scrutiny or attention as have definition, purpose, and content and thus should be taken as indicative rather than as definitive features of the concept of family life education. It is not clear from the literature that family life educators necessarily understand the implications of using or endorsing these principles or that in fact the principles are reflected in family life education practice. Much work remains to be done to further clarify these operational principles.

CURRENT STATUS AND NEW DIRECTIONS

The purpose of this chapter has been to clarify the nature of the concept of family life education based on a critical examination of the literature. It was noted that the issue of definition has been problematic since the inception of the field and that in spite of early attempts to gain a consensus on definition, family life educators have continued to struggle with the meaning of the term. Recent attempts to overcome the limitations of definitions have focused on the use of methods of analytical inquiry to determine what features something must have to be called family life education.

Attention in this chapter has focused on four features of the concept of family life education: rationale, purpose, content, and operational principles. To summarize these features briefly, three different but related rationales (dealing with problems, preventing problems, developing potentials) appear to have been influential in the development of family life education. At the current time, the most appropriate statement of the general purpose or ultimate goal of the field is to strengthen and enrich individual and family well-being, and the Framework for Life-Span Family Life Education (National Council on Family Relations, 1984) is a defensible conception of the content of family life education. The apparent operational principles of family life education indicate that it (a) is relevant to individuals and families throughout the life span, (b) should be based on the needs of individuals and families, (c) is a multidisciplinary area of study and multiprofessional in its practice, (d) is offered in many different settings, (e) takes an educational rather than a therapeutic approach, (f) should present and respect differing family values, and (g) requires qualified educators to successfully realize its goals. Because these operational principles have not been subjected to any scholarly scrutiny, they are indicative rather than definitive principles.

In their analytical study, Thomas and Arcus (1992) indicated that other features of the concept of family life education (such as assumptions and normative beliefs) also require scholarly attention. Others have called for similar scholarly activity. According to Smith, Shoffner, and Scott (1979), one of the factors characteristic of a professional area of study is that it has a differentiating set of assumptions and propositions. The need to articulate the assumptions and propositions of family life education was echoed by Fisher and Kerckhoff (1981).

Discussion here will focus on only one of these issues: What are the assumptions that underlie and thus are central to family life education? At this time, these assumptions appear to be implicit rather than explicit in most of the family life education literature. One of the notable exceptions is found in the work of Hoopes, Fisher, and Barlow (1984), who specify 12 assumptions that they believe underlie all forms of family facilitation (including family life education, family enrichment, and family treatment). Some of their assumptions are about families while others are about family facilitation programs.

Once assumptions about families or about family life education are made explicit, it is possible to examine the assumptions for their justification or credibility. For example, Hoopes et al. make the assumption: "Families proceed through developmental stages" (1984, p. 9). Although this assumption may have made sense at the time their work was published (nearly 10 years ago), more recent work in the study of families suggests that the concept of "proceeding through developmental stages" may no longer adequately describe the diversity of families and of family experience over time. This example illustrates the importance of articulating and examining underlying assumptions. Assumptions that once were appropriate may no longer be so because social conditions and/or the state of knowledge have changed. To what extent are family life education programs still based on this assumption? What does it mean for family life education when the assumptions underlying its practices are no longer warranted?

One of the assumptions that has often been stated explicitly in family life education is that family life education prevents problems. There is little indication, however, that attempts have been made to examine this assumption directly. Most evaluation studies have investigated outcomes such as whether or not participants have learned anything, whether their attitudes or values have changed, whether they have acquired new skills, and so on. These studies appear to be based on the assumption that, if one knows more or has better skills (for example), then one will somehow be more resistant to problems. But does family life education in fact prevent problems? It would appear that the central question that needs to be examined with regard to this assumption is this one: Do family life education participants have fewer problems than do nonparticipants; that is, did taking family life education actually *prevent* problems? (Ideally, this question would be stated even more broadly: How are family life education participants different than nonparticipants?)

What does it mean for family life education if its practices are based on assumptions that are unwarranted or that are no longer warranted because of changing conditions? To claim an outcome that has not been documented or that is outdated may undermine the credibility of the field, may direct energies away from what should be the central questions and issues of the field, and may result in programs that are not as relevant to the lives of families as they might be. Can family life education continue to ignore these central scholarly questions?

Although space limitations preclude the discussion of the other features here, clarification of the concept of family life education will require attention to specifying and examining the basic propositions, the central values, and the normative beliefs of family life education. Attention should also be directed toward some of the tensions that appear to exist in family life education. For example, the literature of the field clearly reflects some tension between educational approaches and therapeutic ones. Is there a legitimate *conceptual* distinction between these two approaches, or do they simply reflect different points along some continuum? How would clarification of this issue influence the nature of family life education?

As well, the literature reflects an apparent tension between the felt needs and problem orientation of many participants in family life education and the discomfort with this problem orientation and the disclaimer expressed by many family life educators that family life education is more than problems. How might this apparent difference influence the nature of the concept of family life education and what happens in its practice?

Further attention also needs to be directed toward the goals of family life education. Although the ultimate goal has been clarified, many questions remain about the subgoals (or lower objectives). Is there some consistent or preferred hierarchy of subgoals that would help to clarify this concept? How diverse may the subgoals be and still be included in family life education?

Thus, while some claims can be made about the nature of family life education, many important conceptual questions remain to be answered. Serious and systematic attention to these questions should not be seen just as a scholarly exercise but as an essential step in the theoretical, empirical, and practical development of the field of family life education.

REFERENCES

Arcus, M. E. (1984, July). *Quality of life: Toward conceptual clarification.* Paper presented at the Beatrice Paolucci Symposium, Michigan State University, East Lansing.

Arcus, M. E. (1986). Should family life education be required for high school students? An examination of the issues. *Family Relations, 35,* 347-356.

Arcus, M. (1987). A framework for life-span family life education. *Family Relations, 36,* 5-10.

Arcus, M. (1990). *Introduction to family life education.* Minneapolis, MN: National Council on Family Relations.

Avery, C. E. (1962). Inside family life education. *The Family Life Coordinator, 11*(2), 27-39.

Avery, C. E., & Lee, M. R. (1964). Family life education: Its philosophy and purpose. *The Family Life Coordinator, 13*(2), 27-37.

Baier, K. (1974). Toward a definition of "quality of life." In R. O. Clarke & P. C. List (Eds.), *Environmental spectrum: Social and economic views on the quality of life* (pp. 58-81). New York: Van Nostrand.

Barozzi, R. L., & Engel, J. W. (1985). A survey of attitudes about family life education. *Social Casework, 66,* 106-110.

Bedau, J. (1979). Social justice and the quality of life. In W. J. Megaw (Ed.), *Prospects for man: The quality of life* (pp. 97-113). Toronto: York University, Centre for Research on Environmental Quality.

Christiansen, G. A. (1958). *An analysis of selected issues in family life education.* Unpublished doctoral dissertation, Michigan State University.

Coombs, J. R. (1989). Attitudes as educational goals. In R. W. Marx (Ed.), *Curriculum: Towards developing a common understanding* (pp. 75-93). Victoria: British Columbia Ministry of Education.

Coombs, J. R., & Daniels, L. B. (1991). Philosophical inquiry: Conceptual analysis. In E. C. Short (Ed.), *Forms of curriculum inquiry* (pp. 27-41). New York: State University of New York Press.

Cromwell, B. E., & Thomas, V. L. (1976). Developing resources for family potential: A family action model. *The Family Coordinator, 25,* 13-20.

Dager, E. Z., Harper, G. A., & Whitehurst, R. N. (1962). Family life education in public high schools: A survey report on Indiana. *Marriage and Family Living, 24,* 365-370.

Darling, C. A. (1987). Family life education. In M. B. Sussman & S. K. Steinmetz (Eds.), *Handbook of marriage and the family* (pp. 815-833). New York: Plenum.

de Lissovoy, V. (1978). Parent education: White elephant in the classroom? *Youth & Society, 9,* 315-338.

Fisher, B. L. (1986, February). *Theory building: Delayed development in family life education.* Paper presented at the Symposium on Family Life Education, Brigham Young University, Provo, UT.

Fisher, B. L., & Kerckhoff, R. K. (1981). Family life education: Generating cohesion out of chaos. *Family Relations, 30,* 505-509.

Fisher, C. D. (1982). Community based family life education: The Family Life Council of Greater Greensboro, Inc. *Family Relations, 31,* 179-183.

Fohlin, M. B. (1971). Selection and training of teachers for life education programs. *The Family Coordinator, 20,* 231-240.

Frasier, R. C. (1967). Beware the elephants. *Journal of Marriage and the Family, 29,* 380-382.

Gaylin, N. L. (1981). Family life education: Behavioral sciences Wonderbread? *Family Relations, 30,* 511-516.

Gross, P. (1985). *On family life education: For family life educators* (2nd ed., rev.). Montreal: Concordia University Centre for Human Relations and Community Studies.

Guerney, B., Jr., & Guerney, L. F. (1981). Family life education as intervention. *Family Relations, 30,* 591-598.

Hennon, C. B., & Arcus, M. E. (1993). Life-span family life education. In T. H. Brubaker (Ed.), *Family relations: Challenges for the future* (pp. 181-210). Newbury Park, CA: Sage.

Herold, E. S., Kopf, K. E., & deCarlo, M. (1974). Family life education: Student perspectives. *Canadian Journal of Public Health, 65,* 365-368.

Hey, R., & Neubeck, G. (1990). Family life education. In D. H. Olson & M. K. Hanson (Eds.), *2001: Preparing families for the future* (pp. 8-9). Minneapolis, MN: National Council on Family Relations.

Hill, R., & Aldous, J. (1969). Socialization for marriage and parenthood. In D. A. Goslin (Ed.), *Handbook of socialization theory and research* (pp. 885-950). Chicago: Rand McNally.

Hoopes, M. H., Fisher, B. L., & Barlow, S. H. (1984). *Structured family facilitation programs: Enrichment, education, and treatment.* Rockville, MD: Aspen Systems Corporation.

Kerckhoff, R. K. (1964). Family life education in America. In H. T. Christensen (Ed.), *Handbook of marriage and the family* (pp. 881-911). Chicago: Rand McNally.

Kirkendall, L. A. (1973). Marriage and family living, education for. In A. Ellis & A. Abarbanel (Eds.), *The encyclopedia of sexual behavior* (2nd ed.). New York: Hawthorne.

Laycock, S. R. (1967). *Family living and sex education: A guide for parents and youth leaders.* Toronto: Canadian Health Association.

Lee, M. R. (1963). How do experts define "family life education?" *The Family Life Coordinator, 12*(3-4), 105-106.

Levin, E. (1975). Development of a family life education program in a community social service agency. *The Family Coordinator, 24,* 343-349.

Litke, R. (1976). Who is to say what should be taught in values education. In J. R. Meyer (Ed.), *Reflections on values education* (pp. 89-110). Waterloo, Ontario: Wilfred Laurier University Press.

McCall, S. (1975). Quality of life. *Social Indicators Research, 2,* 229-248.

Moss, J. J., & Elbert, M. (1987, November). *The affective domain in family life education.* Paper presented at the annual meeting of the National Council on Family Relations, Atlanta, GA.

National Commission on Family Life Education (Task Force of the National Council on Family Relations). (1968). Family life education programs: Principles, plans, procedures: A framework for family life educators. *The Family Coordinator, 17,* 211-214.

National Council on Family Relations. (1970). Position paper on family life education. *The Family Coordinator, 19,* 186.

National Council on Family Relations. (1984). *Standards and criteria for the certification of family life educators, college/university curriculum guidelines, and content guidelines for family life education: A framework for planning programs over the life span.* Minneapolis, MN: Author.

Peters, R. S. (1967). *The concept of education.* London: Routledge & Kegan Paul.

Rodman, H. (1970). *Teaching about families: Textbook evaluations and recommendations for secondary schools.* Cambridge, MA: Howard A. Doyle.

Scheffler, I. (1960). *The language of education.* Springfield, IL: Charles C Thomas.

Sheek, B. W. (1984). *A nation for families.* Washington, DC: American Home Economics Association.

Smith, R. M., Shoffner, S. M., & Scott, J. P. (1979). Marriage and family enrichment: A new professional area. *The Family Coordinator, 28,* 87-93.

Smith, W. M., Jr. (1968). Family life education—Who needs it? *The Family Coordinator, 17,* 55-61.

Soltis, J. F. (1977). *An introduction to the analysis of educational concepts.* Reading, MA: Addison-Wesley.

Somerville, R. M. (1967). The relationship between family life education and sex education. *Journal of Marriage and the Family, 29,* 374-389.

Somerville, R. M. (1971). Family life education and sex education in the turbulent sixties. *Journal of Marriage and the Family, 33,* 11-35.

Sork, T. J. (1988). Ethical issues in program planning. In R. G. Brockett (Ed.), *Ethical issues in adult education* (pp. 34-50). New York: Columbia University, Teachers College Press.

Stern, E. E. (1969). Family life education: Some rationales and contents. *The Family Coordinator, 18,* 39-43.

Tennant, J. (1989). Family life education: Identity, objectives, and future directions. *McGill Journal of Education, 24,* 127-142.

Thomas, J., & Arcus, M. (1991, March). What's in a name? Home economics education or health education or family life education. In *Proceedings of a Canadian symposium: Issues and directions for home economics/family studies education* (pp. 129-141). Winnipeg, Manitoba.

Thomas, J., & Arcus, M. (1992). Family life education: An analysis of the concept. *Family Relations, 41,* 3-8.

The Vanier Institute of the Family. (1971). *Report of family life education survey, Part 2, Family life education in the schools.* Ottawa: Author.

Whatley, A. E. (1973). Graduate students' perceptions of needed personal characteristics for family life educators. *The Family Coordinator, 22,* 193-198.

Wilcox, A. R. (1981). Dissatisfaction with satisfaction: Subjective social indicators and the quality of life. In D. F. Johnston (Ed.), *Measurement of subjective phenomena.* Washington, D.C.: U.S. Department of Commerce, Bureau of the Census, Center for Demographic Studies. Speical Demographic Analysis CDS-80-3.

Wright, L., & L'Abate, L. (1977). Four approaches to family facilitation: Some issues and implications. *The Family Coordinator, 26,* 176-181.

2

The Evolution of Education for Family Life

Maxine Lewis-Rowley
Ruth E. Brasher
J. Joel Moss
Stephen F. Duncan
Randall J. Stiles

> When an historian sets out to tell us what really
> happened at some time in the past . . . he has to
> do more than write a series of happenings; he has
> further to help his readers weigh them up; it is
> description and assessment.
>
> Walsh, 1958, p. 71

THE HISTORICAL UNFOLDING of family life education is presented here in five time-sequential periods selected on the basis of the dynamic relationships between the society, the culture, and the foundational academic areas that created the paradigms of education for family life. The foundational areas include home economics, family sociology, social psychology, social work, and relevant dimensions of marriage and family therapy and parenting education.

This chapter does not provide a comprehensive history of the family life education movement per se. Rather, the intent is to present a historical account of efforts to educate for family life. The examples provided come primarily from a U.S. perspective, but it is assumed that many of the issues and influences are pertinent to other countries as well.

DEVELOPMENT OF EDUCATION

If education can accrue from either life experiences or systematic studies designed to train mental and moral powers, then family life has always been a part of education. Viewed from this perspective, family life education moved, over time, from the informal contexts of everyday living to instruction combining life experiences with planned study in educational institutions, and it necessarily evolved with ties to other educational movements and to a number of disciplines and professions.

As people searched for freer expression in life, they were motivated to experiment with democratic government. Ultimately, this led to questions about who should be educated and what the content of that education should be.

The dominant educational philosophy in the 1700s produced highly selective religious, private, and state schools. These were attended by a preferred minority from a privileged social strata. The favored curricular model was a classical one dominated by philosophical paradigms of textual criticism and scientific thought (Resnick, 1987).

In contrast, when schools developed later to serve the masses, as distinct from the elite, they were expected to (a) teach basic skills, (b) meet manpower needs, and (c) impose a common culture and language upon the population (Resnick, 1987). These three expectations were to become the thrusts of public education. In the evolving two-tier educational system, however, the focus was on white males. Minorities and women were not included, even in the lower tier (Resnick, 1987).

As democratic-political and socioeconomic changes were reflected in the education system, there was opposition from those who were excluded as well as from insightful others who were part of the elite participants in the higher tier. Eventually, the need for formal education for women and for the work of women, especially as it related to children, gained more attention. Along with this came the forerunners of two family life education foundation academic areas: home economics and sociology.

Concurrently, a division between sacred and secular curriculum perspectives took root and grew. Although moral education had traditionally been fundamental in the academic setting, a secular focus for the basic education curriculum began to unfold (Cranney, 1990). This reflected new attitudes in society regarding freedom of individuals and indicated the beginning of a growing emphasis on individual benefits at the expense of family and group interests.

Slowly the realization came that the teaching of one generation by its predecessors might not be adequate. Because of the limited existing knowledge base, models were only beginning to emerge that could direct families in coping with the changing challenges and difficulties. A need to have assistance pushed new developments to the forefront of education for family life.

COALESCENCE: 1776-1860

Formal education for home and family life began to evolve around the provision of food, shelter, and clothing. These historically had been in the woman's realm, and typically women had been socialized to attend first to the well-being of others, particularly children (Thompson, 1988). It is not surprising that, as far as family life education is concerned, the eighteenth century began as a period of women teaching women about women's work. Such knowledge evolved within an interpretive mode of inquiry—ways of knowing built on folk tales, narratives, and intuitive and spiritual experiences.

In the late 1700s, Benjamin Thompson, an internationally renowned physicist, had called for application of science to problems experienced by families in their homes (Quigley, 1969). Before 1800 there had been exchanges of information on child care between female leaders in Europe and the United States (Brim, 1959). As early as 1815, informal groups of parents met in Portland, Maine, to discuss methods of child rearing (Bridgeman, 1930). Mother study groups, called "maternal associations," were organized during the 1820s to discuss child-rearing practices (Sunley, 1955). *Mother's Magazine*, founded in 1832, and *Mother's Assistant*, printed in 1841, were among the first known periodicals dealing with family life (Sunley, 1955).

Home and family subject matter appeared within the formal educational system during the latter part of the eighteenth and the early part of the nineteenth centuries. The beginnings of instruction specifically dedicated to society's traditional expression of women's work became identified as "domestic economy or household economics" (Brown, 1985, p. 182). As experience and association accumulated, domestic science and, later, home economics became the genus.

The first programs were in grades 1 through 4, since formal education for most females ended in the primary grades. Sewing was the nucleus for the early elementary domestic science curricula because monetary support for education of women was limited, and sewing supplies provided by the students sustained the programs. Foods, nutrition, and meal preparation programs were more expensive and less common, and the systematic study of relationships was yet to be envisioned (Quigley, 1969).

Time was needed to amass the academic knowledge base essential for developing and formulating explicit theories and models of education that could serve home and family. In 1837, however, a pioneer program in higher education was established at Mt. Holyoke College in South Hadley, Massachusetts (Craig, 1944). This provided a pattern for similar educational experiments at other institutions.

By 1840 *A Treatise on Domestic Economy* was being written by Catherine Beecher. She followed it in 1842 with her *Domestic Receipt Book*. "Both books went through edition after edition for forty years . . . and assuredly were the beginning of domestic education" (Andrews, cited in Baldwin, 1949, p. 3).

Beecher discussed impoverished home conditions, the nature of work delegated to homemakers, and the lack of education for familial roles. She proposed in *Treatise* that "domestic economy be made a science, equal to other sciences in . . . education [and] . . . be taught as a practical course . . . systematically, like other sciences . . . until it became . . . a specific branch of study" (Beecher, quoted in Quigley, 1969, p. 19).

Problems dominating the earliest academic education for family life were identified in the preface to the third edition of *Treatise*. Beecher wrote, "The author of this book was led to attempt it, by discovering in her extensive travels, the deplorable sufferings of multitudes of young wives and mothers from . . . defective domestic education" (1844, p. 40).

Era précis. Patterns of family life, as evidenced repeatedly over time, are embedded in ongoing social changes that become central to education for family life. Growing concern for such education in the late 1700s and early 1800s was influenced by dominant sociocultural patterns. These set the stage for the informal teachings shared between family members in the home as well as for the establishment of voluntary community and parent education groups and the creation of formal curriculum for the traditional roles of women.

EMERGENCE: 1861-1900

As early as 1861, the urban centers of the East exhibited a growing need for individuals with training in domestic skills. At the same time, the nation's rapid westward expansion compounded the hardships of maintaining home and family. Both situations emphasized the possible benefits of instruction for the work of women.

Meanwhile, the moral education models that had prevailed in the academic setting continued to experience challenges as the empirical-analytic mode of inquiry, with its emphasis on quantitative analysis, advanced physical science methodology. The subject matter area related to women's roles that lent itself best to models of chemistry and physics was foods and nutrition. Increasing knowledge of the effect of nutrition on human growth and development contributed especially to outreach endeavors that focused attention on education for families.

In most private schools, implementation of these models took the form of specific classes for girls, because "one of the political realities of these undertakings was to use the empirically based nutrition linkages to human development to create a demand for . . . instruction [for women] in public schools" (Quigley, 1974, p. 21). In part, this pattern evolved in the East because of the prejudice against coeducation, particularly when it related to subject matter that was traditionally in the woman's domain (Quigley, 1974).

In the West, family education models took a different form. The Morrill Land Grant Act of 1862 became the catalyst for the development of programs in higher education (Quigley, 1974). The act was the first federal legislation supporting an educational delivery system for training in work related to the family (McConnell, 1970). The contribution of the land-grant system to education for the family is beyond estimation:

> No other agency has appreciated the possibilities of the subject so clearly or laid for it such broad and deep foundations. As these colleges were among the first to recognize the need for a scientific basis to education for the home, they have been most insistent that [scientific] standards should be maintained. (Bevier, 1924, pp. 131-132)

In the land-grant college community, there was a concern for the symbolic interaction of the arts and humanities in daily living, and these, as well as the sciences, became an integral part of the developing family life curriculums (Baldwin, 1949). Ultimately, all subject matter central to the holistic nature of family and home was enhanced.

In 1872 Massachusetts passed a statute legalizing domestic science, which was already in practice in that state, for educating young women. This was the first state law to recognize and support studies related to the family in the public school system (Quigley, 1974). From 1875 to 1890, courses in domestic science became a more directed educational focus in public schools nationwide. For example, in 1886 the superintendent of public instruction in Florida encouraged domestic science and industrial education for girls, and in 1898 the first system in the South offering such training was located at St. Louis, Missouri (Craig, 1944).

During the 1870s and 1880s, the unifying of education with other interest groups concerned with family issues was common, and group action became a significant new political force in advancing education for family life. One such early instrumental group was the Kitchen Garden Association of New York, which taught early childhood education in the form of household arts and gardening (Quigley, 1974).

The New York College for Training Teachers, which later became the Teachers College of Columbia University, was an outgrowth of the early Kitchen Garden Association. In 1884 Columbia University developed a program for domestic economy that was centered on both subject matter and method of instruction (Quigley, 1974). This was perhaps the earliest direct attempt to bring together the epistemology and pedagogy of education related to family.

In 1888 five mothers and a New York City school master, Dr. Feliz Adler, formed a study group that led to the 1890 organization of the Society for the Study of Child Nature. In later decades, the initial effort also merged with other movements associated with family life education (Quigley, 1974). Some publications related to children also appeared. One early publication was the National Congress of Mothers' magazine, *Child Welfare*. Another was Holt's (1894) *The Care and Feeding of Children*, which at the turn of the century was the authoritative reference (Bridgeman, 1930).

By 1895, 16 states offered college courses in home economics (East, 1980). In some of these, the curriculum for advanced education in family life centered on training domestic help, but a different image evolved in other private and public institutions. For example, in 1896 the curricula at Utah's Brigham Young Academy (later Brigham Young University) included a lecture series for students and townspeople offering a wide range of topics: American homes, home culture, home decoration, managing money, companionship, parental influence, children, benefits of early childhood training, the rights of children, the health of children, the nature of a child, religious ideas for children, the child as the hope of the nation, and children and play (Poulson, 1975).

The social milieu was such that male as well as female scholars, because of concern for home and family education, became involved in the unfolding of the home economics movement. In 1896 the New York Board of Regents decided to include household science on college entrance exams. Melvil Dewey, director of the state library, invited Ellen H. Richards to Lake Placid, New York, to discuss questions for the exams. Richards had chemistry degrees from Vassar and the Massachusetts Institute of Technology and was interested in household management and the quality of family life (Quigley, 1974).

Dewey and Richards met again in 1898, and Richards was invited to speak before a group concerned with application of science to the study of the home. From this meeting came plans to convene conferences annually at Lake Placid, New York. The Lake Placid meetings were instrumental in making the last years of the nineteenth century a time of clarification on expanded views of education for family, home, and household management orientations. *Home economics* was given formal recognition as the title of education for home and family life in the public school system (*Lake Placid Conference Proceedings*, 1901).

Home economics fostered what was essentially a "social engineering" approach to the prevention of social problems through education for integrating and managing all areas of family life. The model was based on recognition that difficulties encountered by families had repercussions for society, and it evidenced a pattern of academia responding to societal needs through attempted amelioration of family problems. Such attempts were to become a pattern for family life education, and historically this pattern has always preceded a research thrust.

During the same time period that the home economics movement was initiated, and as commitment to and concern for the family in academic settings became increasingly evident to those in higher education, sociologists and other social scientists undertook research specifically related to the family. The first American textbook on family sociology appeared in 1887, written by Charles Franklin Thwing and Carrie F. Butler Thwing, and "elements of change were already in existence that would, in the next three decades, transform the field of interest in the family from moral debate and speculative scholarship to a scientific enterprise committed to gathering empirical evidence about its nature" (Howard, 1981, p. 26).

Scholars with a social reform perspective began to focus empirically and almost exclusively upon divorce as the major moral evil threatening the family. This was important for two reasons: (a) The orientation to quantitative methods recognized divorce as an area requiring statistical study to guide efforts in attempting to determine what might best be done about the problem, and (b) the statistical approach to research on divorce began to create a comfortable environment where men could work with studies of the home and family and not have to seem to be a part of what had been identified as a women's field.

A key figure in this process, Samuel Warren Dike, was by the end of the 1880s "the preeminent family relations expert in the United States" (Howard, 1981, p. 23). Dike attempted to blend social reform and scholarly study, as he argued that divorce was not a family problem to be solved in isolation but was connected to other aspects of home and community life. The challenge, he felt, was to conduct research that would yield the data necessary to provide insight and guidance for future action. His power of persuasion led to decisions in Congress to provide research money, which produced the 1889 publication, *Report on Marriage and Divorce, 1867-1887* (Howard, 1981).

At the same time, there were important contributions from a smaller group of scholars who were concerned with the family as an institution in transition, an evolutionary unit resistant to, yet a captive of, the social environment. These scholars, drawing on qualitative anthropological studies and the work of such writers as Comte, Spencer, Ward, Giddings, and Sumner (Chamblias, 1954), set the stage for the later division of family sociology from social work. The efforts of these sociologists created the framework for new research and literature that contributed to the foundations of family education.

In the aftermath of the Civil War and the depression of 1873, many intellectuals came to view good family life as a product of adequate governmental support. Emphasis was therefore given to various kinds of social reform, including changes in laws and changes in environmental conditions. Programs focusing on parent education and child well-being became major avenues for dealing with pressing societal issues concerning the family.

Era précis. As interest groups organized and became influential, two distinct ideas about family and related education took form during the 1861-1900 period. The first was the home economics perspective, which built on already developing educational programs for the work of women, including family well-being and all dimensions of the home environment. In this approach, home was assumed to be the central paradigm for family education, and any activities therein were key elements. Improvement of the quality of life therefore depended upon educating for the effective management of the home and family. Leaders of the programs envisioned education for family life fashioned after physical science models to be used as a strategy to alleviate problems in the larger society.

A second idea concentrated on connections between problems in family life and problems in society. Leaders saw empirical research as fundamental to accumulating knowledge that could be corrective. Emphasis was on the need for government intercession and support of the reciprocal roles of family and society and encompassed social reform as a driving force, whether looked at from the perspective of the social system (sociology) or from the perspective of the family and its members (social work).

CRYSTALLIZATION: 1901-1920

From 1900 to 1920, the postures of the competing patterns of present-day family life education were established. Howard (1981) identified this period as the progressive era of family sociology and listed as the significant sociological publications before 1910: (a) Willcox's doctoral dissertation, *The Divorce Problem, A Study in Statistics* (1891), the first major sociological study based on the Census Bureau's 1889 report of marriage and divorce statistics; (b) *A History of Matrimonial Institutions* (1904), an elaboration upon the idea of the family as an institution in transition; and (c) Lictenberger's *Divorce: A Study in Social Causation* (1909), the most detailed study of divorce completed up to that time.

Social psychology was the major influence in sociology by 1910, and the social psychological perspective emphasized the family's function as an agent of socialization. This encouraged a tendency to view marriage not as a sacrament but a contract, divorce not as a threat but a symptom, and marriage and family life as needing empowerment in the form of education (Howard, 1981).

By 1920 family sociology had become the major force in academia's family life education programs, and it was to maintain that position for more than two decades. Also in 1920, Cooley's *Social Organization* was published, and it promoted a shift in focus from studying the family as an integral agent of socialization to the study of the function of socialization as it linked the larger society and the family.

Cooley's book was a part of the motivation for higher education's separation of sociology and social work into two fields. Each fostered an empirical emphasis, but pursuits took them in different directions. Social work embraced a model along the lines of medicine and therapy. Its goals emphasized family preservation and viewed the family as fragile and requiring work and study to protect it from extinction. On the other hand, most family sociologists believed that major functions of society were transferable to primary groups, including the family, which was seen as sturdy and enduring.

The separation of social work and family sociology was reflected in arguments about "basic knowledge" as opposed to "interventionistic ideas" and what should be taught and for what purposes (Howard, 1981). Case study approaches and dialectic research were to become definitive contributions of these two fields to family life education.

Paralleling and sometimes building upon the developments in sociology and social work, during this same period home economics incorporated an evangelism that centered on a scientific approach to content areas connected by theoretical foundations with a holistic philosophy (*Syllabus of Home Economics*, 1913). As a result, the American Home Economics Association (AHEA) was organized in 1908 as the first professional organization dedicated specifically to family concerns and issues. The objective, according to the AHEA constitution, was "to provide opportunities for professional home economists and members of other fields to cooperate in the attainment of the well-being of individuals and families" (*Home Economics New Directions*, 1959, p. 6).

To facilitate its purposes of "bringing together widely separated interests and groups and providing leadership for experiencing, promoting, discussing and debating ideas" (Parker, 1980, p. 26), the AHEA founded the first publication in the United States for professionals in family life. Volume 1, Number 1, of *The Home Economics Journal* was published in February 1909 with Benjamin Andrews, of Columbia's Teachers College, as editor (Parker, 1980).

Meanwhile, involvement of volunteers in family education through community organizations increased. The National Congress of Mothers, dedicated to promoting the concepts and practice of "mother-love" and "mother-thought," had been founded in 1897, and in 1908, as it expanded throughout the nation, the group was renamed the National Congress of Mothers and Parent-Teacher Associations (Bridgeman, 1930).

The Society for the Study of Child Nature had also grown to several chapters and by 1908 was consolidated into the Federation for Child Study. Its purpose was to collect and distribute information on children, promote lectures and conferences, conduct research, and develop cooperation with other child study groups (Bridgeman, 1930).

In 1909 the first White House Conference on Child Welfare was held. Soon after, the Children's Bureau was created, and in 1914 it began publishing *Infant Care*, which was directed to parents (Bridgeman, 1930).

The passage of the Smith-Lever act, also in 1914, established the Cooperative Extension Service at land-grant universities in each state and charged it with the responsibility to "aid in diffusing . . . useful and practical information in subjects relating to . . . home" (Rasmussen, 1989, p. 153). David F. Houston, a director of the extension service, reported that, in its first year, home economists visited 5,500 homes and trained 6,000 women to be leaders in educating others (Rasmussen, 1989).

In 1917 the University of Iowa opened the first Child Welfare Research Station in the United States. Other centers were the Institutes of Child Welfare at the University of Minnesota and the University of California, the Yale Psychological Clinic, the National Research Center in Washington, D.C., and the Merrill-Palmer Institute in Detroit (Frank, 1962).

There was much evidence, particularly after 1910, of increased endeavors related to children and their welfare. This period saw the beginning of trends that would support the action of the Scandinavian philosopher, Eller Key, who named the twentieth century "the Century of the Child" (Frank, 1962).

Era précis. The 1900-1920 period was characterized by a variety of programs with different emphases. Social psychology began to affect family life education. Family sociology and social work were established as separate academic areas in higher education. Social work developed its own service arena, which expanded over time from casework with a group emphasis to a variety of interventionistic approaches that competed with psychology's moves in the same direction. Family sociology became the dominant discipline in family life education programs at the postsecondary level, and empirical research, as a driving force of family sociology, also became a major thrust in other family-related disciplines.

Home economics developed a network of specialty areas related to education for family life, and the AHEA was organized. The first professional journal dedicated to concerns and issues associated with family life was published by the AHEA.

The Cooperative Extension Service hired home economists to institute education programs in the home for those who were unable to participate in on-campus higher education. This strengthened a tie between education in general and family life education, as the expansion of postsecondary family-related programs supported the breadth of related teaching at other educational levels in the community.

Parent education and volunteer community groups continued to grow. Society's concern for the welfare of its children moved forward internationally.

EXPANSION: 1921-1950

The years between 1921 and 1950 were dynamic ones for families grappling with the demands of changes resulting from two world wars. New developments in both home economics and family sociology, as well as in social services and other family intervention programs, embodied changes that raised questions about what, how, and by whom concepts and skills related to family were to be taught.

In October 1924 the Child Study Association of America invited 13 smaller organizations to send representatives to a conference. This resulted in the formation of the National Council of Parent Education.

Edna Nobel White, director of the Merrill-Palmer School, was named to chair the organization. The goals were to conduct research, to collect research material for parent educators, to be a research clearinghouse, and to suggest qualifications and guidelines for the training of parents. Eventually, 124 study groups were formed and, because of increased interest from fathers as well as mothers, the organization became known as the National Congress of Parents and Teachers. It grew to include 500 study groups by 1929 (Bridgeman, 1930).

Also in 1924, the National Council on Parent Education had been organized, and parent education appeared firmly established (Kerckhoff, 1964). By this time, 75 major organizations were conducting parent education programs (Brim, 1959).

The Laura Spelman Rockefeller Memorial (1918-1920), later known as the Spelman Fund (1928-1938), was important in supporting parent education. It encouraged the 1924 expansion of the Federation for Child Study into the Child Study Association of America. The primary function of the organization was development and supervision of the use of parent education materials. By 1930 there were 6,000 members dedicated to assisting parents in the rearing of their children (Bridgeman, 1930).

The late 1930s, however, witnessed some dynamic shifts in family education. There was, for example, a marked decrease in parent education activity because professional literature questioned the stability of the family unit and therefore the advisability of pouring government resources into it (Brim, 1959). This coincided with the 1938 ending of the Spelman Fund, which disbanded the National Council of Parent Education and some other parent education organizations.

At the same time, partly in response to the increasing knowledge base and concern of professionals for family well-being, a number of local, state, and national conferences of individuals, from an array of specialized fields, appeared. For example, in 1934

> a Conference on Education for Marriage and Family Social Relations was held in New York City, cosponsored by the American Home Economics Association, the American Social Hygiene Association, and Teachers College of Columbia University. One outcome of this meeting was the organization in 1938 of the National Conference on Family Relations, which later was renamed the National Council on Family Relations (NCFR). (Kerckhoff, 1964, p. 83)

For many, the most important work of this period (Howard, 1981) was Thomas and Znaniecki's family sociological study, *The Polish Peasant in Europe and America* (22nd edition, 1927). This work represents the closure of one era of education for family life and the beginning of another:

> In one sense, the work reflected the rising interest of the Progressive Era in the
> concerns for the loss of community life as a major causality of the process of
> industrialization. . . . In another sense, Thomas and Znaniecki's emphasis
> upon the need to study the internal and subjective processes of social disor-
> ganization anticipated the growing preoccupation [with] . . . internal relation-
> ships of family interaction, rather than the external relationships of the family
> with larger institutions of society. (Howard, 1981, p. 54)

The 1920s and the 1930s also brought into focus the emphasis of Park
and Burgess's book, *Introduction to the Science of Sociology* (1921), which
identified interaction as the essential element of society. Five years later,
Burgess published "The Family as a Unit of Interacting Personalities,"
which suggested viewing the family, like society, as a process whose
essential nature changed with time because "family" was created and
influenced by the individuals within it (Burgess, 1926).

Burgess's idea that various types of behavior were exhibited within
the family led to studies on marriage with a focus on marital maladjust-
ment. It also gave added significance to interdisciplinary approaches
with increased use of subcultural and cross-cultural interviews and case
studies in research. One example of this was Frazier's study of the black
family (Howard, 1981).

The depression of the 1930s brought with it concern for family
handling of stress as seen in the works of Cavan and Ranck (1938), Hill
(1949), Koos and Fulcomer (1948), and others. A family development
approach also appeared (Duvall & Hill, 1948), but the interaction approach still dominated much of family sociology up to World War II.

The war fostered and stimulated small group-related studies within
the military. This contributed to formation of an eclectic base centered
on emerging therapy theory as a sort of educational action.

Parent education continued in the 1940s, but it was seen as a preventive program and its growth emphasized a mental health rather than a
family perspective. Mental health screening during World War II provided data, however, that led to the National Mental Health Act of 1946
and funded state-led community health programs, including parent
education.

Following World War II, anthropological cross-cultural research on
the impact of institutionalization began to diminish the effects of anti-
family literature. This helped to make concern about preparatory education for marriage and parenthood become more visible (Brim, 1959).

Ernest Groves, a sociologist with a psychiatric interest, began to
study the factors that sustained marriages and came to believe that
affection, initially based upon sex but a product of experience and
mutual accommodation as well, was the fundamental quality determining the success or failure of a marriage. Later, Groves, assisted by his

wife Gladys, expanded the work and brought recognition to the University of North Carolina as a center for family life education. As the Groves' work progressed and publications resulted from their efforts, their influence was felt at other centers.

In 1949, following Ernest Groves's death, Reuben Hill, a family sociologist with some interest in psychiatric-therapeutic activity, was brought to the University of North Carolina. Later, Hill elected to move to the University of Minnesota, which, under his guidance, became the leading center in America for family theory and research.

A mixed focus was increasingly evident as professionals educated through the Minnesota and North Carolina programs, and the publications that accompanied their scholarly efforts and interests, moved into home economics and other family life education programs across the nation. For example, Evelyn Duvall, executive secretary of the NCFR, who with Hill had written *When You Marry* (1945), wrote the first text specifically designed for high school family living courses.

Duvall indicated that, over a period of 15 years, she worked with thousands of high school students and collected 25,000 questions asked by the students. With these questions as a base, from 1944 to 1949 Duvall worked with home economics teachers from 25 states and Canada to structure and refine the text, which was titled *Family Living* (1950).

Because of home economics' ties to public education delivery systems, Duvall's book helped set the stage for home economics to replace sociology as the preponderant discipline in family life education (Kerckhoff, 1964). Home economics' position of dominance was enhanced nationally through the publication of specific materials related to family life education and enhanced internationally as home economists, supported by such government programs as the Marshall Plan, established family life education programs worldwide.

Era précis. Because of the influential empirical-analytic research produced in family sociology, that field was the dominant force in family life education during the 1930s and 1940s. The changing configuration of national and international views following World War II, and the accompanying changes in societal norms, were combined with an explosion of science and technology to affect all areas of family life. As a consequence of these dynamics, a reemphasis on prevention became the basis of exceptional growth in therapeutic programs. The influence of specialists with a therapeutic background was felt in all areas of education for family life, especially home economics. By 1950 publications and international projects had once again placed home economics at the vanguard of family life education.

ENTRENCHMENT: 1951-1990

Economic well-being following World War II was reflected in family life education through the 1950s and the 1960s. Increased research money available from government and private foundations magnified opportunities in social reform, therapy, and education.

In the 1950s society's difficulties continued to influence family research. Two issues were at the forefront of questions pertinent to family life education: (a) the increasing divorce rate, a phenomenon that had been so significant in the development of family sociology two decades earlier, and (b) an open focus on differences in sexual behavior standards and the degree of emphasis and nature of the content that should be presented as a part of sex education programs. The latter affected family research in much the same way that divorce had affected it earlier (Howard, 1981).

By 1960, as a consequence of the Korean and Vietnam wars, family and society faced additional new dilemmas: use of illegal drugs, increase in cohabitation, and resistance by some youth groups to existing societal patterns and norms. Virtually all professions concerned with family life education debated these issues and altered approaches and activities, accommodated new ideas, or challenged the criticisms leveled at existing programs.

During this time, the feminist movement became a force in the social, legal, and political world, and there was intensification of the discussion of favoring individual over group rights. Within this context, the family as a unit diminished in strength of focus, and competing groups began a discussion, which has continued into recent decades, about what name should be selected for education for family life and what content should be included (McFarland, 1984; Spitze, 1985; Vail, 1961).

Questions were raised about whether the home economics generalists' approach fixed a role for women as submissive to an authoritarian social structure. A segment of the specialists in home economics units, many with grounding in other fields of study, also questioned applied research and the application of theory to the home setting as well as the provision of education for the role of homemaker. These dynamics later resulted in the change of some department and college names from *home economics* to disparate nomenclatures and contributed to confusion about content and curriculum titles. In removing home economics programs, some universities effectively removed educational preparation for family life from their campuses (Harper, 1981; Harper & Davis, 1986; McFarland, 1984; Vail, 1961).

In spite of these complexities, home economics, which, of the foundational academic areas, is most integral to public education systems, during the early part of this period experienced the greatest growth in its history. A direct result was that large numbers of home economics generalists sought advanced degrees in human development and family relationships, and this was fundamental to important changes in family life education.

Although both generalists and specialists were preoccupied with attempts to intervene and ameliorate recurring problems resulting from the impact upon society of families not assuming appropriate roles, by 1970 a wider separation had developed between the two groups in approaches to academic pursuits, dissemination of knowledge, and rendering of service. Generalists strengthened practical application and eclectic approaches to family life education, while specialists were more concerned with the dialectic building of theory.

The generalist practitioner became more and more dependent upon the specialist for production of research, and the home economics generalist became more and more a specialist in education. Specialists began to replace the generalists in some academic settings. This opened the door for teams of specialists to bring differing perspectives to bear on such issues of concern as divorce, changing sex standards, single heads of household, latchkey children, teen pregnancy, suicide, abortion, blended families, aging, resource management, family violence, ethics, and new linkages between nutrition and human development.

Recession in the 1970s brought significant cutbacks across all levels of education. Federal funding sources gave preference to career and economics education (Border et al., 1983). What had been a haven of growth for family life educators began to ebb away as resources were diverted to meet pressing social needs through avenues other than education. The realignment of monies gave impetus to new directions in secondary schools, where curricula began to be dictated by society rather than by family.

During the decade of the 1970s, however, there was an explosion of basic research with concomitant development of family theory (Holman & Burr, 1980). Both in home economics and in family sociology, the elements were firmly in place by 1951 for the family life education knowledge base to begin expanding rapidly. Continued funding, perennial problems, and growth of generalist programs in the 1960s also set the stage for professional production in the 1970s

unlike anything that had gone before. The Inventory of Marriage and Family Literature shows that about 2 percent of the items in the English language appeared between 1900 and 1928; from 1929 to 1940, about 6 percent appeared; between 1941 and 1971, 67 percent appeared. In the years between 1972 and 1976, there appeared 25 percent of all articles and books. In other words, up to 1940, the historian had to deal with 10 percent of the publications: 90 percent of all existing family sociology has been written and published since 1940. The grand total for 1900 to 1976 [was] 25,557 items. (Mogey, cited in Howard, 1981, pp. viii-ix)

The report to which Mogey referred was drawn not just from sociology but also from social work, home economics, psychology, and other journals with implications for the family. The themes of the writers also reflected change. "Counseling or therapy, followed by education, was the orientation of most articles, and interest in individual outcomes rather than group effects clearly distinguished the family sociologist from others in the discipline of sociology" (Mogey, cited in Howard, 1981, p. ix).

A focus on prevention by professionals in most family-related disciplines resulted in calls for family service agencies to take a more active role in community family life education (Ortof, 1970) and to provide educational programs that could assist in the empowerment of families, both in their own right and as an adjunct to therapy (Carder, 1972; McPherson & Samuels, 1971; Walz, 1975). These services had routinely been staffed and managed by individuals with social work backgrounds, who provided assistance to families primarily through counseling (Simon, 1976). In 1978 the Council on Social Work Education sponsored a series of five teaching institutes, which continued into the 1980s, in an effort to prepare social workers to offer more effective preventive services (Bowker, 1983).

In 1977 the Coalition of Family Organizations (COFO) was formed by the NCFR, AHEA, AAMFT, and Family Service America (FSA). The primary purpose of COFO was lobbying for social policy in support of family. Steven Priester, AAMFT deputy executive director, noted:

Families are the key for improving the educational success of children; they are crucial for planning and delivering care for the frail elderly; they are essential resources in attempting to help youth in trouble. When families are working well, they carry out responsibilities essential for the functioning of society. When they are in trouble, the government must act in their place. (COFO Family Policy Report, 1987, p. 1)

Some sociologists believed that conscious efforts to keep the sociology of marriage and family closely tied with mainstream sociology would increase postsecondary students' understanding of sociological theory applied to the family and enhance recognition of the way such theories explain a wide range of human behavior. Several texts published in the 1970s used the family as a basis for understanding general principles about social organization and human interaction. Examples are Winch's *The Modern Family* (1971), Skolnick's *The Intimate Environment* (1973), and Scanzoni's *Men, Women, and Change* (1976). Other texts for family life courses at the university level, such as Burr's *Successful Marriage: A Principles Approach* (1976), were equally embedded in sociological research, but they were more practical and "functional" than theoretical and used research findings to produce propositional ideas for use in family and nonfamily relationship settings.

Family sociologists also made innovative contributions to methodology in education for family life. For example, Gillespie (1977) introduced the use of a simulated family technique; Lehtinen (1977) described the use of student-developed reports of their own family experiences; and Debenham and Smith (1979) developed MATESIM, a computerized simulation of mate selection.

Some home economists and others recognized the limitation of viewing the family's behavior and development only from the perspective of the family life cycle. Multidisciplinary research was strongly encouraged by the attention given to a theoretical connection between human ecology and individual and family development (Andrews, Bubolz, & Paolucci, 1979).

Also in the 1970s, social exchange theory, by drawing together economic, psychological, and other ideas, influenced research and affected family systems theory and process analysis. In addition, middle range theories and models contributed to groups with special educational needs and to particular topics. A challenge to provide better linkages between research and application was made as the new decade began (Holman & Burr, 1980).

For a brief period in the early 1980s, family life education was engrossed in defining and delineating parenting education because a rationale for mandating parent education classes at the national, state, and local levels peaked at that time. Divorce and separation, nontraditional family forms, alternative approaches to parenting, child abuse, pro-life versus pro-choice perspectives of abortion, genetic manipulation of the fetus, and other problems strengthened and supported the petition.

Parenting education had experienced great growth from 1951 to the 1980s. Behavior modification had become widely accepted by parent educators as had Gordon's (1978) *Parent Effectiveness Training* and Dreikurs's (1964) Adlerian approach with *Children: The Challenge*. Group approaches were dominant methods of parenting instruction, and the nurturant socialization of children was defined as one of "the main tasks of families" (Hicks & Williams, 1981, pp. 580-584).

Establishing criteria for certification of parenting specialists became a concern for family therapists as well as family life educators in both the secondary and the postsecondary systems. In the mid-1980s certification programs were adopted by several professional associations, including the AHEA, NCFR, and American Association for Marriage and Family Therapy (AAMFT).

Also in the 1980s, therapeutic units, which had struggled in prior decades, began to thrive as money from government and insurance companies became available to support both the establishing of clinics and the professional treatment of patients. Increasing numbers of specialists with clinical training became involved in university departments preparing family life educators, and marriage and family enrichment programs with a therapeutic educational focus appeared in clinics nationwide.

Guerney and Guerney (1981) presented a pervasive argument that all family life educators should be interventionistic, and David and Vera Mace, therapists who came to the United States from England, began extended work in marriage enrichment, with the idea that preparatory education was not enough (Mace, 1982).

As global perspectives changed from East-West to North-South, responsibility for shared beliefs and understandings of the ethical challenges of daily living gained attention (Brown, 1989; Brown & Paolucci, 1979; Strom & Plihal, 1989). Visibility was given to the need for both professional action and professional preparation of family life educators.

Some scholars (Arcus, 1980; Warner & Olson, 1981) saw the overemphasis on individualism in the society as a compelling consideration and argued that family life education should become more concerned with moral issues and should stress formal education focused on ethical dimensions of behavior within the context of the family. Exploration began of the development of morals and ethics and the extent to which society should intervene therapeutically and educationally in people's lives.

Within family-related organizations such as the NCFR, AAMFT, and AHEA, professionals asked: Will there emerge a new type of labeling that ignores family? Will the primary concern of society remain individual, support nonkin relationships, and focus on interactions and processes outside the family? What will be the implications of these dynamics for family life education?

Within the larger society, some earlier trends began to be reversed as opposition to individualistic extremes was reflected in professional organizations, on the news, and in the streets. Those who believed in stopping the movement toward individualism lobbied court decisions about abortion and other family-related matters and argued for education to incorporate more of the affective elements of family relationships, which, some felt, had not received adequate attention in individualized models.

Concurrently, the perplexity of the work/family interface was another issue related to individualism that affected family life education. The context of the family and who was available in the home to spend time with the children altered significantly as the number of mothers in the paid labor force who had children in the home increased dramatically. Bird, in *The Two Paycheck Marriage* (1979), had written that the long-term implications of both parents being in the labor force were "absolutely unchartable . . . the cumulative consequences will only be revealed in the 21st or 22nd century" (p. xiii).

The movement during the 1980s was more than a women's issue. It brought to the forefront discussions related to such topics as employer policy variations, including paid maternity and paternity leave, paid personal days for family matters, flexible hours, and part-time employee benefits. As the world of business and government became alerted to *family well-being*, affecting production and profit through the *working well-being* of employees, a climate was created in which some businesses and corporations moved to provide employee benefits in the form of family-related programs.

In some cases, this redirected attention to the models of small group dynamics developed in the 1940s and 1950s, and home economics' social engineering and sociology's social exchange approaches to family life education had opportunities to expand at the work site. This blending of therapeutic, educational, and corporate mentalities began to present an attractive image for those seeking careers related to family life education in both the public and the private spheres.

The merging of the 1980s into the 1990s reflected continued frustration with recurring problems and a lack of definite solutions. Research in the empirical/analytic mode was not diminished, but dialogues among some family life educators centered on interrelating ways of knowing and being as well as the need for critical explications (Hultgren & Coomer, 1989). Many graduate programs concerned with training future family life educators became centers of high-level debates reflecting the differing philosophies of scholars concerned with epistemological assumptions of the field and the direction that educational efforts should take those assumptions (Christensen, 1992).

Era précis. From 1951 to 1990, some of what had been traditionally important in family life education became controversial, and programs that had emerged promoting certain aspects and viewpoints repostured and then restated their contributions. Areas that had originated as subject matter specialties in home economics and sociology became competing and allied fields of their predecessors.

Scholars articulated a need for affective as well as moral and ethical components of family life education, and those with competing conceptions of theory and practice debated the qualities of good research and the need for critical theory. Concerns with ethical and moral education increased, and some groups tried to reverse historical trends that had strengthened individual models at the expense of group models. National coalitions formed from separate professional organizations in an effort to affect public policy for the good of the family. The corporate world began to foster family support programs as employee incentives. Global perspectives brought consideration of shared comprehensions and actions. Public and professional discussions of family-related issues were ever present.

ASSESSMENT

Family life education has always been an interesting and dynamic phenomenon and a locus of concern for many who believe in a need to treat problems and provide instruction that could, in the context of family, enable people to be responsible, caring, and conscientious and allow individuals to reach their maximum potential. Family life education will always be a focus for those who recognize the family's paramount role in ameliorating problems in society through proper socialization of family members.

Historically, the nature of family life education changed as the social-political-economic order of the United States changed. A "working compromise" between individuals and families was present during the founding years of the nation, with the compromise tending to favor families. Family life education, as it evolved, was supportive of that perspective. As the nation expanded, however, the democratic and liberal republic nourished a separation of the sacred and the secular along with an emphasis on individual rights at the expense of the family group. Family life education has therefore been partly shaped by periods of reaction.

As has been true historically, family life education will probably continue to be incorporated into a variety of educational enterprises.

Future changes will occur consistent with emotional preferences and working compromises of various groups. Coalitions of individuals, families, businesses, and governments, interacting with what the legal system adjudicates and interprets, could prevent costly conflicts and result in better preparatory education for family professionals. Cognizant of their own biases and preferences, professionals could then choose the work setting that would most complement their individual philosophies and preparation and maximize individual contributions.

Remembering the past and looking to the future, the immediate decades will probably give attention to

(a) *teams of specialists and/or generalists,* recognizing that family life educators do not work in isolation and combining innovative training and staffing possibilities, such as therapeutic-corporate manager-home economics, or family resource management-organizational behavior-early childhood educator, or human development-physician's assistant-family finance specialist teams;

(b) *refined theory and research,* building a knowledge base established by both the empirical/analytic perspectives of the early family sociologists and the interpretive approaches that gave meaning to initial home economics education efforts for home and family but in addition using critical suppositions responsive to empowerment of families;

(c) *intervention in private and/or public spheres,* strengthening the linkage between the contributions of the family and the consequences for society through building upon the preventive philosophy that was the foundation of the original ties between home economics and education and that are now embraced by most family life educators; and

(d) *global, in addition to national, family policies* made possible by communication and technological advances and humanitarian educational programs that refocus attention upon the cross-cultural home economics education models of the 1940s and 1950s and interact with social, political, and economic systems in ways that are proactive as well as problem centered.

REFERENCES

Andrews, M., Bubolz, M., & Paolucci, B. (1979). An ecological approach to the study of the family. *Marriage and Family Review, 3,* 29-49.

Arcus, M. (1980). Value reasoning: An approach to values education. *Family Relations, 29,* 163-171.

Baldwin, K. E. (1949). *The AHEA saga.* Washington, DC: American Home Economics Association.

Beecher, C. E. (1840). *A treatise on domestic economy.* Boston: Source Book.

Beecher, C. E. (1842). *Domestic receipt book.* Boston: Harper.

Beecher, C. E. (1844). *A treatise on domestic economy* (3rd ed.). New York: Harper.

Bevier, I. (1924). *Home economics in education*. Chicago: J. B. Lippincott.

Bird, C. (1979). *The two paycheck marriage*. New York: Rawson, Wade.

Border, B. A., et al. (Eds.). (1983). *Nontraditional home economics: Meeting uncommon needs with innovative plans* (Home Economics Teacher Education Yearbook). Bloomington, IL: McKnight.

Bowker, J. P. (Ed.). (1983). *Education for primary prevention in social work*. New York: Council on Social Work Education.

Bridgeman, R. P. (1930). Ten years' progress in parent education. *Annals of the American Academy of Political and Social Science, 151*, 32-45.

Brim, O. G., Jr. (1959). *Education for child rearing*. New York: Russell Sage.

Brown, M. M. (1985). *Philosophical studies of home economics in the United States, our practical intellectual heritage* (Vol. 1). East Lansing: Michigan State University.

Brown, M. M. (1989). What are the qualities of good research? In F. Hultgren (Ed.), *Alternative modes of inquiry in home economics research* (Home Economics Teacher Education Yearbook, pp. 257-297). Peoria, IL: Glencoe.

Brown, M. M., & Paolucci, B. (1979). *Home economics: A definition*. Washington, DC: American Home Economics Association.

Burgess, E. W. (1926). The family as a unit of interacting personalities. *Family, 7, 6*.

Burr, W. R. (1976). *Successful marriage: A principles approach*. Homewood, IL: Dorsey.

Carder, J. H. (1972). New dimension to family agency from family life education. *Social Casework, 53*, 355-360.

Cavan, R. S., & Ranck, K. H. (1938). *The family and the depression*. Chicago: University of Chicago Press.

Chamblias, R. (1954). *Social thought from Hammurabi to Comte*. New York: Holt, Rinehart.

Christensen, B. (1992). *Utopia*. San Francisco: Ignatius.

COFO Family Policy Report. (1987, June). [COFO memo]. Washington, DC: COFO Editorial Board.

Cooley, C. (1920). *Social organization*. New York: Scribner.

Craig, H. T. (1944, June). The history of home economics (part 1). *Practical Home Economics*, pp. 245-246, 269-270, 272, 275.

Cranney, G. (1990, December). *History of reading in the colonial period of the United States*. Notes presented at a Reading Methods Seminar, Provo, UT.

Debenham, J., & Smith, G. (1979). MATESIM: Simulating decision making in marriage formation. *Teaching Sociology, 6*, 147-166.

Dreikurs, R. (1964). *Children: The challenge*. New York: Meredith.

Duvall, E. M. (1950). *Family living*. New York: Macmillan.

Duvall, E., & Hill, R. (1945). *When you marry*. New York: D. C. Heath.

Duvall, E. M., & Hill, R. (Eds.). (1948). *Women's foundations*. New York: Macmillan.

East, M. (1980). *Home economics: Past, present and future*. Boston: Allyn & Bacon.

Frank, L. K. (1962). The beginnings of child development and family life education in the twentieth century. *Merrill-Palmer Quarterly of Behavior and Development, 8*, 7-28.

Gillespie, J. B. (1977). Simulated family: Sociology of family courses. In *American Sociological Association Project in Undergraduate Teaching: Approaches to undergraduate teaching*. New Rochelle, NY: Change Magazine.

Gordon, T. (1978). *Parent effectiveness training*. New York: P. H. Wyden.

Guerney, B., Jr., & Guerney, L. F. (1981). Family life education and intervention. *Family Relations, 30*, 591-598.

Harper, L. J. (1981, Spring). Home economics in higher education: Status and trends, 1980. *Journal of Home Economics 73*, 14-18.

Harper, L. J., & Davis, S. L. (1986, Summer). Home economics in higher education, 1968 to 1982: Analysis and trends. *Journal of Home Economics*, 6-17, 50.

Hicks, M. W., & Williams, J. W. (1981). Current challenges in educating for parenthood. *Family Relations, 30,* 579-584.

Hill, R. (1949). *Families under stress.* New York: Harper.

Holman, T. B., & Burr, W. R. (1980). Beyond the beyond: The growth of family theories in the 1970s. *Journal of Marriage and the Family, 42,* 729-741.

Holt, L. E. (1894). *The care and feeding of children: Catechism for the use of mothers and children's nurses.* New York: Appleton.

Home economics new directions. (1950). Washington, DC: American Home Economics Association.

Howard, R. (1981). *A social history of American sociology, 1865-1940.* West Port, CT: Greenwood.

Hultgren, F., & Coomer, D. (Eds.). (1989). *Alternative modes of inquiry in home economics research* (Home Economics Teacher Education Yearbook). Peoria, IL: Glencoe.

Kerckhoff, R. K. (1964). Family life education in America. In H. T. Christiansen (Ed.), *Handbook of marriage and the family* (pp. 881-911). Chicago: Rand McNally.

Koos, E. L., & Fulcomer, D. (1948). Families in crisis. In *Dynamics of family interaction.* New York: Kings Crown.

Lake Placid Conference on Home Economics proceedings of the first, second, and third conferences. (1901). Geneva, NY: American Home Economics Association.

Lehtinen, M. W. (1977). Sociological family analysis. *Teaching Sociology, 4,* 307-314.

Mace, D. R. (1982). *Close companions: The marriage enrichment handbook.* New York: Continuum.

McConnell, E. (1970, September). The history of home economics. *Forecast for Home Economics,* pp. F-86, F-87, F-134.

McFarland, K. (1984, April). Name change! If not home economics, what alternative? *What's New in Home Economics,* pp. 3-13.

McPherson, S. B., & Samuels, C. R. (1971). Teaching behavioral methods to parents. *Social Casework, 52,* 148-153.

Ortof, S. S. (1970). The family agency as community educational activists. *Social Casework, 51,* 28-34.

Park, R. E., & Burgess, E. W. (1921). *Introduction to the science of sociology.* Chicago: University of Chicago Press.

Parker, F. J. (1980). *Home economics: An introduction to a dynamic profession.* New York: Macmillan.

Poulson, V. B. (1975). *History of College of Family Living: Ladies Work Department to College of Family Living.* Provo, UT: Brigham Young University, College of Family Living.

Quigley, E. (1969). *Introduction to home economics.* New York: Macmillian.

Quigley, E. (1974). *Introduction to home economics* (2nd ed.). New York: Macmillan.

Rasmussen, W. D. (1989). *Taking the university to the people.* Ames: Iowa University Press.

Resnick, L. (1987). *Education and learning to think.* Washington, DC: V. H. Winston.

Scanzoni, J. H. (1976). *Men, women and change.* New York: McGraw-Hill.

Simon, D. S. (1976). A systematic approach to family life education. *Social Casework, 57,* 511-516.

Skolnick, A. (1973). *The intimate environment.* Boston: Little, Brown.

Spitze, H. (1985). A rose by any other name would not be a rose. *Illinois Teacher, 29,* 44.

Strom, S., & Plihal, J. (1989). The critical approach to research. In F. Hultgren & D. Coomer (Eds.), *Alternative modes of inquiry in home economics research* (Home Economics Teacher Education Yearbook; pp. 185-210). Peoria, IL: Glencoe.

Sunley, R. (1955). Early nineteenth-century American literature on child-rearing. In M. Mead & M. Wolfenstein (Eds.), *Childhood in contemporary cultures*. Chicago: University of Chicago Press.

Syllabus of home economics. (1913). (Prepared by the Committee on Nomenclature and Syllabus). Washington, DC: American Home Economics Association.

Thomas, W. I., & Znaniecki, F. (1927). *The Polish peasant in Europe and America* (22nd ed.). New York: Knopf.

Thompson, P. (1988). *Home economics and feminism*. Prince Edward Island, Canada: Home Economics Publishing Collective.

Thwing, C. F., & Thwing, C. F. B. (1887). *The family: An historical study*. Boston: Lee and Shepherd.

Vail, G. (1961). [Keynote address, founding Alpha Tau Chapter of Omicron Nu, Provo, UT].

Walsh, W. H. (1958). *Philosophy of history*. New York: Harper.

Walz, T. H. (1975). The family, the family agency, and post-industrial society. *Social Casework, 56*, 13-20.

Warner, C. T., & Olson, T. D. (1981). Another view of family conflict and family wholeness. *Family Relations, 30*, 493-503.

Winch, R. F. (1971). *The modern family* (3rd ed.). New York: Holt, Rinehart & Winston.

3

The Professionalization of Family Life Education

Mary Jo Czaplewski
Stephen R. Jorgensen

IN HIS REVIEW of family life education in America, Kerckhoff (1964) identified three major issues and concerns in the professionalization of family life education. First, there was a lack of formal training in family life education, with many educators (specifically family life education teachers) trained in some other subject matter area but recruited into the field because of local circumstances. Formal training in family life education at that time was primarily at the graduate level, and most family life educators were dependent upon in-service training for both their preparation and their updating.

Problems in the recruitment and retention of family life educators were related to a second concern at the time, which focused on the progress of family life education toward professional status and on the establishment of specific standards and codes for the field. The latter was seen to be of particular importance, because, as Longworth (1952) stated, "Failure to establish requirements for the [state] certification of teachers of family living may eventually jeopardize the growth of the program" (p. 103).

Finally, the diverse backgrounds of family life educators were also recognized as an issue, as many different professional organizations claimed the allegiance of family life educators. Although this led to divided loyalties among some family life educators, still, according to Kerckhoff (1964), the National Council on Family Relations (NCFR) came to be seen as the "parent organization" for family life education, attracting individuals who had diverse disciplinary backgrounds but who shared a common interest in and concern for families.

Somerville identified some of the same professionalization issues in her 1971 decade review of family life education. She noted that two of the obstacles facing family life education at the time were the competition among disciplines for major responsibility in formulating and implementing family life programs and the lack of professionalization (i.e., inadequate teacher preparation opportunities and the lack of any established standards for family life and sex education). Because few broad preservice preparation programs were available, in-service education workshops were the primary force for preparing educators. She also identified legislation either mandating or prohibiting programs as a major force during the decade and suggested that, "legislatively, the field of family life education was wide open."

Attention to these issues of professionalization is of importance to family life education because of the basic assumption in the field that the family life educator plays a pivotal role in the success of family life programs (e.g., Fohlin, 1971; National Commission on Family Life Education, 1968). In fact, the educator may be the most important element in a family life program because it is ultimately the educator who develops and implements a program and who interacts directly with program participants.

In this chapter, the current status of the professionalization of family life education is examined. Attention will be given to the training or preparation of family life educators, to models of professionalization (accreditation, certification, and licensure), and to ethical issues in family life education. The chapter concludes with a discussion of some current and future issues that confront family life education in its progress toward greater professionalization.

PATTERNS OF PROFESSIONALIZATION

Various scholars have described the development of professions as following a pattern of sequential steps. These scholars appear to agree that professions evolve through similar stages (Caplow, 1954; East, 1980; Hayes, 1948; Weigley, 1976; Wilensky, 1964). Kerckhoff (1964) concluded that there was considerable difference of opinion among family life educators about the progress of family life education toward professional status. According to the framework provided by East (1980), the progress of family life education toward professional status can be measured by eight criteria.

1. *The activity becomes a full-time paid occupation.* There are thousands of full-time paid and degreed people practicing family life education at various educational levels and in various settings in the United States and abroad.

2. *Training schools and curricula are established.* Many departments and schools have been established at undergraduate and graduate levels in family life education and family studies. The first Ph.D. program in family life education was established by Ernest R. Groves in 1962 at Columbia University in New York.

3. *Those who are trained establish a professional association.* The established professional association most consistently supportive of the development of the knowledge base and practitioners of family life education and that has played a key role in its definitions is the National Council on Family Relations.

4. *A name, standards of admission, a core body of knowledge, and competencies for practice are developed.* A core body of knowledge and standards for practice have been established by the National Council on Family Relations through a voluntary certification process. Debate about professional name and breadth of the field continues, however.

5. *Internal conflict within the group and external conflicts from other professionals with similar concerns lead to a unique role definition.* Sex education, family therapy, and other subspecializations have given impetus to attempts at establishing a unique role for those who are family life educators. These unique roles have yet to be clearly defined, however.

6. *The public served expresses some acceptance of the expertise of those practicing the occupation.* Family life educators, though ambiguous about certain subareas such as sex education, which remains to be clarified, have been accepted in some states as having special expertise.

7. *Certification and licensure is the legal sign that a group is sanctioned for a particular service to society and that it is self-regulated.* Through the NCFR's Certification of Family Life Educators program and in various states that license family life educators to teach in the public schools or at county levels, this group is beginning to be recognized. For example, in Minnesota, parenting/family life teachers must now be licensed.

8. *A code of ethics is developed to eliminate unethical practice to protect the public.* This code is still in the developmental stages among U.S. practitioners.

It is clear that family life education is a new field and one that is moving toward the "professional" end of the continuum. Pressing issues still need resolution because of the number of characteristics that have influenced its development as a profession. Some issues are more socially volatile than those confronting other professional domains. According to Darling (1987), family life education is not free of value debates, nor is it a purely factual subspecialization delivered only in the traditional formal educational settings. The inclusion of sensitive issues such as sexuality, family violence, parental values, divorce, and remarriage has moral and ethical implications not encountered by many other professions.

Definitions of family life education often vary in terms of content, goals, teaching methods, timing of delivery, and audience (see Chapter 1). Debate continues as to the disciplinary home of family life education. Delivery by home economists, social scientists, psychologists, clergy, social workers, and others makes it difficult to determine its proper home despite the fact that family studies departments at the college and university levels appear to be the most logical places for these programs.

Further discussion and developments regarding the context of family life education must continue to take place before it can attain full status as a profession.

THE PREPARATION OF FAMILY LIFE EDUCATORS

One of the key components of any profession is the preparation of those who practice the profession. It is assumed that a major indicator of the health and viability of a profession is the degree to which practicing professionals are prepared with the requisite knowledge and skills to practice effectively and to accomplish the goals and objectives of the profession.

A review of the literature of family life education reveals that, although there are many beliefs and preferences regarding how family life educators should be prepared (see Flaherty & Smith, 1981; Luckey, 1981; Womble & Yeakley, 1980), a commonly accepted model for the preparation of family life educators is lacking (Thomas, 1989). Indeed, as Fisher and Kerckhoff (1981) have pointed out, family life educators have been prepared under myriad pedagogical theories, teaching methodologies, and subject matter orientations. Moreover, apart from outlining requirements for an appropriate knowledge base in family life education, relatively little has been written about the preservice preparation of family life educators. Instead, as suggested earlier, the emphasis has been placed on the role of in-service training in the preparation of family life educators.

To some extent, this state of affairs is not surprising, given the range and diversity of content areas, potential audiences, and disciplinary homes characteristic of family life educators. The complexity and sensitive nature of the content of family life education indicate, however, that careful consideration should be given to the development of particular skills and abilities during professional preparation (Darling, 1987; Fohlin, 1971).

The formal and informal procedures by which family life educators have been prepared will not be reviewed in this chapter. Rather, the focus will be on two aspects of professional preparation: (a) the paradigms or theoretical perspectives guiding educator preparation and their relevance for family life education and (b) the subject matter considered to be essential in the preparation of family life educators.

Teacher Education Paradigms and Family Life Education

Thomas (1989) used three predominant paradigms or theoretical perspectives of teacher education to analyze the stated beliefs and preferred practices as these are reflected in the literature concerned with the preparation of family life educators. Her analysis is reviewed here to illustrate how a clearly conceptualized professional preparation program for family life educators is currently lacking and to raise questions about possibilities for the development of such a program in the future.

Thomas based her analysis on the three paradigms of teacher education identified by Zeichner (1983): (a) behavioristic, (b) personalistic, and (c) inquiry oriented. Each paradigm or perspective embodies particular views of the learner, of society, of knowledge, of the educator, and of the purpose and process of education itself. Collectively, these views influence the organization and practices of educator preparation programs. The beliefs and assumptions underlying each perspective are briefly reviewed in relation to preferred family life education preparation practices.

The Behavioristic Paradigm

The behavioristic paradigm of teacher preparation is based on the stimulus-response model of psychology and reflects a technical orientation to learning in which the learner is viewed as a "passive consumer in the acquisition of knowledge" (Thomas, 1989, p. 5). Educators are viewed as technicians who impart specialized knowledge, skills, and competencies to the learner. This knowledge is viewed as a commodity to be acquired from the educator upon whom the learner is dependent, and it is assumed that learners use the knowledge gained from the educator to better fit into the existing social order. According to Tanner and Tanner, the behavioristic paradigm "connotes a kind of mechanistic function for education in which the learners are to be manipulated and shaped and in which their destiny is not of their own making" (1975, p. 118). In this paradigm, the preparation of educators is structured, formal, and relatively rigid, with emphasis placed on teaching methodologies and techniques and directed toward skill mastery and acceptance of the status quo in society.

Although Thomas (1989) found a number of examples of the behavioristic paradigm in the family life education literature, these examples were most often used in combination with other paradigms. Flaherty and Smith (1981), for example, recommended a "systems framework" for training sex educators in which teaching effectiveness would be evaluated in relation to specific measurable goals for classroom performance. Management and mastery of facts are paramount, and pre- and posttest knowledge and attitude scores are often the measure of training effectiveness. Other examples included recommendations that training for family life and sex educators include competency in teaching skills (Luckey, 1967; National Council on Family Relations, 1984) and the mastery of subject matter content as well as a thorough grounding in classroom methodology (Schulz & Williams, 1969). The combination of the behavioristic paradigm with other paradigms suggested that few family life educators view this as a central paradigm in the field.

One advantage of the behavioristic paradigm is generally considered to be the use of measurable outcomes in evaluating the success of programs (i.e., increases in knowledge, changes in attitudes). As Thomas (1989) pointed out, however, critics of this paradigm have argued that such approaches stifle personal growth and the development of sensitivity to moral, ethical, and political concerns. She noted that, because such concerns are pervasive in family life education, to treat them with indifference in the preparation of family life educators is potentially harmful to the total enterprise (Hartnett & Naish, 1980; Zeichner, 1983). It is also unlikely that attitude and value changes can be measured in behavioral terms. (See Chapter 5 for further discussion of this point.)

The Personalistic Paradigm

This paradigm of teacher preparation is based on humanistic psychology and phenomenology and views personal growth and self-actualization as central to learning. Attention is given to the needs of the learners, who are accorded an active role in the educational process (that is, education is seen as more than a one-way transmission of information from educator to learner). Although the mastery of factual information is considered to be important in this paradigm, it is equally (if not more) important that the educational process involve development of the "total person." In fact, knowledge is not viewed as fixed or static; rather, it is a subjective phenomenon. The personalistic paradigm considers how both educators and learners construct and organize their own personal realities and make autonomous choices based on these realities. Knowledge is seen to be a personal subjective phenomenon best tapped experientially. The learning environment is relatively unstructured, and the learner is encouraged to reflect upon his or her own thoughts and feelings.

According to Thomas (1989), teacher preparation programs that follow this paradigm portray the teacher as a "role model for the learner" (Sergiovanni, 1982, p. 137) and emphasize the development of autonomy, self-direction, and psychological maturity. Rarely does this paradigm promote a specific prescribed set of techniques or teacher behaviors. Rather, teachers are encouraged to discover for themselves the most appropriate means of relating to students and functioning as educators (Zeichner, 1983).

Thomas (1989) identified a number of examples of the personalistic paradigm in the family life education literature. This was most apparent in the concern that family life educators gain insight into their own feelings and attitudes about the subject matter of family life education (e.g., Arcus, 1979; Fohlin, 1971; Juhasz, 1970; Schulz & Williams, 1969). Luckey (1967) has described teacher training programs that prepared educators to gain such insight, and this goal is also reflected in more recent teacher preparation "models" (e.g., National Commission on Family Life Education, 1968; National Council on Family Relations, 1984; Pennsylvania Department of Education, 1969; Reed & Munson, 1976; Yarber & McCabe, 1981).

The personalistic paradigm is appealing to family life education because of its focus on the individual as a total person and on the development of healthy attitudes, values, and behavior patterns. As Thomas (1989) pointed out, however, this feature of the paradigm might also be its weakness. She argued that societal expectations regarding the participation of teachers in the educational process might be incompatible with what the teacher and/or the students believe should be covered and how it should be taught. It is possible that giving teachers and students too much freedom to pursue their own perceived needs and interests may result in family life education programs that are neither morally justified nor socially useful in accomplishing certain valued goals of family life education. It is questionable whether children and adolescents in particular are always in the best position to structure their own family life education experiences because they may not have had the relevant life experiences necessary to make such judgments, that is, to define what it is that they need to learn and to know.

Another potential weakness of the personalistic approach lies in its subjective focus on personal growth, self-awareness, and the evolution of program goals (in contrast to rationally derived a priori goals). This paradigm renders difficult the evaluation of measurable program outcomes and may be less amenable to evaluation research in the educational setting.

The Inquiry-Oriented Paradigm

The inquiry-oriented teacher preparation paradigm reflects an interactive or reciprocal view of the learner and the environment: The learner influences the environment and the environment influences the learner. This paradigm recognizes that, as a member of society, the individual has a responsibility to contribute in socially productive ways and thus it stresses the need for learners to develop critical thinking skills. Both family life educators and learners in family life programs are expected to draw upon cognitive and affective resources to reflect critically upon life situations and current social conditions. Knowledge is used to gain insight into issues and to solve socially relevant problems.

Inquiry-oriented teacher preparation emphasizes that existing reality is but one of many possible realities. It is the educator's responsibility, through the application of the skills of critical inquiry, to help foster a social reality that is conducive to the personal development and well-being of the members of a society. Educators are encouraged to continually monitor their own teaching behavior in terms of its effect on children, parents, the school, and the community, in ways that are morally and ethically justified.

Thomas (1989) found examples of the inquiry-oriented paradigm in preparing family life educators in the works of Arcus (1979), Hamburg (1968), Luckey (1967, 1968), and McFadden (1981). These authors stressed that educators must develop an awareness of local school and community conditions and work effectively within a particular social context. Additionally, educators must be prepared to help learners explore and understand diverse values and points of view without imposing one particular view on them (see Chapter 4 for further discussion on this issue).

As with the behavioristic and personalistic paradigms, the inquiry-oriented paradigm also has its limitations (Thomas, 1989). It may be difficult in this paradigm to evaluate teacher preparation programs in terms of their effectiveness and outcomes. Zeichner (1983) has referred to this paradigm as "fostering a disposition toward critical inquiry—a critical spirit" (p. 6). Thomas (1989), however, asked: How does one measure a critical orientation or a disposition toward such an orientation? And if one accepts the notion that family life education programs should deal with relevant issues in a critical, reflective manner, upon whose terms is "relevance" defined?

An Eclectic Approach to Preparation

Although there are numerous references in the family life education literature to the three paradigms described above, it is not clear that these paradigms have been critically examined or used in the development of specific preparation programs for family life educators. Indeed, a major limitation in the literature is the lack of attention to specific models for teacher preparation, whether or not these models are based on some justified theoretical approach. This is an area in need of major attention in family life education.

In the absence of such models, the preparation of family life educators appears to reflect some "eclectic" approach. Thomas (1989) has summarized the major elements of professional preparation for family life education (regardless of paradigm) as these emerged from her review of the literature. These major elements include

(a) knowledge in a variety of specific content areas;

(b) individual and group communication skills;

(c) using and evaluating family life materials and resources;

(d) appreciation of the multiplicity of contextual settings in which family life programs operate and of the influences these community characteristics exert on the type and nature of program offerings;

(e) insight into one's own feelings, attitudes, and self-perceptions;

(f) skill in creating a questioning atmosphere to encourage the development of critical thinking;

(g) skill in dealing with the formation of social attitudes and values; and

(h) ability to translate relevant research findings from a variety of disciplines into meaningful concepts for use in family life programs.

Although these elements are well supported in the literature, the extent to which they are indeed essential for family life education and can be attained in preparation programs for family life educators has not been subjected to systematic examination.

The Content of Family Life Education

The above review of teacher preparation paradigms has addressed the different ways in which educators may be prepared to enter the profession of family life education. These paradigms reflect different philosophical and theoretical orientations that an educator might bring to an educational setting as well as the manner in which ideas, facts, and values might be approached in family life programs. Although each paradigm holds a general view of the nature of knowledge, it clearly cannot address issues of specific content or subject matter.

A number of efforts have been made to clarify the subject matter content necessary for the preparation of family life educators (e.g., Committee on Educational Standards and Certification for Family Life Educators, 1970). The most recent formulation is that developed by a task force of the National Council on Family Relations (1984) as a part of the development of a certification program for family life educators. At the current time, the content areas deemed to be most important in the preparation of family life educators are listed in Table 3.1. Although this listing specifies the content to be included in a preparation program, it does not specify a particular curriculum or model to be followed. Rather, potential family life educators might obtain appropriate preparation in a variety of ways (formal course work in a college or university, preservice and in-service educational opportunities, fieldwork, self-study).

Although there is general agreement on the necessary content areas for the preparation of family life educators, a number of questions and issues relevant to preparation programs still require some attention.

1. Should preparation programs prepare specialists or generalists in family life education? While it is well recognized that some family life educators (e.g., public school teachers) require breadth in preparation in all of the content areas of family life education, others (e.g., specialists in sexuality education) have greater need for depth in only some content areas. What does this mean for designing appropriate and relevant family life education preparation programs? Is it possible to meet the needs both for breadth and for depth, and, if so, how is this best accomplished?

2. Do the diverse settings in which family life education may be offered make a difference in designing preparation programs? For example, are

TABLE 3.1. Family Life Education Substance Areas for Certification by NCFR (1984)

Families in society	Includes the study of various family structures and functions; sociocultural variations (social class, ethnicity, religion), dating, courtship, and marital choice; kinship (intergenerational relations); cross-cultural understanding of minority families; changing gender roles; current and future demographic trends; family history; the reciprocal influence of work and family roles; and the reciprocal influence of the family, as an institution of society, with other institutions (governmental, educational, religious, and economic)
Family dynamics	Includes internal family processes, such as communication and conflict management, stress and stress management, decision making and goal setting, family crises, and families with special needs (e.g., adoptive, migrant, foster, blended, and low-income families as well as military families and families with handicapped members)
Human growth and development	Includes study of human development across the life span, including social, emotional, physical, cognitive, personality, and moral development
Human sexuality	Includes study of reproductive physiology and biological aspects of sexuality, emotional and psychological aspects, sexual behavior and values, family planning, sexual response, sexual dysfunction, and the relationship between sexuality and interpersonal relationship development
Interpersonal relationships	Includes study of interpersonal skills, such as communication, problem solving, conflict management, self-disclosure, and listening; understanding love and intimacy; and effectively relating to others with concern, respect, responsibility, and sincerity
Family resource management	Includes study of such concepts as goals, resources, planning, decision making, and implementing as well as changing family resource management concerns over the family life cycle and across different family structures (e.g., single parents, blended families, dual earners)
Parent education and guidance	Includes study of the parenting process, rights and responsibilities of parents, parental roles over the life cycle, and variations in parenting practices

TABLE 3.1. (*continued*)

Family law and public policy	Includes study of historical development of family law; laws relating to marriage, divorce, family support, child custody, child protection and rights, and family planning; and public policy as it affects the family (e.g., civil rights, tax laws, social security, and economic support laws)
Ethics	Includes critical examination of ethical issues and questions, how attitudes and values are formed, recognition of diversity of human values and the complexity of value choice in contemporary society, understanding the social consequences of value choices, and recognition of ethical implications of social and technological changes
Family life education	Includes study of philosophy and principles of family life education; program planning and implementation; evaluating materials, students, and program effectiveness; sensitivity to other people and to community concerns and values; and recognizing the relationship between one's personal values and the various areas of family life education

the salient content areas different for educators in formal university or school settings than they are for educators who may operate in less formal settings such as churches, community agencies, or other settings for adult education?

3. Similarly, are there important differences in the potential audiences to which family life education programs may be targeted that might influence appropriate models of preparation in family life education? Should preparation programs be different for those who will deal with children and youth, with adults, and with the elderly?

The content areas shown in Table 3.1 were identified by the task force of the National Council on Family Relations (1984) based on the belief that the areas listed are linked, both theoretically and empirically, and that some exposure to and understanding of each of these areas is essential whether one is a specialist or a generalist in family life education. Nevertheless, the potential influence of the above issues on the development of family life education preparation programs presents major challenges for those who are involved in the development and evaluation of these programs. At the current time, these issues have not been the focus of systematic attention or investigation, and thus understanding of the most appropriate models for preparation is limited.

MODELS OF PROFESSIONALIZATION

Perhaps the most important quality expected of a professional practitioner in any discipline is competence. As far back as ancient Greek and Roman times, credentialing has been used as a form of quality assurance to the public consumer of professional services. For example, Roman Emperor Frederick II in the thirteenth century initiated the first credential for medical practice (Gilley & Eggland, 1989). For more than 40 years in American society, professional certification has been employed to distinguish competent practitioners from those who are not. Educators, lawyers, therapists, medical doctors, and public accountants are expected to have some type of credential that presents them in the public "eye" as a practitioner with an independent "seal of approval."

Intensifying the movement toward certification in the past decade has been the increasing service orientation of society. This trend has encouraged a rapid movement of individuals into training programs in many areas, leading to a supply of professionals that may exceed the demand for them. The result is increased competition for a limited number of positions and a desire to distinguish oneself as a professional with competencies above and beyond others in the field.

Compounding matters is evidence that public trust in certain professionals has eroded in recent years. For example, periodic surveys of occupational prestige indicate that lawyers are sometimes ranked with "used car" salesmen and that medical doctors are no longer accorded the status in which one would unequivocally trust them with one's life. Thus consumers are now asking to see additional credentials to assure the competence of professional practitioners.

According to a 1988 study of the American Society of Association Executives (ASAE), more than 450 professional and trade associations in the United States offer certification programs. (It is assumed that similar patterns occur in other countries.) These organizations have recognized that the rapid expansion of knowledge and technology has created a situation where updating of knowledge and skills is required so as to maintain one's competence at an acceptable level.

Three major processes of professionalization have been identified: licensure, accreditation, and certification (Bratton & Hildebrand, 1980). These processes differ from each other in (a) the recipient of the credential, (b) the certifying body, and (c) the degree of required volunteerism.

Licensure

With licensure, the individual is the recipient of the credential. Professional licenses are granted by a political body such as the state or provincial government because it is in the state's interest to protect its citizens from harm by incompetent practitioners. A license is generally required for practice and gives the individual holder the right to engage in a specific occupation or profession, to use a particular title, or to perform a specific function.

Some states that require licensure to teach early childhood family education in the public schools mandate an academic core of courses in order to teach (for example, Minnesota). Because of the complexity of the field, time and financial costs, and state autonomy for educating its citizens, licensure of family life educators in all states does not appear likely in the foreseeable future.

Accreditation

Accreditation is granted to professional programs (schools, colleges, universities, institutions) rather than to individuals. Such accreditation is granted by a professional association or agency to those programs that meet established qualifications and educational standards. These standards are maintained through an initial, then periodic, evaluation and then subsequent periodic reviews of the program. Accreditation is generally voluntary, except in cases where it is linked to licensure requirements.

The objectives, common elements, and benefits of accreditation have been identified by the American Society of Association Executives (1988), following a survey of hundreds of professional associations. The objectives of accreditation include

(a) creating an impetus for organizational self-improvement and stimulating general improvement of professional standards,

(b) offering evaluation and education on a voluntary basis as opposed to by government regulation,

(c) providing recognition of good performance and motivation to maintain and improve that performance, and

(d) protecting the interests of the general public as well as assisting prospective users in identifying acceptable institutions, programs of study, or services.

Because of the costliness, legal implications, and competitive nature of the accreditation process, it has been recommended that professional associations carefully consider all aspects of the decision to develop such a program (e.g., effective procedures to maintain operations on a professional basis, technical assistance for self-studies). Financial management of any accrediting operation must be in accordance with published policies and procedures, at reasonable fees, and in conformity with antitrust laws.

At the current time, no accrediting body approves preparation programs for family life educators. The American Home Economics Association (AHEA) accredits a broader core of academic program components, including family studies and human development. The American Association for Marriage and Family Therapy (AAMFT) accredits marriage and family therapy programs.

Certification

Certification is a voluntary credential granted by a nongovernmental professional association or agency to those individuals meeting the qualifications and criteria established by the professional association. According to the recent survey of professional organizations conducted by the American Society of Association Executives (1988), the objectives of certification programs are

(a) raising and maintaining the standards of the profession,
(b) encouraging self-assessment by offering guidelines for achievement,
(c) identifying individuals with acceptable knowledge of principles and practices of the profession and related disciplines,
(d) recognizing those with demonstrated high levels of competence and ethical fitness for the profession, and
(e) improving performance in the profession by encouraging participation in a continuing program of professional development.

Galbraith and Gilley (1987) identified the benefits of certification, many of which apply to family life education. They concluded that the greatest benefit of certification for the individual practitioners is that it clearly articulates the expectations of the profession, thus enabling them to perform their professional roles more effectively. This results in higher self-esteem for the certified individual, increased respect and recognition in the profession, increased remuneration and job benefits, and increased professional credibility due to a continuing analysis and evaluation of the individual's competence against standards established by the profession.

Certification can also benefit the certifying organization in that it provides structure and continuity to the field (Galbraith & Gilley, 1987).

The profession can better monitor the quality of practitioners in the regulation and restriction of entry into the profession. Member interest in continuing education provided by the certifying association is also stimulated. In some cases, academic programs preparing certification candidates are improved by the development of guidelines, course work, internships, and practicum experiences. In addition, it provides a vehicle for the orderly and efficient collection and consolidation of the body of knowledge of the profession.

Certification has potential drawbacks as well. Dissension in the profession is possible if some practitioners feel threatened, especially if procedures and implications of certification are ambiguously defined. If a field is multidisciplinary, as is the case with family life education, common core competencies may be difficult to isolate and define with an adequate level of consensus. In such circumstances, valid and reliable measurement of such competencies becomes an issue. A certification program can be costly if it is to effectively differentiate competent practitioners from others in a fair and nondiscriminatory manner in compliance with antitrust requirements. Written examinations, performance evaluations, and self-assessment documentation are three options for evaluation, but all are difficult to validate. Record-keeping, marketing, legal expenses, and other general operating costs all conspire to make certification an expensive process. Antitrust regulations prohibit discriminatory membership restrictions.

CERTIFICATION PROGRAMS IN FAMILY LIFE EDUCATION

Although several other professional associations certify in related fields of family life education, the National Council on Family Relations (NCFR) has maintained a certification program since 1984. Currently it is the only program specifically certifying family life educators across a broad range of content areas. The NCFR's certification purposes are fourfold (NCFR, 1984): (a) to evaluate the competencies of individual family life educators, (b) to raise and maintain professional standards in the field of family life education, (c) to identify the core body of knowledge as a guide for family life educators, and (d) to provide guidelines for the development of curriculum in the field of family life education. Applicants for certification are required to meet various criteria, including documentation of academic preparation and experience in 10 core content areas, current employment as a family life educator, and an ongoing record of professional development. No examination is required, but certification may be renewed after a 5-year interval and with documentation of continued professional development and practice.

The development of this credentialing program evolved from decades of research and study of family life education. A national commission published the report, "Family Life Education Programs: Principles, Plans, Procedures" (National Commission on Family Life Education, 1968), and criteria for the education of family life teachers were adopted in 1970 (Committee on Educational Standards, 1970). Standards of practice were developed and approved in 1978 (NCFR, 1984). In 1982 college and university curriculum guidelines were approved and a framework for planning and evaluating family life education programs over the life span was published (NCFR, 1984). The consultative process, field testing, and documentation of this multidisciplinary effort culminated in the certification program.

Other organizations also certify educators in more narrowly defined family life areas. The American Home Economics Association (AHEA, 1988) initiated the certification of home economists in 1986 and provides a broad, multidisciplinary credential that includes (but is not limited to) competencies in human development, family studies, communication, family policy, resource management, and education. There appear to be many similarities between the NCFR and AHEA certification programs in their emphasis on a broad perspective of family life education.

Since 1982 the American Association for Sex Educators, Counselors and Therapists (AASECT) has certified sex educators, counselors, and therapists, linking these professionals in an environment of professional training programs and conferences. This certification is linked to valid state licensure in related disciplines, such as psychology, medicine, nursing, social work, and marriage and family therapy. This program differs from that of the NCFR in that its focus is a more narrowly defined physiological conception of human sexuality, excluding such dimensions of family life education as relationship development, parenting, and resource management.

The National Board for Certified Counselors (NBCC), initiated in 1982 by the American Association for Counseling and Development (AACD), identifies counselors who have become voluntarily certified and maintains a registry of certified practitioners.

Social workers are certified by the Academy of Certified Social Workers (ACSW), a program of the National Association of Social Workers (NASW).

Finally, the American Association for Marriage and Family Therapy (AAMFT) accredits academic training programs in marital and family therapy and requires an extended period of supervisional practice before certification as a therapist is obtained. This subspecialization of the family field focuses on mental health and marriage and family interventions.

ETHICAL ISSUES IN THE PROFESSIONALIZATION OF
FAMILY LIFE EDUCATION

Ethics has been defined as "philosophical inquiry into the principles of morality, of right and wrong conduct, of virtue and vice, and of good and evil as they relate to conduct" (Ladd, 1978). As a branch of philosophy, ethics is concerned with philosophical thinking about morality and moral problems and arises when "we pass beyond the stage in which these rules are so internalized that we can be said to be inner-directed, to the stage in which we think for ourselves in critical and general terms . . . and achieve a kind of autonomy as moral agents" (Frankena, 1973, p. 4). As these statements indicate, the terms *ethics* and *morality* generally refer to the same thing, with the term *ethics* coming from the Greek and *moral* from the Latin (Arcus, 1986). (For more detailed explanations of ethics and morality, see, for example, Boyd, 1979; Frankena, 1973; Ladd, 1980; Peters, 1967.)

There are several reasons that ethics is important in family life education (Arcus, 1987). First, ethics has been identified as one part of the Framework for Life-Span Family Life Education, and it has also been listed as one of the curriculum areas for the certification of family life educators as established by the National Council on Family Relations (see Table 3.1; NCFR, 1984). Second, in their everyday living experiences, all individuals must make personal and social choices about critical questions and dilemmas in human experience. Because many of these questions and dilemmas are related to the subject matter of family life education, family life educators must be prepared to deal with these questions in the practice of family life education. Finally (as suggested earlier in this chapter), all professionals are held to be more or less accountable as professionals for their actions because of the potential impact of their actions on the lives of others. This accountability of professionals for their practice has led to concerns, both historically and more recently, about developing a code of ethics for family life educators.

According to the Professional Ethics Project of the American Association for the Advancement of Science (AAAS; Chalk, Frankel, & Chafer, 1980), codes of ethics may serve several purposes: to meet legal requirements, such as for the registration of a profession; to provide inspiration to members of a profession, encouraging them to act according to some specified set of ethical ideals; to alert members of a profession to ethical aspects of their work; to provide guidance for members in dealing with ethical problems and issues that may arise in their work; and to serve as a disciplinary code to enforce particular rules and to protect the integrity of the profession. Codes of ethics may also serve "nonethical" purposes such as serving as a status symbol for a profession or helping to protect the monopoly of a profession (Arcus, 1986).

Many professional organizations have adopted codes of ethics for members in the practice of their profession. As early as 1848, the American Medical Association adopted such a code (Jacobs, 1983). By 1926 over 300 service and professional associations used codes of ethics to foster ethical conduct by their members. This is the essence of professional self-regulation. Ethical regulation can be achieved either by the private sector as a voluntary mechanism or by public agencies such as federal, state, and local governments. Clearly, many professional associations have chosen the former route.

Although family life education has existed since the turn of the century (see Chapter 2), there is no universally accepted code of ethics specifically designed for family life educators. This does not mean, of course, that family life educators are not accountable to any code of ethics, because many family life educators are also members of other associations that have adopted (and sometimes enforce) codes of ethics for their members. These include organizations such as the American Association for Marriage and Family Therapy, the American Home Economics Association, the National Association for the Education of Young Children, and the National Association of Social Workers. As well, family life educators may work in settings that are governed by general codes of ethics. For example, most researchers, including family life education researchers, are obligated to ethical codes regarding research on both human and animal subjects; family life educators in government settings may be covered by ethical codes regarding conflicts of interest; and family life education teachers may be regulated by codes of ethics that apply to all teachers.

In spite of the presence of these other codes of ethics, however, there is concern that family life education develop its own code of ethics. Even if there is no legal obligation for a code of ethics, such codes are seen as desirable, indicating that the profession has "come of age" as a profession and providing some visible evidence of the concern of the profession for its scholarly and professional accountability (Arcus, 1986).

If family life education is to develop its own code of ethics, several issues will need to be addressed. According to the AAAS Professional Ethics Project (Chalk et al., 1980), the first step is to determine the appropriate goals and functions of the code. If the code is designed simply to meet some legal requirement, then almost any set of statements will be sufficient. If, however, "the code is intended to be a disciplinary and thus a quasi-legal document, then statements must be carefully selected and worded, not only to address major ethical situations facing members of the association, but also to make it very clear what these members may do, must do, and must not do in these situations" (Arcus, 1986, p. 67).

At the current time, this kind of groundwork for a code of ethics in family life education has not been carried out. For example, little attention has been given to specifying the central ethical values of family life education and to gaining sufficient consensus on these values so that they may, in fact, serve as the basis of a code of ethics. Little attention has been given to the identification of the major ethical issues and problems faced by family life educators in their practice. Levy (1978) has suggested that codes of ethics are meaningless outside of the context of the specific roles, functions, and beliefs of a profession. If this is true, then it may not be possible to develop a single code of ethics for family life education that will be appropriate for those who practice in diverse settings such as schools, churches, community agencies, and businesses.

Other issues must also be addressed. For example, many important terms used in codes of ethics (e.g., *respect, loyalty, integrity*) are seldom defined and may be interpreted differently by family life educators. If statements in the codes are too general, then it may not be possible to determine in fact what professional action is permitted or prohibited. Because statements in codes of ethics reflect the ethical values of the profession, it is inevitable that some of these statements will come into conflict with each other. In such a case, when it is not possible to implement one statement without violating another, what is a professional to do? Reamer (1982) has addressed such issues in the field of social work, and his work may have relevance for family life education.

In developing codes of ethics, it is also important to distinguish between conduct that is unprofessional and conduct that is unethical; that is, it is important that codes of ethics address professional ethics (matters of right and wrong and good and bad in professional conduct) rather than professional etiquette. Many existing codes of ethics have been criticized because they emphasize relationships with professional colleagues and the protection of the reputation of the profession (both matters of professional etiquette) rather than safeguarding the interests of clients, subjects, or society as a whole (Chalk et al., 1980; Levy, 1976).

Finally, as family life educators develop ethical codes for members of the profession to follow, it is important to understand the legal ramifications of doing so. If regulatory codes of ethics are used, for whatever reason, to discipline or expel professional family life educators from an association or to strip an individual of certification status, then certain laws will apply (Webster, 1979). Alleged violators of ethics codes must be informed in writing of the nature of the charge and the proposed sanction; they must be given an opportunity to respond to charges; and they must be afforded due process (i.e., a hearing or other acceptable mechanism for filing an appeal; Jacobs, 1983). Codes of ethics should be enforced in a fair and impartial manner; that is, codes of ethics must also be ethical.

Family life education as a young and developing profession is just beginning serious discussion of ethical codes. It is thus appropriate to raise critical questions rather than offering prescriptive answers. The Family Discipline Section of the NCFR has begun such a study. It will be necessary to recognize in advance that issues will be complex, that lessons can be learned from other professions who have struggled through the process, that the strengths inherent in the profession can be of value if reflective and critical analysis takes place, that involvement at all levels of the profession will be necessary, and that ethical concerns must ultimately be responsive to the families and individuals served by the profession.

FUTURE CHALLENGES FOR THE PROFESSIONALIZATION OF FAMILY LIFE EDUCATION

Although family life education programs in one form or another have existed for decades, the profession itself in many ways has not matured as rapidly as others. It has remained somewhat fragmented, with multiple specializations professionally insulated from each other (Fisher & Kerckhoff, 1981). It has an uncertain identity in formal and informal educational systems as well as among its own practitioners. A number of legal issues have yet to be settled in regard to the credentialing of programs and individuals, and widely accepted codes of ethics have been slow in coming. There is no single professional association that represents the range and diversity of family life education content areas and that serves as an advocate for the family life education profession. The National Council on Family Relations has, more than other organizations, made significant contributions to the professionalization of family life education through research and, most recently, the development of family life education certification.

The professionalization of family life education can be enhanced by more carefully articulated programs in higher education to train educators in the various content areas. This will entail further development and use of a conceptual framework that will integrate the disciplines and content of family life education. Performance standards for teachers, as well as students, need to be developed, evaluated, and refined to assess the effectiveness of teacher training and student learning in a more reliable manner than is currently accepted. This will require further study and discussion of the timing of preservice and in-service teacher education. The potential benefits of family life education must be more clearly linked to predefined program goals (e.g., the reduction of teenage sexual activity or pregnancy, more effective parenting behavior, or stronger, more fulfilling interpersonal relationships) in a way that shows such education to be good for society by fostering the development of individuals and their families (for a different perspective on this point, see Chapter 5). This will require thoughtful study of the critical role played by family members as educators. Programs of accreditation and certification must be expanded and improved to cement the quality assurance aspect of the profession. Empirical evaluations must be used to show the real and potential benefits of family life education. Finally, it is important that one or more professional associations concerned with family life education assume a stronger position of leadership in building the professional image of the family life educator, in enhancing the credibility of the profession, and in effectively "marketing" the profession in a way that will allow it to become a more integral part of the fabric of modern society.

Accomplishing these tasks will enhance the credibility of the profession in the eyes of the public and relevant social institutions, such as the systems of public and private education for children and adolescents. Clearly, family life education is not seen as a subject as essential for youth as mathematics, English, history, or social studies. As long as policy formulators and educational administrators perceive family life education to be nonessential in the total educational process, the development of the profession in this important arena will be limited. The family life education profession simply must find avenues that will enhance its image as a legitimate profession in the public eye.

Professional family life educators in less formal settings than those offered by the schools face a similar dilemma. Individuals and families will not choose to participate in family life education programs unless the offerings are perceived to be potentially useful. Here, too, marketing, public relations, and the leadership of nationally respected professional associations will be needed to provide a greater impetus for potential clients to seek out and to use family life education.

The advancements made in the past several years in the professionalization of family life education have been remarkable. Nonetheless, much remains to be done to enhance the professional image of the family life educator, to increase the demand for the services that this individual can provide, and to place professional family life educators in a position to create the kind of significant positive impact on society that they are truly capable of creating.

REFERENCES

American Home Economics Association. (1988, September). *Certification of home economists: Professional development unit guidelines and certification renewal policies.* Washington, DC: Author.

American Society of Association Executives. (1988). *Policies and procedures in association management.* Washington, DC: Author.

Arcus, M. E. (1979). Inservice education in family life education. *Canadian Journal of Education, 4,* 43-52.

Arcus, M. E. (1986). A code of ethics for the Canadian Home Economics Association. *Canadian Journal of Home Economics, 26*(2), 66-69.

Arcus, M. E. (1987, November 16). *Education in ethics for family life educators: Goals, strategies, and problems.* Paper presented at the National Council on Family Relations Annual Conference, Atlanta, GA.

Boyd, D. A. (1979). An interpretation of principled morality. *Journal of Moral Education, 8,* 110-123.

Bratton, B., & Hildebrand, M. (1980). Plain talk about professional certification. *Instructional Innovator, 25*(9), 22-24, 29.

Caplow, T. (1954). *The sociology of work.* New York: McGraw-Hill.

Chalk, R., Frankel, M. S., & Chafer, S. B. (Eds.). (1980). *AAAS Professional Ethics Project: Professional ethics activities in the scientific and engineering societies.* Washington, DC: American Association for the Advancement of Sciences.

Committee on Educational Standards and Certification for Family Life Educators. (1970). Family life and sex education: Proposed criteria for teacher education. *The Family Coordinator, 19*(2), 183.

Darling, C. A. (1987). Family life education. In M. Sussman & S. Steinmetz (Eds.), *Handbook of marriage and the family* (pp. 815-833). New York: Plenum.

East, M. (1980). *Home economics: Past, present, and future.* Boston: Allyn & Bacon.

Fisher, B. L., & Kerckhoff, R. K. (1981). Family life education: Generating cohesion out of chaos. *Family Relations, 30,* 505-511.

Flaherty, C., & Smith, P. B. (1981). Teacher training for sex education. *Journal of School Health, 51,* 261-264.

Fohlin, M. B. (1971). Selection and training of teachers for life education programs. *The Family Coordinator, 20,* 231-240.

Frankena, W. K. (1973). *Ethics* (2nd ed.). Englewood Cliffs, NJ: Prentice-Hall.

Galbraith, M. W., & Gilley, J. W. (1987). Professionalization and professional certification: A relationship. In *Proceedings of the 28th Annual Adult Education Research Conference* (pp. 96-102). Washington, D.C.: American Society of Association Executives.

Gilley, J., & Eggland, S. A. (1989). *Principles of human resource development.* New York: Addison-Wesley.

Hamburg, M. W. (1968). Sex education in the elementary school . . . teacher preparation. *National Elementary Principal, 48,* 52-56.

Hartnett, A., & Naish, M. (1980). Technicians or social bandits? Some moral and political issues in the education of teachers. In P. Woods (Ed.), *Teacher strategies* (pp. 255-273). London: Croom Helm.

Hayes, W. J. (1948). The place of sociology in professional education. *Social Forces, 26*, 292-298.

Jacobs, J. W. (1983). Vehicles for self regulation: Codes of ethics, credentialing, standards. In *Selected materials in legal aspects of professional credentialing*. Washington, DC: Jacobs, Leighton, Conklin, Lemov, and Bruckley.

Juhasz, A. M. (1970). Characteristics essential to teachers in sex education. *Journal of School Health, 40*, 17-18.

Kerckhoff, R. K. (1964). Family life education in America. In H. T. Christensen (Ed.), *Handbook of marriage and the family* (pp. 881-911). Chicago: Rand McNally.

Ladd, J. (1978). The task of ethics. In W. T. Reich (Editor-in-chief), *Encyclopedia of bio-ethics* (Vol. 1, pp. 400-407). New York: Free Press.

Ladd, J. (1980). The quest for a code of professional ethics: An intellectual and moral confession. In R. Chalk, M. S. Frankel, & S. B. Chafer (Eds.), *AAAS Professional Ethics Project: Professional ethics activities in scientific and engineering societies* (pp. 154-159). Washington, DC: American Association for the Advancement of Science.

Levy, C. S. (1976). *Social work ethics*. New York: Human Sciences.

Levy, C. S. (1978, July). In search of a professional code of ethics. *NASW News, 23*(7), 6-7.

Longworth, D. S. (1952). Certification of teachers of family living: A proposal. *Marriage and Family Living, 14*, 103-104.

Luckey, E. B. (1967). Family life and/or sex ed? *Journal of Marriage and the Family, 29*, 377-380.

Luckey, E. B. (1968). Sex education and an in-service training program. *Family Coordinator, 17*, 89-95.

Luckey, E. B. (1981). Higher education: Instruction, research, and service. *Family Relations, 30*(4), 631-636.

McFadden, J. R. (1981). Family life education and university outreach. *Family Relations, 30*, 637-642.

National Commission on Family Life Education. (1968). Family life education programs: Principles, plans, procedures: A framework for family life educators. *The Family Coordinator, 17*, 211-214.

National Council on Family Relations. (1984). *Standards and criteria for the certification of family life educators, college/university curriculum guidelines, and an overview of content in family life education: A framework for planning life span programs*. Minneapolis, MN: Author.

Pennsylvania Department of Education. (1969). *Recommended standards for sex education teachers*. Harrisburg: Author.

Peters, R. S. (1967). *Ethics and education*. Glenview, IL: Scott, Foresman.

Reamer, F. G. (1982). *Ethical dilemmas in social service*. New York: Columbia University Press.

Reed, D. A., & Munson, H. E. (1976). Resolution of one's sexual self: An important first step for sexuality educators. *Journal of School Health, 46*, 31-34.

Schulz, E. D., & Williams, S. R. (1969). *Family life and sex education: Curriculum and instruction*. New York: Harcourt, Brace.

Sergiovanni, T. J. (1982). *Supervision of teaching*. Alexandria, VA: ASCD Yearbook Committee.

Somerville, R. M. (1971). Family life and sex education in the turbulent sixties. *Journal of Marriage and the Family, 33*, 11-35.

Tanner, D., & Tanner, L. (1975). *Curriculum development: Theory into practice*. New York: Macmillan.

Thomas, J. (1989). *Alternative paradigms of teacher education and the preparation of family life educators: Using theory to guide practice.* Unpublished manuscript, University of British Columbia, Vancouver.

Webster, G. D. (1979). *Law of associations.* New York: Matthew Bender.

Weigley, E. S. (1976). The professionalization of home economics. *Home Economics Research Journal, 4,* 253-259.

Wilensky, H. L. (1964). The professionalization of everyone? *American Journal of Sociology, 70,* 142-146.

Womble, D. L., & Yeakley, E. B. (1980). A review of the academic preparation of some Indiana secondary school family life educators and the state's new certification requirements. *Family Relations, 29*(2), 151-153.

Yarber, W. L., & McCabe, G. P. (1981). Teacher characteristics and the inclusion of sex education topics in grades 6-8 and 9-11. *Journal of School Health, 51,* 288-290.

Zeichner, K. M. (1983). Alternative paradigms of teacher education. *Journal of Teacher Education, 34*(3), 3-9.

4

Values and Family Life Education

Margaret E. Arcus
LeRoi B. Daniels

VALUES HAVE LONG BEEN recognized as a theme in family life education and as a problem confronting family life educators (Darling, 1987; Kerckhoff, 1964; Rodman, 1970; Somerville, 1971). Questions have been raised about the role of values in family life education and about the appropriate responses of family life educators to various values issues and concerns. What values should (or should not) be included in family life education programs? Should educators share their personal values with participants? What is the best way to handle controversial values questions? How should family life educators deal with potential differing values among the various family life education stakeholders—parents, children, the community, the state, the family life educator, and the field itself?

In spite of the importance and centrality of values in family life education, inadequate attention has been given to addressing these (and other) values questions. Thomas and Arcus (1992), for example, have identified the need to examine the normative beliefs of family life education as a part of clarifying the concept of family life education. According to Somerville (1971), family life educators have continued to have difficulty examining value systems objectively, and Rodman (1970) has suggested that schools in particular often bungle the opportunity to teach values. As well, family life educators have continued to be troubled by value judgments (e.g., Arcus, 1980; Pollis, 1985), and little work has been done on important ethical concerns and standards in the field

(Leigh, Loewen, & Lester, 1986). Thus, at the current time, there appears to be a major need in family life education to address more systematically the values content of family life education.

The purpose of this chapter is to review the literature on values and values education so as to provide perspectives and insights that might assist family life educators in addressing the central values issues in family life education. The chapter will address three major topics: (a) a brief historical overview of the role of values in family life education, (b) a clarification of several central aspects of the concept of values, and (c) a review and critique of major approaches to values education. The chapter will conclude with a brief discussion of several key issues and challenges related to the values content of family life education.

THE ROLE OF VALUES IN FAMILY LIFE EDUCATION

As described elsewhere in this handbook (see Chapters 1 and 2), family life education in North America developed around the turn of the century in response to felt social needs. In his review of family life education in America, Kerckhoff noted that early efforts in family life education had "many of the aspects of a reform movement" and were "designed to correct a bad situation" (1964, p. 898). This bad situation had resulted from the perceived inadequacies of families in dealing with social change and was reflected in an apparent loss of social control over family members, especially children and youth. According to Kerckhoff, at least some people at the time believed that there were better ways to do things in families and that these better ways were known and should be taught to individuals and families. Underlying this belief was a strong assumption that everyone (or at least everyone who counted) believed the same things, and the literature of the time included many relatively unchallenged assertions about the rightness or wrongness of family behaviors. In this context, the task for family life education was simply to convince people to do these "right things" (and presumably avoid the wrong things), and then "the divorce rate would drop, children would be reared properly, and the institution of the family would be saved" (Kerckhoff, 1964, p. 898). Thus values (i.e., the right things) were "part and parcel of the field from the beginning" (Kerckhoff, 1964, p. 898).

As family life education developed as an educational specialty, however, greater emphasis was placed on the use of scientific findings, and values came to be seen as both an issue and a problem. Christensen (1964), for example, distinguished between what he called the legitimate and the illegitimate "intrusions" of values into social science. According to Christensen, legitimate values in social science included accepting the scientific method as a valid approach to truth, selecting research problems that have potential utility, using values as data in research, and determining the best means to a chosen end. Values that were illegitimate (i.e., not legitimate) included such things as the values of subjects that got in the way of research instruments or those of the social scientists themselves who valued other things (i.e., had a reform orientation) more highly than they did science. Although not all family scholars were in agreement on the role of values in the social sciences (some, for example, believed that social scientists had an *obligation* to assume active leadership in helping to shape action for the benefit of society), the positivistic view of science as "value free" came to predominate in the family field. In this positivistic view, values were seen as noncognitive, emotive, and relativistic or personalistic in nature and thus not subject to any rational examination or validation (e.g., Christensen, 1964).

The presence in family life education of both a reform orientation concerned with improving family living and a "scientific" orientation that saw values as illegitimate or inappropriate has presented several problems for family life educators, with discussions and debates revolving around several broad questions (Kerckhoff, 1964): Should values be taught in family life education? Whose values (or which values) should be taught? Can we teach values? How can values be taught? Some believed that teaching values was "both desirable and unavoidable" (Bowman, 1957, p. 325), while others suggested that values should not be taught in family life education as there was no one value system upon which all could agree (Kerckhoff, 1957). As long as family life educators remained unclear about whether or not values belonged in family life education, they were also unclear about the remaining questions: what values (if any) to teach, and when and how to go about teaching them.

At the current time, there are several indications that values have been accepted as an appropriate and inevitable part of family life education. The National Commission on Family Life Education (1968), for example, noted that those working in family life education should be able to assist in the formation of social attitudes and values and should help both youth and adults to clarify their own views and expand their thinking beyond their own value structures. A position paper on family life education prepared by the National Council on Family Relations (1970) stated that the importance of personal integrity and family responsibility should be emphasized in family life education and that programs should reflect awareness of and sensitivity to the variety of moral viewpoints present in the field (although the position paper did not indicate what these various viewpoints were). More recently, the

Framework for Life-Span Family Life Education has identified ethics as one of seven major topic areas in family life education (Arcus, 1987; National Council on Family Relations, 1984). (This framework is reproduced in the Appendix of this volume.)

Further indication of the acceptance of values as a central part of family life education may be found in the many programs and curriculum guides that include goals and experiences dealing with values. Typical values goals and objectives include clarifying personal and family values; understanding how values influence human behavior; recognizing diversity in personal and family values and accepting these value differences; examining value systems; satisfying needs in ways beneficial to self, family, and society; and developing critical thinking skills. It should be noted that, although these indicate some of the explicitly stated goals of family life education programs, there are likely other values in these programs that are implicit or hidden rather than explicit. In family life education, typical values assignments and experiences related to these goals include completing values questionnaires, ranking values on checklists, clarifying values through exercises and activities, debating values issues, and examining case studies for evidence of values and value conflicts.

Although the above indicates the apparent acceptance of values in family life education, the "remaining questions" identified earlier still require attention: What values, if any, should be taught in family life education? When and how should family life educators go about teaching them?

THE NATURE OF VALUES

Clearly, values have a central role in family life education. In spite of this important role, however, there appears to be both confusion about and discomfort with the concept of values. Many family life education documents, for example, have used the terms *values, attitudes,* and *opinions* interchangeably, and at least some educators appear to assume that *any* talk about values is the same as values education. As well (as noted earlier), some family life educators have been troubled by value judgments and how to handle them within family life education programs (Arcus, 1980; Pollis, 1985). Although some of this discomfort and confusion may reflect complexities inherent in the nature of values, at least some may indicate a misunderstanding of that nature.

In many ways, this confusion should not be surprising. The concept of values is frequently used both in the social sciences and in education, but it has seldom been treated as a subject for careful analysis (Daniels,

1975). Rather, scholars have developed what Scheffler (1960) called "stipulative definitions"; that is, an author stipulates that, for his or her own purposes, the term will be defined in a particular way, regardless of how others might use the same term. Although these stipulative terms can be meaningful in the context of an individual author's work, the variety of definitions has resulted in considerable ambiguity and inconsistency in the use of the term. Rescher (1969) has developed a short list of definitions of *values* that indicates both the variety and the "looseness" with which this term is used in the scholarly literature.

It is not possible to provide here a full account of the nature of values. Rather, the intent is to summarize some of the aspects of values that appear to have particular relevance to family life education. First, the major features of the concept of values will be identified, and these will be distinguished from related concepts such as attitudes, opinions, and tastes or preferences. Second, the different kinds of values will be explained, in particular those kinds of values most central to family life education: moral/ethical, cultural, religious, and personal. Third, attention will be given to the nature of value judgments, as such judgments have often been problematic for family life educators. Finally, reference will be made to the different levels of analysis of values that are possible and to the significance of this for family life education.

The Concept of Values

It is important to recognize that the term *values* may be used in several different ways (Daniels, 1975). For example, it may be used as a verb to indicate that one holds something in high regard ("I value cooperation"), or it may be used as an adjective to express the concept of worth ("That is a wise decision"). As well, *values* may be used as a noun to ascribe features to individuals or groups ("Her values are conservative ones"). As will become apparent later in this chapter, all of these uses may be found in family life education. Confusion among family life educators regarding these uses will also become apparent.

According to Daniels, the concept of values is a "psycho-normative concept"; that is, it is a concept used "to inform us about certain psychological traits or states of people, and to indicate the normative stances of the person—how he or she appraises and evaluates the world" (Daniels, 1975, p. 21). Rescher has described values (traits and stances) as "things of the mind that have to do with the visions people have of 'the good life' for themselves and their fellows" (Rescher, 1969, p. 4). Baier also has stated that the subject matter of values is "the good life and how to come closer to it" (Baier, 1965, p. 57). Thus values are expressed using concepts

that judge things with respect to their worth and that are "core conceptions of the desirable within every individual and society" (Rokeach,
1973, p. 2).

Two elements are involved in talk about values: (a) an evaluative
claim that some state of affairs is good or worthwhile (or bad or worth-
less) and (b) an empirical claim that realizing this state of affairs will
bring about some favorable (or unfavorable) difference to oneself and/or
to others. Some might claim, for example, that family life education is a
good thing (an evaluative claim) because it improves family communication or because it prevents family violence (both empirical claims).
Others might, of course, claim that family life education is a bad thing
because it causes conflict between parents and children. Any serious
attempt at values education will need to give attention to both of these
elements—that is, to whether or not the implied evaluations are justified
or defensible and to whether or not the empirical claims are true (Daniels,
1975). Attention to both of these elements will also be important in
dealing with the value-laden and often political context of family life
education.

Other Psycho-normative Concepts

Values are often confused with other psycho-normative concepts
such as attitudes, beliefs, emotions, and feelings (Daniels, 1975). This is
not surprising because these concepts share some of the same features
and thus are to some extent enmeshed with each other. Of most concern
in family life education is the confusion between the concept of values
and the concepts of attitudes, opinions, and preferences.

The concepts of values and attitudes are similar in that the analysis
of each involves both empirical and normative claims. What distin-
guishes them is illustrated by the following:

> When we ask "What's your attitude toward abortion?" we usually don't
> mean, "What's your moral attitude toward abortion?" or "What's your eco-
> nomic attitude?" Instead we want to know your on-the-whole evaluation of
> abortion. Unlike values, which must involve evaluations from some one point
> of view [as will be seen below], attitudes involve **summary** evaluations. In
> fact, if we simply say "My attitude toward X is Y," the listener will take us to
> be offering our evaluation, **all things considered.**" (Daniels, 1975, p. 31)

Thus, while values indicate evaluations made from some *one* specific
point of view (e.g., a moral, legal, or economic point of view), attitudes
reflect a person's *summary* evaluations.

There is another pervasive view of values, which is that all values are relative. This is sometimes expressed by saying that values are merely matters of opinion—unlike, it is typically argued, claims made in the sciences. It may be useful here to contrast "holding an opinion" with "knowing something." To know something implies that one believes something and that one has what one regards as sufficient evidence to support it (Scheffler, 1965). If one's claim to know is challenged *and* if one is uncertain about the supporting evidence, however, then a typical response is to say something like, "Well, that's my opinion." To say that something is an opinion is to avoid claiming that one has adequate evidence. One can have opinions about either empirical or values issues. In other words, "to know" as contrasted with "to have an opinion" cuts across the distinction between empirical and value claims. The "know-opinion" contrast has to do with whether or not there is adequate evidence for the claim—whether it's an empirical or a value claim. The "empirical-value" contrast has to do with the kind of claim being made. Values claims or empirical claims may be either knowledge claims or expressions of opinion. Not all value claims are opinions.

Statements expressing values may also be confused with statements of taste or of preference. To say that a certain family life education program is successful or that a certain family life educator is ineffective is to make a value claim about, respectively, the program and the educator. To say, however, that one likes the family life program or dislikes the family life educator does not say anything at all about either the program or the educator. Rather, it says something about the speaker, namely, that the speaker likes the program and does not like the educator. It is, in fact, an empirical claim about the speaker. To hold that value claims are simply claims of taste or preference is to confound value and empirical claims. Clearly, values and preferences are interrelated, but an individual's values and preferences may not always be consistent. One may believe, for example, that smoking is bad for one's health (indicating that smoking has a negative value) but like to smoke anyway.

To summarize the distinctions among these psycho-normative concepts: making a value claim says something positive or negative about the subject under discussion; having an attitude indicates a person's summary view of a particular thing; and expressing a preference provides information about the person who expresses the preference. Thus giving an opinion or expressing an attitude is not the same as assigning value or worth to an object or to an action for some kind of reason. These concepts are different, and these differences must be recognized if efforts at values education are to be sound and relevant.

These distinctions are of considerable importance because values require things of those who hold them. According to Rokeach (1973), values press claims and make demands on both one's thoughts and one's actions and thus have some "authority" over the individual. Holding a value represents a commitment to certain kinds of aims and calls for certain kinds of conduct. To hold the value of honesty or of equality, for example, requires that one think and act in ways that reflect these values.

Thus, not only are one's values more than personal opinions or preferences, they are in fact guides that help one to orient choice and judgment and that play an important role in one's deliberation and decision making. Because one's values make demands and are used to orient and justify choices, they obviously shape one's life in important ways and have important consequences for human behavior. It should be noted that, in addition to this "forward-looking" role of values (to guide goal-directed and anticipatory behavior), values may also be "backward-looking" in that they may be used to justify or explain one's past behavior (Williams, 1973).

Kinds of Values

There are many different kinds of values (e.g., Association for Values Education and Research, 1978). Although it is not possible to provide an exhaustive list here, some of the most important kinds include moral and ethical values, religious values, aesthetic values, health values, economic values, legal values, cultural values, educational values, personal values, and prudential values. Most of these kinds of values are relevant to the purposes and the subject matter of family life education.

Most of these kinds of values are also obvious and self-explanatory: Aesthetic values have to do with beauty; health values have to do with safety and nutrition; and so on. Because one of the major operating principles in family life education is to "respect differing individual and family values" (see Chapter 1), however, special attention needs to be given to moral and ethical values and to the relationship of moral and ethical values to cultural, religious, and personal values.

Moral and Ethical Values

Although many family life educators (as well as many family life education participants) are often uncomfortable with the word *moral* (perhaps because it carries overtones of repression and guilt), the words *ethics* and *morality* essentially mean the same thing and can be used interchangeably (Frankena, 1973; Lacey, 1976). These terms pertain to human conduct and character and generally refer to those actions that it makes sense to describe as right or wrong or good or bad and that are concerned with actions likely to have helpful or harmful effects on the lives of others (Ladd, 1978). Moral/ethical values are expressed in principles or rules of right conduct, for example, "we ought to tell the truth" and "we ought to keep our promises" (Gert, 1966; Schulte & Teal, 1975). Although no systematic attention has been given to identifying and justifying specific values central to family life education, one can infer from the literature of the field the importance of moral and ethical values such as personal integrity, tolerance for diverse viewpoints, social responsibility, respect for persons, and equality. (See, for example, the Framework for Life-Span Family Life Education in the Appendix.)

The key point of ethics and morality is to go beyond personal self-interest to consider equally and impartially the rights and the interests of all involved in a situation. The intention here is to rule out favoritism or preference for any one group or individual over another (Coombs, 1975). For example, it would be unacceptable that an accused be judged in a court controlled by her or his relatives, even if there were no law against this. Further, although there are no laws against it, many recognize the immorality of the enormous disparity of resources between the "First World" and the "Third World." Each of these examples is immoral because it involves unwarranted favoritism; in the former, the special interests of some take precedence over fairness; in the latter, millions of people are put at risk while others prosper.

A second intention, equally important, is to consider whether or not potential harm to some people can ever be justified. Coombs (1980) has referred to this as the "moral hazard" of a situation. The situation of the Third World is a clear case of moral hazard for the First World. Within family life education, there are many opportunities to discuss issues involving moral hazard. For example, violence against women and children, racism, the marginalization of gays and lesbians, and the treatment of indigenous peoples all involve moral hazard and clearly are relevant to what happens in families.

It is not possible to elaborate more fully on moral and ethical values here but, for more detailed explanations, see Boyd (1979), Frankena (1973), and Thiroux (1986).

Cultural Values

In one sense, every value is a cultural value, because the central way in which one acquires values is by acquiring a language, and language is a public cultural artifact. Among other things, language is used to express commitment to certain values, and it would be difficult to imagine a culture that does not contain, for example, legal, economic, aesthetic, moral, and intellectual values.

Two important points about cultural values are significant to family life education. First, all cultures will have some commitment both to a set of dominant ideals and to a set of greatest fears. In general, the relevance and purpose of moral principles in a particular culture is to facilitate the attainment of the dominant ideals (e.g., to attain equality or familial continuity) and the avoidance of the greatest fears (e.g., to avoid exploitation or the loss of autonomy). Family life educators who work with multicultural groups (and nearly all groups are multicultural ones) will need to be aware of and sensitive to not only expressions of cultural differences but also how these differences represent cultural attempts to accomplish their ideals and to avoid their fears. (See Chapter 7 for a discussion of the implications of multicultural societies for family life education.)

Second, because cultures do not remain stagnant, there are likely to be conflicts within the culture about its dominant ideals and fears. Some of these conflicts will have to do with topics central to family life education (e.g., Which ideal is more important—loyalty to family or personal autonomy?). Because these intracultural conflicts are sensitive issues and often problematic for families, family life education programs that do not prepare individuals to deal rationally with these changing ideals and fears are bound to be inadequate. (Some specific examples of these intracultural conflicts, particularly as they are expressed in parent-adolescent relationships, are described in Chapter 7.)

Religious Values

The relationship between religion and family life education is discussed extensively in Chapter 8. The intent here is not to repeat the broader themes and issues of that chapter but to focus more narrowly on the relationship between religious and moral/ethical values. Although there are many differences among religions, a number of features appear to be common to many of them: (a) a belief in a supreme being or set of beings; (b) a set of concepts (usually a very complex set) that refer to the postulated relationships between the supreme being(s) and humans; (c) a belief in some sort of life after physical death; and (d) a moral system, that is, a notion of ideals and of fears. These features have important implications for family life education.

First, it is clear that many moral concepts and religious concepts such as respect for persons will overlap (see Chapter 8), leading at least some people to believe that moral/ethical values and religious values are the same thing. Such a belief results in potential misunderstandings, however, because at least some religions may have a different view of what counts as justification of moral principles than will be found, for example, in books on ethics. Thus some religions hold that moral principles have weight *because* they are "commandments" of one or more supreme beings rather than because they are parts of an autonomous way of viewing human relations and human actions.

Obviously, family life educators will need to be sensitive to these potentially different beliefs, but it need not result in an impasse where the educator can do nothing. What is crucial is a willingness on the part of the educator to be open-minded (Hare, 1979) and to be both willing and able to set an example of careful and balanced consideration of issues that are central to family life education and, indeed, to the lives of all.

Second, the fact that most religions contain a moral system provides an opportunity for family life educators to explore at least some of these systems (e.g., examining their moral concepts and beliefs, recognizing how these beliefs may be debated within the religious community, clarifying the principles they embody) and how these systems affect family life. Such exploration can enlighten all individuals, regardless of their particular religious beliefs.

Personal Values

Much of the attention to values in family life education appears to be directed toward what is usually referred to as developing an understanding of one's own personal values and of learning to respect the personal values of others. Hamm (1985) has made an important distinction between public or social morality and private or personal morality that has relevance for family life education.

According to Hamm, social moral judgment has to do with interpersonal behaviors and "addresses itself to basic human needs and fears, wants and desires, which are either to be satisfied or avoided . . . and is a precondition for human beings to have a choice at pursuing quality of life in its many forms" (Hamm, 1985, p. 41). Some of the basic principles that are necessary for social morality include (a) justice as fairness (impartiality, nondiscrimination); (b) non-maleficence (restraint from harming or injuring others); (c) minimal beneficence (the moral responsibility to consider others' interests and to assist them in satisfying their basic needs); (d) freedom (no right to interfere with others in what they want to do *without justification*); and (e) honesty (truthfulness and nondeception). In Hamm's view, social morality refers to those things that are "good for all" and has as its summary notion respect for others.

Hamm has suggested that, although personal morality shares some of the same features as social morality, personal moral judgments are in fact intended to commend something or prescribe it only for oneself, that is, to address those things that have to do with "my good" rather than with good for all. The summary notion in personal morality is self-respect. According to Hamm, "When it comes to the crunch private morality must give way to social morality" (Hamm, 1985, p. 45). This has important implications for family life educators who are concerned about the role of their personal values in family life education.

Hamm (1985) has claimed that this distinction is an important one because the subject matter and the strategies required for teaching social morality and personal morality are different. In general, teaching social morality requires serious and systematic attention to the rules and principles of social morality, while education for personal morality requires some kind of values clarification, although not the "mindless activities" engaged in by those who use the Values Clarification approach (Raths, Harmin, & Simon, 1966). Rather, systematic efforts are required to help participants "gain insight into themselves at the very deepest level" (Hamm, 1985, p. 57).

Value Judgments

As noted in the introduction to this chapter, value judgments have often been problematic for family life educators, probably because of the earlier beliefs that social science (and thus family life education) was value free. It is the essence of education, whether in family life education or in other fields, however, to be surrounded by and enmeshed in value questions that require judgments. Value, or normative decisions must be made by educators all the time. When resources are limited, whose needs (e.g., those of single parents or those of the elderly) should be given priority? Must an educator include content (e.g., sex education) even if he or she is uncomfortable with it? Should a particular program (e.g., marriage preparation) be required for everyone? All of these are versions of a simple question: Should I do X? In every case, a value judgment is being called for, whether this judgment is made with full awareness or from ingrained habit.

Although there are many ways to classify value judgments, in this chapter the distinction will be made between value assessments and value prescriptions. Value assessments are claims that some thing, person, or action is good, bad, unhealthy, and so on. The general form for simple value assessments is "x is v," where x is the thing being evaluated and v is the value term used to do the evaluating. Examples of value assessments include the following: "That program is effective." "Those policies are unfair." "His research is sound." Value prescriptions, on the other hand, are directed toward persons and tell them what they should or should not do, such as the following: "Don't steal the money." "You ought to take care of your elderly relatives." "Pay your taxes on time."

Value judgments, whether value assessments or value prescriptions, have a common set of assumptions. In offering a value judgment, one operates from at least the following set of interrelated assumptions:

1. One assumes that the thing being evaluated (person, action, event) has features that enable one to decide whether it's good, bad, expensive, decadent, or whatever. Thus, for it to make sense to judge a family life education program to be good or a particular person to be evil, there must be features of the program or of the person that can be observed and used as the basis for assessment. In assessing a program, one would be interested in such things as accuracy and relevance of content, impact, cost, and so on. In judging people as good or evil, one is primarily concerned with assessing their *actions* in terms of *social* morality, that is, their actions toward people other than themselves.

2. But having features that can be observed is not the only basis for value judgments. One must also presuppose that there are values (embodied in standards, rules, principles, maxims, and so on) with which the thing or person being assessed either is or is not in accord. A person who routinely lies, cheats, and seeks to harm others fails to meet minimum standards of morality and thus he or she may well be immoral.[1] As noted earlier, if one holds the value of honesty, then one is strongly committed to being honest. It is because one is making judgments based upon one's values that those judgments are called *value* judgments.

3. Thus, when a person makes a value judgment about some thing or person, that person judges that the features of the thing or the person conform or do not conform with certain values to which the person making the judgment is committed. A person will have a pro attitude toward a thing or a person *because* it meets the values to which the person is committed; he or she will have a negative attitude when the thing or person fails to meet the standards implicit in the value.

4. Things and persons can be assessed from different value points of view, and these assessments may differ. For example, a person may be both beautiful and evil. In the first instance, the person is assessed from an aesthetic point of view; in the latter, from a moral point of view. What

differentiates the points of view is what is relevant in making and defending a value judgment. Roughly speaking, things relevant to the aesthetic point of view are those things having to do with the form of something. With the moral point of view, it is not form that matters but actions—how that person treats other people. To say that there are different points of view is another way of saying that there are different kinds of values. And, as stated earlier, most of these have relevance for family life education.

Because of widespread skepticism, cynicism, or confusion about the nature of value judgments, it is important to stress the difference between value judgments and other expressions with which they are often confused. Perhaps the most pervasive confusions come from confounding value judgments with expressions of preference. This confusion is endemic, for example, in what is misleadingly called *Values Clarification*, which is not about values at all; rather, it is about tastes and preferences. As noted earlier, expressions about what a person likes are about the person, not about other persons, things, or actions. Value judgments can be about us; that is what conscience is all about. But, more commonly, value judgments are about the vast variety of things, actions, and people of the world.

Thus it should not be surprising that family life educators have a difficult task in dealing with the values content of family life education. These educators are expected—and it could not be otherwise—to help students discover a great range of points of view that people can take toward important and complex issues. And, even more difficult, they are expected to deal in a defensible way with issues in a climate where the basic understanding of what counts as a value issue is frequently misunderstood.

Levels of Analysis

According to Rokeach (1973), the concept of values is meaningful at all levels of social analysis. Although family life education tends to emphasize personal and family values, organizations, institutions, and societies can also be said to have values. All cultural groups, religions, the broader society, business institutions, governments, and indeed fields of study and practice such as family life education have values, whether these values are implicit or explicit.

The significance of different levels of values for family life education lies in the fact that the values of these different levels may come into conflict. Obviously, individuals may hold personal values that conflict with the values of their family, their church, or the broader society. As well, family life educators themselves may find that the values of the family life education field conflict with some of the values of their particular religion. An important implication of this conflict among levels of values is that educational efforts must assist individuals in learning to balance and to reconcile these value conflicts.

An additional implication emerges from the beliefs of many philosophers, futurists, and others that the problems and challenges of the future require greater attention and commitment to shared and socially beneficial values. This suggests a need for family life education to address more thoughtfully levels of values in addition to personal and familial ones.

APPROACHES TO VALUES EDUCATION

Although talk about values education is now relatively common, there is considerable misunderstanding of what counts as values education. At one time or another, many ways have been promulgated for handling values issues: to ignore them, to teach a given set of values, to allow students to clarify their own values, to enhance students' abilities to reason about values, and so on. Some of these have resulted in specific programs or models designed to provide values education, although not always under that label. This section provides a brief overview and critique of four major approaches typically used in family life education. In this discussion, evaluation studies carried out on each of the four models is summarized. This section concludes with a discussion of the potential implications that "postfoundationist" views of ethics might have for values education.[2]

Ignoring Values

As suggested earlier, some have believed that values have no place in family life education and therefore that the best way to handle values is to ignore or omit them altogether (in any educational setting but most particularly in school settings). In such circumstances, there would be no program guides or lessons explicitly labeled as values education; that is, there would be no acknowledged values education curriculum.

The absence of values education labels, however, does not mean that no education about values is occurring. There are many value-laden aspects in the "hidden curriculum"—those things that participants may learn about but that are not explicitly stated in any program guide. For example, in school-based family life education, a classroom that emphasizes group work not only teaches things about cooperation, but students may also learn whether or not fair play is important and what behaviors will be rewarded or punished. Additionally, students learn about values from school policies, as, for example, when unmarried pregnant adolescents are not allowed to attend regular classes or when certain controversial publications are banned.[3]

Indoctrination and Inculcation

Early approaches to values in family life education might be termed *indoctrination*, wherein certain specific values were believed to be right and were thus taught to family life education participants as the truth (Kerckhoff, 1964). This approach to values is now in disrepute (although it may still be in use, either implicitly or explicitly), and to label anything as indoctrination tends to damn it in the eyes of the educational community.

It is important, however, not to run the risk of misusing the term *indoctrination* simply to connote disapproval of any kind of education one dislikes or with which one disagrees. Indoctrination in at least one form consists of misrepresenting the credibility of the subject being taught, either by representing something as true when it is actually ill-founded or by imparting knowledge without fairly or accurately indicating its level of credibility (Hall & Davis, 1975). For example, "If certain religious believers want their faith presented as 'the truth' rather than as one of a number of alternatives, then it is *they*, and not the educators, who are proposing indoctrination" (Hall & Davis, 1975, p. 42).

Indoctrination is judged to be wrong both educationally *and* morally because it hinders or thwarts the intellectual process that any individual has the right to exercise freely and autonomously (at least in societies based on these freedoms) and thus diminishes the freedom of human thought and action.

> If the indoctrination of factual information is in question, then men [*sic*] have a right by virtue of their intelligence to confront not only some one chosen theory but also the whole available range of information and opinion and to make up their own minds. If the indoctrination of moral beliefs and judgments is in question, then, . . . people have a right to make their own moral decisions without having their intellectual efforts thwarted, pressured, or coerced. (Hall & Davis, 1975, p. 28)

According to Hall and Davis, educators can avoid indoctrination by ensuring either that knowledge is universally unobjectionable (a difficult criterion to meet) or by ensuring that participants are presented with the

existing alternatives on a somewhat equal basis, according to the degree
of support that exists for the various alternatives.

Hall and Davis have argued that, in rejecting indoctrination as a
viable strategy for values education, it is important not to confuse
indoctrination with the direct inculcation of social behaviors (e.g., honesty, respect for persons) that occurs in the rearing of young children.
They hold that "we should really only talk about the possibility of
indoctrination when youngsters are psychologically mature enough to
make their own decisions" (Hall & Davis, 1975, p. 30). Because the
education of children cannot wait until they are mature enough to
decide for themselves, social training that occurs before the developmental stage at which they are ready to make moral decisions is both
necessary and inevitable and therefore, they claim, should not be called
"indoctrination." Such training may be detrimental, but it may be misleading to call it "indoctrination." (More will be said about indoctrination below.)

Values Clarification

To avoid what is viewed as indoctrination, many have come to
believe that the best way to handle values is to allow individuals (particularly students) to think through and develop values for themselves.
This alternative is found most clearly in Values Clarification (Raths et al.,
1966). It is probably the most commonly used values education program
in family life education.

According to the Values Clarification approach, values are a private
and personal matter, individually derived (that is, developed by thinking things through for oneself), relative and situational, and not amenable to any objective evaluation. Raths et al. claim that, for something to
be a value, it must meet seven criteria: (a) chosen freely, (b) chosen from
among alternatives, (c) chosen after thoughtful consideration of the
consequences of each alternative, (d) prized and cherished, (e) affirmed,
(f) acted upon, and (d) repeated (Raths et al., 1966).

One of the advantages of Values Clarification is that its techniques
are simple and easy to use and many students have reported the activities to be "fun." This approach requires little educator training or preparation of participants. Its potential merits include its openness for
discussion purposes (e.g., Daniels & Oliver, 1977) and its encouragement of the consideration of values (although the realization of such
potential depends to a great extent upon the skills and the openness of
the educator).

Although Values Clarification has been one of the most popular and commercially successful values education programs (Stewart, 1976), its acceptance (in family life education and indeed in education more generally) has been for the most part unreflective and uncritical. However, serious questions have been raised about its limitations, both theoretically and pedagogically.

Theoretically, Values Clarification has been criticized as an inadequate and internally inconsistent concept of values, for its emphasis on personal preferences and tastes rather than on values, for its extreme relativism, and for its failure to confront the central questions of normative ethics (Stewart, 1976). An examination of two of the seven criteria for values illustrates the inadequacy of these criteria as an account of values. Regarding the first criterion, values don't need to be chosen freely to be a value. Many values are acquired simply by living in a society, often with no awareness that the values have been acquired. The second criterion (choosing among alternatives) is nothing more than a statement of the conditions under which it makes sense to say that someone has a *choice*. Without alternatives, it is logically impossible to have a choice. Similar criticisms may be made of the remaining criteria for values.

There is a serious hidden message in Values Clarification—which constant use of the materials may give to educators and to their students—and that is the message that there is no difference between expressions of preference and value judgments (precisely the confusion discussed earlier in this chapter). In Values Clarification, no criteria are provided to enable one to assess the merits of various value claims; no advice is given to help one to recognize the structure of value arguments or even to become aware that there is such a structure; and no recognition is made of the crucial roles of principles, standards, and rules in dealing with morally hazardous situations. Thus Values Clarification is inadequate as a strategy for *values* education.

Pedagogically, Values Clarification techniques, in and of themselves, have provided "little or no stimulation for students to progress beyond the level they find themselves clarifying" (Schulte & Teal, 1975, p. 233). No tools are provided to help examine values or to deal with problems of values conflict (either values conflicts between persons or conflicts within an individual's value system). In addition, Stewart (1976) has expressed concerns about the potential for peer pressure and "coercion to the mean," and Daniels and Oliver (1977) have suggested that little that is serious or worthwhile is communicated through such activities. Thus Values Clarification is also an unlikely vehicle for values *education*.

(For critiques of Values Clarification, see Daniels & Oliver, 1977; Hamm, 1989; Lockwood, 1978; Schulte & Teal, 1975; Stewart, 1976.)

At the current time, there is little evidence that Values Clarification works as values education (Hamm, 1989; Lockwood, 1978; Stewart, 1976). Most studies of Values Clarification are methodologically flawed, limiting the kinds of claims that can be made for its effectiveness. There is little evidence that it lessens value confusion and some concern that, in fact, it may contribute to value confusion because it raises value questions but provides no tools for dealing with them. It is also unclear whether any changes that occur are the result of the Values Clarification approach itself or whether such changes are the result of something else, such as a caring and supportive environment or the fact that some specific attention was given to values, regardless of the kind of approach used.

Kohlberg's Cognitive Moral Development

Although less common than Values Clarification, there is some evidence that Kohlberg's model of moral development (Kohlberg, 1978) is also used in family life education (Englund, 1980). This model is predominantly concerned with moral judgments and with a posited developmental sequence of cognitive moral thought. Kohlberg has identified stages of moral development that he claims are universal in all cultures and that are invariant in their sequence (that is, all individuals proceed through the stages in a certain order). In Kohlberg's model, each "higher" stage of reasoning is not only a different kind of reasoning but also a better kind of reasoning. He argued that, to acquire this better reasoning, one must be exposed to reasoning at a level one stage above one's current stage of reasoning. The primary pedagogical device in Kohlberg's model is the discussion of moral dilemmas.

Although the Kohlberg approach is a considerable improvement over Values Clarification, several theoretical and pedagogical criticisms have been raised about this approach to moral education. Theoretically, Kohlberg's approach has been challenged because it fails to conceptualize moral education adequately[4] and because its almost exclusive concern with justice ignores other important moral principles (Fraenkel, 1976; Hamm, 1989). Nicolayev and Phillips (1979) reviewed research on the Kohlberg approach and found the claims of logical necessity to be untenable, considerable counterevidence regarding the assertion of invariance, and even the stage assumption to be unwarranted (because in fact many people straddle the stages). Thus they claimed that there is good reason to believe that the "hard core" of the Kohlberg approach is implausible. Theoretical questions must also be raised about Kohlberg's notion that the moral *content* of his theory is universal. Given the enormous diversity of cultures and moralities, this type of universality seems unlikely.

The pedagogical concerns about the Kohlberg theory have to do with the use of dilemmas, whether in the paper and pencil versions or via slides, discussion groups, and so on. Apart from the artificiality of these methods and the possible failure of participants to see the potential relevance to their own lives, the use of dilemmas presents a serious problem for educators. A central assumption of Kohlbergian theory is that people "move" from one stage to another if, and only if, they are presented with arguments that are one stage "above" their own current stage. Several important questions related to this assumption must be raised. How is an educator to establish these stages for each of the several individuals enrolled in a family life education program? Once established, how are these potentially different stages to be remembered? How does an educator present program participants with the appropriate one-stage-above challenges, especially when these participants are likely at different stages? And given that some educators may be at lower stages themselves, how does (for example) a stage 3 teacher present a stage 5 argument to a stage 4 student (Fraenkel, 1976)?

According to Lockwood (1978), research on the Kohlberg approach to moral education has indicated that Kohlbergian discussions may promote some development of reasoning, although not all subjects have advanced consistently, and it is not clear whether those advances that were noted were enduring or ephemeral ones. Increases in stage development were most typically found in the lower stages (stages 2 and 3), with little effectiveness in stimulating reasoning beyond stage 4 (Lockwood, 1978). In his review, Fraenkel (1976) noted that many subjects showed no stage movement as a result of Kohlbergian moral education and also that claims that this approach to moral education improved learning skills or self-esteem were unwarranted.

Value Reasoning

It has been suggested that the "value reasoning" approach to values education is relevant to family life education (Arcus, 1980). This approach is intended to help develop both one's inclination and one's ability to reason well about values issues (Daniels & Oliver, 1977). In value reasoning, systematic attention is given to engaging participants in reasoning about moral questions and to introducing them to concepts that will enable them to analyze and to test proffered value arguments.

Reason is seen as the key arbiter of values disputes (Hersch, Miller, & Fielding, 1980). Some of the major aspects involved in the value reasoning approach include distinguishing between factual and value claims, gathering and testing factual evidence, justifying reasons for making value judgments, and principle testing. One account of these steps may be found in the values education materials developed by the Association for Values Education and Research (1978).

There are several advantages to this approach. Value reasoning is clearly relevant to family life education, given the kinds of goals and objectives identified earlier for family life education (e.g., to learn to think critically). Daniels and Oliver (1977) have claimed that this is the most defensible approach to values education because it is most likely to have educational potential. Further, Hersch et al. (1980) have suggested that this approach is most beneficial for coming to terms with complex policy issues and for examining value conflicts. Finally, value reasoning provides a systematic way to engage family life education participants in an examination of important values questions and issues.

One of the difficulties with value reasoning in family life education is that such reasoning is a very complex process, and many family life educators may lack adequate preparation for this approach. There is also some concern that value reasoning materials may be used simply as exercises to occupy participants in relatively mundane ways. As with the Kohlberg approach, students of value reasoning may also fail to see the relevance of this process to real-life examples.

Little attention has been given to evaluative studies of this approach to values education. Thus it is not clear how well or under what conditions students of this approach might learn the process, nor is it clear whether skills in value reasoning will be transferred to real-life values dilemmas.

Values Education in a "Post-foundationist" Era

This chapter has thus far focused on what *has been* or currently *is* the case in values education. The purpose here is to focus on the apparent threat to rational values education posed by a pervasive movement variously called "postmodernist," deconstructionist," or "post-foundationist" (Crowley, 1988; Ellis, 1989; Reading, 1991). The current intellectual climate in literature, philosophy, sociology, education, political theory, and feminist studies is heavily influenced by these ideas (Hekman, 1990; White, 1991). While the movement(s) are far too complex to do justice to them here, they bear on values education because they hold that no arguments can be produced that provide a foundation for ethics—or for science or any other form of understanding. Some have concluded therefore that we must adopt radical relativism in science and in ethics (see the Spring 1992 *Curriculum Inquiry* issue). If this conclusion holds, then there can be no distinction between education and indoctrination. At least one effort has been made to show that this conclusion need not follow (Coombs, 1985). Because the argument is complex, only the briefest sketch can be provided here.

The standard account of what indoctrination means was offered by Snook (1972). He argued that there are at least four ways to consider what it is that makes something indoctrination: the *content* of what's taught (it must be "doctrinal," i.e., contain value claims); the *effects* on learners (they come to hold value beliefs for bad or inadequate reasons); the *method* used (such as the intensive and pervasive propaganda used in Nazi Germany); and the *intentions* of the educator (e.g., to get learners to hold unfounded value beliefs).

With these distinctions in mind, Coombs (1985) argued as follows. With respect to what indoctrination means, he argued that the effects on learners are crucial and that what is central in those effects is the attitude of the student toward what she has learned. If she holds a particular doctrine or set of doctrines in a manner such that she doesn't even consider the possibility of being wrong, or that the doctrine could be conceived of by others in a different yet plausibly legitimate way, then the person is almost certainly an indoctrinated person. What is crucial in such a case is to introduce this person to second order concepts, "concepts for thinking *about* moral concepts and rules [which provide] ... resources for criticism and reform" of the doctrines she has accepted (p. 9). The content, then, of values education would be in part such second order concepts.

With regard to the means of education, Coombs distinguished between "goal-based" and "rights-based" values education. In the former, those carrying out the education have particular goals, such as the acquisition of particular sets of moral beliefs by learners. On the other hand, rights-based values education "is neutral with regard to the goals which individuals or societies may pursue, but it is very much concerned with how persons and their interests are treated in pursuit of those goals" (p. 11).

Coombs then showed that within a society, especially a multicultural society, it is in the interests of all groups that the rights of all individuals be respected and concluded that if "there is good reason for everyone in our pluralistic society to prefer the [rights-based] tradition of moral reason both for themselves and other members of society, then there are good reasons for grounding our programs of moral education in this tradition" (p. 12).

The upshot is that, although one can hold that indoctrination is bad, anti-foundationist arguments mean that one cannot give an unshakable argument in favor of any of the standard value reasoning approaches. But the appropriate response is not to adopt ethical relativism (as in Values Clarification). It is, instead, to focus on various values traditions within a rights-based program of values education.

VALUES ISSUES IN FAMILY LIFE EDUCATION

Although the past several decades have seen the development of several ways in which to provide values education, there are still a number of related critical issues in family life education. Each of these will be discussed briefly here.

Schools as Settings for Values Education in Family Life Education

Values are central to the controversy surrounding family life education in the schools (Arcus, 1986). Opponents of family life education often claim that it violates family values, that teachers cannot handle value differences in the classroom, and that, in fact, it is not possible to teach values in the schools. These claims are difficult to substantiate. Although there is little empirical evidence, anecdotal evidence would suggest that sensitive and trained teachers *can* handle value differences and that values *can* be taught in the classroom setting (see Arcus, 1986).

Some, such as Rodman (1970), have claimed that the job of the school is scientific inquiry, not moral authority. While he has recognized that there is a place for the teaching of "universal values" in the school, he has also claimed that the schools often bungle the opportunity to teach these values. While it is true that schools should not necessarily impose moral authority on their student population, as suggested above, it is possible to inquire about values in a systematic and scientific way. The distinction made by Hamm (1985) between public or social values and private or personal values appears to be relevant to this issue.

The Training of Educators

The literature of family life education is replete with suggestions for educators about their role in values education: "Those working in the field should be able to deal effectively with their own feelings and attitudes; should be able to help youth and adults clarify their own concepts and expand their thinking beyond their own value structures;

and be capable of dealing with the formation of social attitudes and values" (National Commission on Family Life Education, 1968, p. 212). Advice given to educators (or requirements placed upon them) include the need to present and respect different family values, the need to be aware of and sensitive to various moral viewpoints, and the challenge not to impose codes or rules but to evoke capacities for responsible human reasoning and conduct and for attaining fulfilling interpersonal relationships.

Little is known about how family life educators are prepared for dealing with values content but, in general, it is claimed that, "with inadequate teacher preparation, it is not unexpected that teachers often show an inability to examine value systems objectively" (Somerville, 1971, p. 25). Given the centrality of the educator in family life education, it would appear that this is an area in need of considerable attention.

Parental Prerogative

As noted above, one of the central debates in family life education in school settings has to do with the issue of parental rights or the prerogative of parents to educate their children about family living. According to Arcus (1986), some have objected to family life education in the schools because they believe that educating the young about family life is a parental prerogative. These individuals claim that attempts by schools to provide this education and attempts by the state to require it usurp traditional parental rights. Proponents are likely to agree that the family is the best place to learn about family living but have pointed out that many families do not carry out this responsibility (particularly with respect to sexuality education), because they lack sufficient knowledge, are uncomfortable with the subject, or lack motivation for the task.

Proponents of family life education tend to believe, along with Somerville, that "it is only in relatively simple societies that the family can fulfill the total educational function" (Somerville, 1971, p. 24). In more complex societies, other agencies, such as schools and churches, also have important roles to play in education for family life. Proponents of family life education are also likely to acknowledge that, although parents have the right to be involved in and influence the education of their children, this right is not one of censorship or final control. Children, particularly adolescent children, also have rights of their own—including a basic right to education. When the rights of the parents to decide about the lives of their adolescent children come into conflict with a child's right to education and to information, whose rights are to take precedence, who decides, and on what basis?

Blustein (1982) proposed a "moral theory of parenthood," which sheds some light on the issue of parental prerogatives in family life education. He noted that the rise of industrialization resulted in a number of broad social and economic changes that challenged the assumption that there would be an orderly and predictable transmission of occupation and status from parent to child. Because it could no longer be assumed that children would live in the same relatively unchanging milieu as their parents, "new ways of educating the young and a new conception among parents of their parental responsibilities" were needed (Blustein, 1982, p. 4). According to Blustein, "Education for a predetermined social role may have made sense in a world without cultural change, but when social roles themselves are in flux, it is unreasonable for parents to aim for a particular outcome of their children's choices. They should rather seek to develop their children's capacity to make choices in a certain way, namely, autonomously" (Blustein, 1982, p. 4).

Blustein pointed to certain tensions that are embedded in the notion of parental autonomy as well as tensions between the concept of parental autonomy and that of children's autonomy. Briefly, parental autonomy refers to the right of parents to raise their children as they believe to be appropriate and is a particular instance of the individual "right to privacy" enjoyed by citizens in a free society. This right of parents to privacy protects both their own interests as parents and the interests of their children. It is presumed that at least some parental autonomy is necessary for adults to be willing to take on the responsibilities of parenthood. Parental autonomy is also in the interests of the children in that it may help to ensure that they will have the environment necessary for healthy growth and development.

Children also have interests of their own, however, and these interests do not always coincide with those of their parents:

> Parents quite understandably want their children to share their most important values, to participate with them in some forms of life that rest on and develop around common values. This is not, however, the primary end of childrearing, for the maintenance of family life, satisfying as it may be to parents, should not take precedence over the rights and interests of the children who take part in it. (Blustein, 1982, p. 7)

According to Blustein, parental rights to privacy are justified only insofar as they are not inconsistent with the performance of their parental responsibility to develop their children's capacity for autonomy. Although parents may take their own interests into account in carrying out their parental duties, it is not appropriate for them to do so *instead* of carrying out their parental responsibilities. The personal needs and goals of parents must be adjusted to the legitimate needs and demands of their children.

In Blustein's view, it is not adequate to say that children lack the capacity for rational decision making or that their choices may not be fully autonomous. Even if this were true, children should have as much freedom as is compatible with the child's current needs, the long-range objectives of the parents, and the interests and the safety of others. Children, as children, have a right to self-determination, and it is only when their wants and desires are taken into account that they can come to understand that there are good reasons for acting in one way rather than another or for engaging in intentional or purposive behavior. (It should be noted here that Blustein is saying that children's wants and desires need to be taken into account, not necessarily granted. A child's wants and desires should not be exalted to caprice.)

Thus, in Blustein's view, parents do not have the unlimited right to determine choices for their children, particularly their adolescent children. Rather, their parental authority is restricted so that their children can develop their own capacities for autonomous choice. It is the parents' duty to create the conditions under which children may develop this capacity.

SUMMARY AND CONCLUSIONS

This chapter has examined the theme of values in family life education. It noted that the importance and centrality of values in the field are evidenced in several ways: in the role of family life educators (e.g., to assist in the formation of social attitudes and values); in the goals of the field (e.g., to accept value differences, to develop critical thinking skills); in the content of family life education (e.g., ethics as a major content area); and in the learning experiences used (e.g., values questionnaires and checklists, debates about issues). Given the pervasiveness of values in family life education, it is essential that family life education scholars and practitioners begin to approach this theme in a more serious and systematic way.

Although values are an important theme in family life education, they have also been a troublesome theme. Many important values questions have been raised throughout the chapter: What values should (or should not) be included in family life education programs? Should educators share their personal values with participants? What is the best way to handle controversial values questions and to deal with value judgments? What are the normative beliefs of the field? How should family life educators deal with potential differing values among the various family life education stakeholders—parents, children, the community, the state, the family life educator, and the field itself? It was not the intent of this chapter to answer these and other values questions but to clarify important features of the concept of values relevant to addressing these questions. In particular, values were distinguished from attitudes, opinions, and preferences; different kinds of values and their interrelationships were explained; the central assumptions underlying value judgments were identified; and different levels of analysis were identified. Family life educators must give greater attention to these distinctions and clarifications to ensure that they are better informed about the nature of values and thus are likely to be more effective as they deal with the central values questions of family life education.

Of major importance to family life education are pedagogical questions: how best to educate about values. Several major approaches to values education relevant to family life education were described and critiqued. Of major concern to the authors is the predominance in family life education of an approach to values education (Values Clarification) that has been soundly criticized both theoretically and pedagogically. It is of concern not only that this approach has been criticized, but that family life educators appear not to be aware of this important body of educational literature. If family life education is to improve its practices relative to values education, then it is essential that family life educators become more critical and reflective about the approaches that they use. This will require that family life educators go beyond the bodies of knowledge traditionally used in family life education to gain new insights and perspectives on old questions.

Finally, family life education needs to give greater attention to levels of values in addition to personal and familial ones. As articulated throughout other chapters in this volume and its companion (Volume 2 of the *Handbook of Family Life Education*), questions of justice, of sharing resources, of responsibility, of care and concern for others are of increasing importance in contemporary society. Family life education has major contributions to make toward education for these social values, and it is time that family life education began to meet this challenge.

NOTES

1. The words *may be* are used because some social circumstances for a person may be so awful that their actions are, if not commendable, at least understandable and forgivable.

2. Several other approaches have been developed for values education but are not discussed in this chapter (see Hersh et al., 1980). These include Shaver's rationale building (Shaver & Strong, 1976), McPhail's "lifeline" model (McPhail, Ungoed-Thomas, & Chapman, 1975), Hamm's virtues approach (Hamm, 1989), and Wilson's moral education approach (Wilson, 1973).

3. For a discussion of these issues, see *The Hidden Curriculum and Moral Education: Deception or Discovery?* (Giroux & Purpel, 1980).

4. Perhaps the chief critique of Kohlberg has been made by feminists. There is now a large body of literature on this, but Gilligan's (1982) was the seminal work. See also Noddings (1984).

REFERENCES

Arcus, M. (1980). Value reasoning: An approach to values education. *Family Relations, 29,* 163-171.

Arcus, M. (1986). Should family life education be required for high school students? An examination of the issues. *Family Relations, 35,* 347-356.

Arcus, M. (1987). A framework for life-span family life education. *Family Relations, 36,* 5-10.

Association for Values Education and Research. (1978). *The elderly* (Teachers manual). Toronto: Ontario Institute for Studies in Education.

Baier, K. (1965). *The moral point of view.* New York: Random House.

Blustein, J. (1982). *Parents & children: The ethics of the family.* New York: Oxford University Press.

Bowman, H. A. (1957). Teaching ethical values through the marriage course: A debate (pro). *Marriage & Family Living, 19,* 325-330.

Boyd, D. (1979). An interpretation of principles morality. *Journal of Moral Education, 8,* 110-123.

Christensen, H. T. (1964). The intrusion of values. In H. T. Christensen (Ed.), *Handbook of marriage and the family* (pp. 969-1006). Chicago: Rand McNally.

Coombs, J. (1975). Concerning the nature of moral competence: The teaching of values in Canadian education. *Canadian Society for the Study of Education, 2,* 7-20.

Coombs, J. (1980). Attainments of the morally educated person. In D. B. Cochrane & M. Manley-Casimir (Eds.), *Development of moral reasoning.* New York: Praeger.

Coombs, J. (1985, November). Is indoctrination necessary for moral education: The AVER answer. Paper presented at the annual meeting of the Association for Moral Education, Toronto.

Crowley, S. (1988). *A teacher's introduction to deconstruction.* Urbana, IL: National Council of Teachers of English.

Daniels, L. B. (1975). Psycho-normative concepts and moral education research. *Yearbook of the Canadian Society for the Study of Education, 2,* 21-36.

Daniels, L. B., & Oliver, C. (1977). Values education in Canada: An introduction and current assessment. In H. A. Stevenson & J. D. Wilson (Eds.), *Precepts policy and process: Perspectives on contemporary Canadian education.* London, Ontario: Alexander, Blake Associates.

Darling, C. A. (1987). Family life education. In M. B. Sussman & S. K. Steinmetz (Eds.), *Handbook of marriage and the family* (pp. 815-833). New York: Plenum.

Ellis, J. M. (1989). *Against deconstruction.* Princeton, NJ: Princeton University Press.

Englund, C. L. (1980). Using Kohlberg's moral developmental framework in family life education. *Family Relations, 29,* 7-13.

Fraenkel, J. R. (1976). The Kohlberg bandwagon: Some reservations. In D. Purpel & K. Ryan (Eds.), *Moral education . . . It comes with the territory* (pp. 291-307). Berkeley, CA: McCutchan Publishing Corporation. A Phi Delta Kappa Publication.

Frankena, W. K. (1973). *Ethics* (2nd ed.). Englewood Cliffs, NJ: Prentice-Hall.

Gert, B. (1966). *The moral rules.* New York: Harper & Row.

Gilligan, C. (1982). *In a different voice: Psychological theory and women's development.* Cambridge, MA: Harvard University Press.

Giroux, H., & Purpel, D. (Eds.). (1980). *The hidden curriculum and moral education: Deception or discovery?* Berkeley, CA: McCutchan.

Hall, R. T., & Davis, J. U. (1975). *Moral education in theory and practice.* Buffalo, NY: Prometheus.

Hamm, C. M. (1985). Moral education and the distinction between social and personal morality. *Westminster Studies in Education, 8,* 37-58.

Hamm, C. M. (1989). *Philosophical issues in education: An introduction.* Philadelphia: Falmer.

Hare, W. (1979). *Open-mindedness and education.* Montreal: McGill-Queen's University Press.

Hekman, S. J. (1990). *Gender and knowledge: Elements of a post-modern feminism.* Boston: Northeastern University Press.

Hersch, R. H., Miller, J. P., & Fielding, G. D. (1980). *Models of moral education: An appraisal.* New York: Longman.

Kerckhoff, R. K. (1957). Teaching ethical values through the marriage course: A debate (con). *Marriage & Family Living, 19,* 330-334.

Kerckhoff, R. K. (1964). Family life education in America. In H. T. Christensen (Ed.), *Handbook of marriage and the family* (pp. 881-911). Chicago: Rand McNally.

Kohlberg, L. (1978). The cognitive-developmental approach to moral education. In P. Scharf (Ed.), *Readings in moral education* (pp. 36-51). Minneapolis, MN: Winston.

Lacey, A. R. (1976). *A dictionary of philosophy.* London: Routledge & Kegan Paul.

Ladd, J. (1978). The task of ethics. In W. T. Reich (Ed.-in-chief), *Encyclopedia of bioethics* (vol. 1, pp. 400-407). New York: Free Press.

Leigh, G. K., Loewen, I. R., & Lester, M. E. (1986). Caveat emptor: Values and ethics in family life education and enrichment. *Family Relations, 35,* 573-580.

Lockwood, A. (1978). The effects of Values Clarification and moral development curricula on school age subjects: A critical review of recent research. *Review of Educational Research, 48,* 325-364.

McPhail, P. J., Ungoed-Thomas, R., & Chapman, H. (1975). *Lifeline.* Niles, IL: Argus Communications.

National Commission on Family Life Education (Task Force of the National Council on Family Relations). (1968). Family life education programs: Principles, plans, procedures. *The Family Coordinator, 17,* 211-214.

National Council on Family Relations. (1970). Position paper on family life education. *The Family Coordinator, 19,* 186.

National Council on Family Relations. (1984). *Standards and criteria for the certification of family life educators, college/university curriculum guidelines, and content guidelines for family life education: A framework for planning programs over the life span.* Minneapolis, MN: Author.

Nicolayev, J., & Phillips, D. C. (1979). On assessing Kohlberg's stage theory of moral development. In D. B. Cochrane, C. M. Hamm, & A. C. Kazepides (Eds.), *The domain of moral education* (pp. 231-250). New York: Paulist Press.

Noddings, N. (1984). *Caring: A feminine approach to ethics and moral education.* Los Angeles: University of California Press.

Pollis, C. A. (1985). Value judgments and world views in sexuality education. *Family Relations, 34*, 285-290.

Raths, L. E., Harmin, M., & Simon, S. (1966). *Values and teaching.* Columbus, OH: Charles E. Merrill.

Reading, B. (1991). *Introducing Lyotard: Art and politics.* New York: Routledge.

Rescher, N. (1969). *Introduction to value theory.* Englewood Cliffs, NJ: Prentice-Hall.

Rodman, H. (1970). *Teaching about families: Textbook evaluations and recommendations for secondary schools.* Cambridge, MA: Howard A. Doyle.

Rokeach, M. (1973). Introduction. In M. Rokeach (Ed.), *The nature of human values* (pp. 1-11). New York: Free Press.

Scheffler, I. (1960). *The language of education.* Springfield, IL: Charles C Thomas.

Scheffler, I. (1965). *Conditions of knowledge.* Chicago: University of Chicago Press.

Schulte, J. M., & Teal, S. M. (1975). The moral person. *Theory into Practice, 14*(4), 224-235.

Shaver, J., & Strong, W. (1976). *Facing value decisions: Rationale building for teachers.* Belmont, CA: Wadsworth.

Snook, I. A. (1972). *Indoctrination and education.* London: Routledge & Kegan Paul.

Somerville, R. M. (1971). Family life and sex education in the turbulent sixties. *Journal of Marriage and the Family, 33*, 11-35.

Stewart, J. S. (1976). Problems and contradictions of values clarification. In D. Purpel & K. Ryan (Eds.), *Moral education . . . It comes with the territory* (pp. 136-151). Berkeley, CA: McCutchan.

Thiroux, J. P. (1986). *Ethics: Theory and practice* (3rd ed.). New York: Macmillan.

Thomas, J., & Arcus, M. (1992). Family life education: An analysis of the concept. *Family Relations, 41*, 3-8.

White, S. K. (1991). *Political theory and postmodernism.* New York: Cambridge University Press.

Williams, R. M., Jr. (1973). Change and stability in values and value systems: A sociological perspective. In M. Rokeach (Ed.), *Understanding human values: Individual and societal* (pp. 15-46). New York: Free Press.

Wilson, J. (1973). *Moral thinking: A guide for students.* London: Heinemann.

5

Programs in Family Life Education
Development, Implementation, and Evaluation

Jane Thomas
Jay D. Schvaneveldt
Margaret H. Young

MOST FAMILY LIFE educators spend substantial time in activities related to program development, implementation, and evaluation. They develop curricula and plan courses of study; they assess needs and select resources and learning activities; and they generally attempt to obtain some feedback concerning the effectiveness or perceived usefulness of programs.

Despite this considerable program activity, however, little attention in family life education has been directed specifically to the theoretical underpinnings of program development, implementation, and evaluation. Of particular concern is the limited consideration and use of educational theory that might strengthen family life programs. This lack of attention to educational theory represents a significant omission, for, as Fisher and Kerckhoff (1981) asserted, theoretical and conceptual advancement in the field cannot be adequately achieved until the knowledge base is expanded to include research and theory from related fields such as education.

The purpose of this chapter is to review the assumptions and current practices associated with family life education programs and to critique these practices using educational theory and research. Individual family life programs will not be reviewed, nor will practical guidelines for the processes of development, implementation, and evaluation be provided. The chapter concludes with implications for family life education programs and suggests several ways that educational research and theory might better inform the study and practice of family life education.

Before reviewing educational theory and research on programs, however, it is important to clarify the term *program*. This term is potentially problematic as it may be defined and interpreted in a variety of ways (Jackson, 1992). Some have defined the term quite narrowly and have used it to refer to a specific curriculum or course of study devoted to a particular topic (e.g., a sexuality education curriculum or a couples communication program). Others have defined the term more broadly and consider it to encompass everything that participants might experience under the auspices of a particular facility or institution, that is, all of the courses or curricula that are offered by a community agency or within a school setting.

Further confusion has been generated by the traditional use of the term *program* to refer to educational opportunities in settings other than schools (such as community centers and religious institutions), while the term *curriculum* has typically been associated with education in schools. In the educational literature, however, the terms *program* and *curriculum* are generally used synonymously. This chapter will follow that practice and will use the terms *program* and *curriculum* interchangeably to refer to an intended course of study that may be either broad or narrow in scope and that may be offered in any setting.

HISTORICAL PERSPECTIVE

It is useful to begin this discussion with a brief clarification of the different interpretations of the concept of curriculum, because these interpretations reflect the evolution of research and thinking about educational programs during the past several decades (e.g., Fullan & Pomfret, 1977). As will become evident later in the chapter, these various interpretations have significant implications for the issues and practices associated with program development, implementation, and evaluation (Coombs & Daniels, 1991).

Most conceptions of curriculum fall into one of three general categories: curriculum as content, curriculum as experience, and curriculum as plan. The view of curriculum as content depicts curriculum as a list or outline of subject matter and focuses on the organization of knowledge.

The notion of curriculum as experience emphasizes the experiences of program participants as the program is put into practice. Curriculum as plan acknowledges a relationship between what is taught and how it is taught and focuses on planning for instruction. (For further elaboration of these categories, see Jackson, 1992; Tanner & Tanner, 1980.)

Much of the early writing and study about educational programs was concerned with curriculum making or program development (curriculum as content). Questions related to what should be taught and how were of central importance, and during the first half of the twentieth century an extensive literature on program development ensued (Schubert, 1984). During this time, interpretations of curriculum gradually shifted from the early emphasis on curriculum as content to curriculum as plan. In the past two decades, however, research attention has shifted to an examination of how programs are actually used and to the study of program effectiveness. This new direction emerged at least in part because program evaluations undertaken in the 1970s had raised questions about what occurred when new programs were introduced into educational settings (Fullan & Pomfret, 1977). This new direction also drew increased attention to the notion of curriculum as experience.

While there is little agreement in the educational literature about which of these three views is the preferable and most appropriate portrayal of the concept of curriculum, there is some consensus regarding the major components of programs. Werner and Aoki (1979) claimed that, regardless of how the word *program* is defined, all programs in use embody several basic elements. These include the intents (the purposes or goals of the program), the activities (what participants do to accomplish program intents), and the resource materials (artifacts with which program participants interact in realizing the planned program goals). As well, programs either explicitly or implicitly include an evaluation component.

In the following sections, family life education practices regarding three program processes—development, implementation, and evaluation—will be reviewed and critiqued using insights from relevant educational research and theory. Although these processes are integrated ones, each will be discussed separately.

DEVELOPMENT OF PROGRAMS

In general, the term *program development* is used to refer both to the actual construction of program documents and to the influences on decision making that gave rise to the program in the first place (Gay, 1991). Zais (1976), however, has made a useful distinction between what he referred to as the development of programs and the design of programs. In his view, program *development* is the broader term, concerned with the forces that contribute to the origin of programs and that shape their evolution over time, including social, political, and economic movements, the implementation of policies or laws, and the actions of groups and individuals (Cuban, 1979; Fullan, 1991). Program *design* is a narrower term, concerned with producing a plan for the program, and refers to the practical tasks associated with designing a curriculum (e.g., Posner & Rudnitsky, 1986). In program design, one specifies and justifies what should be taught, to whom and under what circumstances, determines the ends or goals of the program, and prescribes the means for achieving the ends (Walker & Soltis, 1986; Werner & Aoki, 1979). While Gay (1991) suggested that "the two enterprises overlap and occur conjunctively" (p. 294), in this chapter program development and program design will be discussed separately.

Program Development and Design in Family Life Education

Program Development

Concern for program development in family life education has been evident in various literature about the influence of social, economic, and political forces that have shaped the evolution of family life programs over time (e.g., Darling, 1987; Kerckhoff, 1964). For example, the emergence of family life programs in the latter part of the nineteenth century was largely influenced by social changes associated with industrialization and urbanization. These movements resulted in alterations to traditional family patterns, the role of the family as the primary socializing agency, and the role of women in families, and they provided the impetus for introducing some form of education that could ostensibly preserve and strengthen North American families. Similarly, educational reformers affiliated with the progressive education movement during the early 1900s believed that education could assist in strengthening families by preparing young people (particularly girls) for their future lives as family members. Eventually these reformers were instrumental in introducing programs for teaching child development and family relations in North American schools (Darling, 1987; Kerckhoff, 1964). An elaboration of these various forces is provided in Chapter 2 on the evolution of family life education, and they will not be discussed further here.

Program Design

Much of the writing about program design in family life education has discussed the content and rationales for family life programs (e.g., Allen & King, 1970; Stern, 1969). This writing has examined the nature of content included in courses that are called family life education, the incidence of various topics in family life programs, and the justifications for offering family life programs in educational settings. Some of the literature has also provided specific guidelines for program design (e.g., Hoopes, Fisher, & Barlow, 1984; Sheek, 1984).

These writings indicate that program design in family life education tends to emanate from a "Tylerian" model of program design (see Tyler, 1949). The Tyler model provided a method for program design based on four sequential steps, each of which is concerned with a central design question: (a) State aims and objectives. (What educational purposes should be sought?) (b) Identify content and learning experiences. (What educational experiences might attain these purposes?) (c) Outline plans for instruction. (How can these experiences be effectively organized?) (d) Specify evaluation strategies. (How can the achievement of purposes be determined?)

To summarize Tyler's (1949) model briefly, educational aims and objectives are ultimately intended to "bring about significant changes in the students' patterns of behavior" (p. 44) and are determined by considering both the characteristics of the learners and the subject matter in relation to the educational philosophy of the program developer. Collectively, these initial considerations constitute the program rationale, which explains and justifies the development of the program. The objectives state the desired changes in learner behavior as a result of instruction; the learning activities develop these behavioral changes; and evaluation tests for the acquisition of new behaviors. If necessary, program objectives are assessed and revised in light of the evaluation findings.

The Tyler model has been influential in family life education programs in several ways. First, as noted above, most program design in family life education suggests a Tylerian model. For example, Hoopes et al. (1984) not only provided guidelines for developing family facilitation programs that specify the development steps noted above, but they also included 15 examples of such programs that quite clearly reflect the model proposed by Tyler. Sheek's (1984) discussion of designing school-based family life education programs also used Tyler's development model. He suggested, for example, that the program developer should "conduct a needs assessment . . . establish objectives, select and organize the content material, review and select . . . resources" (p. 25). Similarly, in their training manuals for family life educators, Gross (1984) and Wagman and Cooper (1981) advocated the use of Tyler's program development steps, including the generation of goals and objectives, the selection of activities and resources, and the identification of evaluation strategies.

Second, the Tyler model is evident in family life education in the considerable attention devoted to program rationales. Most of these program rationales are based on either a formal or an informal needs assessment. Such assessments are used to provide data about the potential program participants and to justify developing a program with a particular emphasis. Indeed, the National Commission on Family Life Education (1968) recommended that an important first step in establishing family life programs is assisting "the groups concerned to assess the needs of children, youth, adults and families in the community, and to select priorities" (p. 212). (Specific examples of the development of program rationales based on needs assessment can be found in the work of Levin, 1975; Smith, 1968; see also Hoopes et al., 1984.)

Third, Tyler's notion of behavior change as the essence of education is apparent in many family life programs. For example, Mace (1981) proposed that family life education is centrally concerned with "learning for doing," where knowledge is "systematically stored information . . . [that] . . . students will draw upon" in modifying their behavior in family and interpersonal relationships (p. 601). Similarly, Gross (1984) indicated that family life education programs are based on the premise that "knowledge and understanding can be used . . . to influence both attitudes and behavior" in individuals and families (p. 6). Guerney and Guerney (1981) suggested that such behavior change is accomplished through "intervention"; that is, family life education is really concerned with "people changing," where change in "knowledge, attitudes/values, behavior" is the central goal (p. 592). They indicated that, in achieving this goal, family life educators must "teach behavior" or provide "skill training" in certain behaviors (p. 597). Many family life education programs appear to focus on such teaching of specific skills and behaviors (e.g., see Harman & Brim, 1980; Repucci & Herman, 1991).

Finally, the Tyler model has been influential in family life education programs in the extensive use of behavioral objectives. This classification of educational objectives emerged from Tyler's concern for education as behavior change and was further developed and refined by a number of educational scholars (e.g., Bloom, 1956; Krathwol, Bloom, & Masia, 1964). Behavioral objectives are used to specify precisely what learners must be able to do to demonstrate their attainment of educational objectives (e.g., students will be able to identify the characteristics of functional relationships; students will be able to demonstrate effective communication skills) and are easily measurable and identifiable for the purpose of evaluation.

Insights From Educational Research and Theory

Two important bodies of educational literature provide important insights into the design of programs. The first of these critiques and raises questions about the Tyler model. In the second body of literature, attention is focused on the underlying assumptions of programs rather than on steps in program design.

The Tyler Model

The educational literature is replete with descriptions of models for effective program design. While these models frequently differ in some of the terminology used and in the sequence of steps or activities associated with designing a program, most are fundamentally based on Tyler's model (e.g., Posner, 1988; Walker & Soltis, 1986). It is not surprising therefore that the Tyler model for program design is widely used in all fields, including family life education.

Despite such widespread use, however, the Tyler model has been the focus of considerable criticism in the educational literature. Of particular concern to some educational theorists has been the appropriateness of equating behavior change with education (e.g., Macdonald & Wolfson, 1970; Peters, 1967). Some writers have suggested that an emphasis on behavior change as evidence of learning does not account for the possibility that some unintended learning might occur as a result of instruction or educational experiences (e.g., Kliebard, 1977; Macdonald & Wolfson, 1970). Macdonald and Wolfson (1970) argued that a behavior may be deceptive as a criterion of learning. For example, individuals may act in an expected manner although they have not learned it, or behavior may be dependent on situational demands but not integrated into independent action, or behavior may be a "chance occurrence or a temporary response" (p. 120). Moreover, it is possible that one may not act (behave) in the expected manner even though learning has occurred.

Tyler's focus on behavioral objectives in education may also have perpetuated the mistaken belief that cognitive and affective learning occur separately and that the behavioral indications of these learnings will be different and therefore easily measurable. As Peters (1967) has pointed out, affective development occurs concurrently with cognitive development. Attitudes and emotions have a cognitive core, and one cannot have feelings or attitudes without having them directed toward something that one knows about or has beliefs about. For example, if one has certain information about insects (e.g., insects are poisonous), one might develop feelings of fear or anxiety about insects. Similarly, one's emotional response to poetry or literature is based on one's cognitive understanding of it. Thus all emotions have a "cognitive aspect" and all cognitions have an "emotive aspect," and "development of feeling and attitude is part and parcel of development of knowledge and understanding" (Hamm, 1989, pp. 40-41).

Underlying Assumptions

During the past two decades, some educational writers have begun to examine the assumptions underlying the decision making associated with program design. According to these writers, the selection and organization of program components embody assumptions about teaching and learning, the nature of knowledge, and the role of the educator and give rise to differing perspectives on the purposes of educational programs in general (e.g., Eisner, 1985; Miller & Seller, 1990).

Miller and Seller (1990) proposed three such program perspectives: transmission, transaction, and transformation. In the transmission perspective, learners are viewed as passive consumers of knowledge, with *knowledge* equated with the subject matter or content to be learned and *knowing* equated with mastery of facts and skills. In this perspective, the purpose of education is the transmission of facts, skills, and values as preparation to fit into society. In contrast, the transaction perspective depicts learners as active, autonomous, and capable of rational thought and problem solving. Knowledge is considered to be produced through inquiry, and the purpose of education is the development of cognitive skills and abilities and the use of knowledge in problem solving. In the transformation perspective, learners are characterized by diversity and uniqueness, while also sharing some common social needs and concerns. Knowledge is developed through social interaction and is considered to have a personal element. The intended purpose of education in this perspective is to facilitate personal and social change. Miller and Seller acknowledged that, although these perspectives portray the differing philosophical views (i.e., underlying assumptions) that predominate in program development, they are not mutually exclusive.

These three perspectives highlight the extent to which the general educational purposes of programs might vary and suggest alternative conceptions of the various program components and of their relationship to each other. For example, the selection of knowledge (or content) and the organization of learning activities in a program will embody a particular theory of how knowledge is developed and how something is learned. The transmission perspective implies a behavioral theory of learning, in which knowledge is the acquisition of behaviors and learning is behavior change (e.g., see Phillips & Soltis, 1985). In contrast, the transformation perspective implies a "constructivist" theory of learning, in which knowledge is developed through experience and learning occurs as individuals actively construct meaning in light of their past experiences (e.g., Driver & Oldham, 1986; Phillips & Soltis, 1985).

Similarly, while the transmission perspective implies no distinctions among learners of different developmental stages, the transformation perspective suggests that the developmental stage of learners may be an important consideration in program planning. Indeed, some research indicates that a learner's developmental life stage does have implications for what and how something is learned (e.g., Phillips & Soltis, 1985). As Egan (1979) commented: "At each stage we make sense of the world and experience in significantly different ways . . . these differences require that knowledge be organized differently to be most accessible and educationally effective at each stage" (p. 7).

Critique of Family Life Education Practice

Although the Tyler model has been the focus of considerable critique within education, its use has been largely unquestioned in family life education. Because the inherent limitations of the Tyler model have potentially significant implications for the field, its extensive use in family life education program design should be reconsidered. For example, while it is generally agreed that family life education is concerned with effecting change in behavior, it does so through the development of knowledge and understanding, that is, the development of justified beliefs and of the capacities required to arrive at these beliefs (see Thomas & Arcus, 1992). Programs that emphasize skill development or training in specific behaviors cannot properly be called education, because being educated requires not only "knowing how" but also "knowing that." Thus educational efforts in family life education may be limited when they are confined to the narrow conception of behavior change as implied in behavioral objectives associated with the Tyler model for program design.

Similarly, distinctions between cognitive and affective development in family life education have been discussed extensively (e.g., Mertens, 1991; Moss & Elbert, 1987; Wright & L'Abate, 1977). Given what is currently known about the relationship between cognition and affect, a more productive focus for such discussion would be to analyze how cognition and affect interact to influence behavior and how this interaction could be integrated explicitly into family life education programs to encourage dispositions toward particular behaviors.

There has also been little examination of the underlying assumptions in family life programs. Thomas (1988) reviewed the stated aims and purposes of family life education and found some evidence of both the transaction and the transformation curriculum perspectives described by Miller and Seller (1990). For example, learners in family life education were characterized as autonomous and capable of rational decision making, while knowledge was presumed to be used to facilitate the development of personal autonomy and responsible decision making. Although autonomy in family life education was generally related to individual development in families, it could also extend to a consideration of social concerns for families in general, where knowledge may then be used in both personal and social transformation.

Most descriptions of family life programs reflected what Miller and Seller (1990) referred to as a transmission perspective, however. Stern (1969), for example, described family life education as dealing "with people . . . primarily on a cognitive and information exchange level. . . . [Family life education] . . . works primarily with the cognitive component of behavioral and emotional functioning" (p. 40). Similarly, Hoopes et al. (1984) considered family life education to "provide useful information to participants about relevant content and skill areas . . . to increase the participant's knowledge" (p. 14). Although most writers acknowledged the potential use of knowledge in decision making and problem solving as a means for achieving personal transformation, with the exception of the Framework for Life-Span Family Life Education (National Council on Family Relations, 1984), there was generally little explicit reference to the potential for social critique and transformation through family life education. This dissonance between a conception of family life education for personal and social transformation and a perception that family life education is information giving and skill development potentially undermines the ultimate goals of the field. As Thomas and Arcus (1992) indicated, clarity of purpose in family life programs is crucial to realizing these goals.

The preceding suggests that many family life education programs embody the assumption that learning is equivalent to behavior change and knowledge acquisition. The "personally lived" nature of most family life education content suggests, however, that considerations of the learners' prior experiences should be central in program conceptualization. In this regard, the constructivist theories of learning noted earlier potentially have considerable relevance for the design of family life programs; that is, program design would need to account for the differing perceptions, meanings, and understandings (based on differing life experiences) that learners bring to the family life education setting. As Cheung and Taylor (1991) have argued, "Although the end points [goals of a program] may be . . . clearly focused in terms of their socially justified status, there may well be a variety of routes towards these end points" (p. 36), depending on the students' personal understanding of what is to be learned.

Similarly, while the recently developed guidelines for family life education programs over the life span indicate a concern for the developmental stage of learners (Arcus, 1986), they appear to be based on developmental theories rather than on any specific theories of learning. An important contribution to the framework would be to examine it from the perspective of learning theories. Such research might determine the extent to which meeting "the educational need of individuals and families which are generated by . . . normative and nonnormative developments" (Hennon & Arcus, 1993) over the life span correlates with a student's ability to learn certain concepts at particular developmental life stages.

IMPLEMENTATION OF PROGRAMS

Once programs have been designed, their introduction and subsequent use in educational settings are frequently referred to as program implementation. In reality, however, implementation is only one of several stages associated with the introduction of an educational program (Berman, 1981). These stages include the initiation or adoption of a program (planning for program use), implementation itself (use of the program in question), and institutionalization (the future stability of the program in use). Implementation therefore specifically refers only to the actual use of a program, the activities of users as they employ a program, or what the program actually consists of in practice (e.g., Fullan, 1991).

Program Implementation in Family Life Education

There has been very little study of program implementation in family life education. What exists in the literature examines issues related to the initiation or adoption of a program rather than to its actual use. In particular, family life education historically has been concerned with overcoming public opposition to programs when they were first proposed or introduced and with dealing with political issues that either facilitated or hampered the introduction and eventual implementation of programs. (For specific examples of political issues related to the introduction of family life programs, see Muraskin, 1986; Zaccone, 1986.)

Insights From Educational Research and Theory

The educational literature on program implementation has particular relevance for family life education. This literature indicates, for example, that the social and political context into which a program is introduced is a potential influence on program implementation, and support at the adoption stage has significant implications for eventual use of the program (Fullan, 1991). Thus the attention devoted to these concerns in family life education is justifiable. These factors represent a limited understanding of the nature of implementation, however. This view of implementation potentially obscures some important issues that may influence the continuation or stabilization of a program over time and may ultimately have implications for program effectiveness. In this regard, assumptions about implementation are particularly significant.

Fullan (1982) identified two perspectives of implementation. The fidelity ("programmed") perspective is based on the assumption that programs should be implemented and used as intended by the developer and that a central task during implementation is to encourage those using the program to implement it "faithfully in practice." Concerns associated with implementation are thus focused on the extent to which the actual use of the program corresponds to the intended or planned use.

In contrast, the adaptation ("evolutionary") perspective is based on the assumption that, in practice, programs are altered or adapted by users to fit the needs and constraints of their unique situations. From this perspective, issues surrounding implementation are centered on the situational factors associated with introducing a program and identifying and analyzing the ways in which the program is changed as it is implemented (see Berman, 1981; Fullan, 1982).

This latter perspective of implementation has been the focus of much educational research during the past two decades. This research has confirmed that programs in use may differ substantially from programs as they were intended in documentary form and that programs are adapted rather than adopted (e.g., Fullan, 1982). Program adaptation is related not only to the characteristics of the educational setting in which the program is used but also to the educator's beliefs about the program itself. Indeed, Ben-Peretz (1990) indicated that educators "function as . . .

selective agents who act as critical mediators in implementation and who may introduce major modifications in their curriculum" as they filter program intents through their own unique perspectives (p. 114).

The research on programs in use has also provided insight into the "hidden" curriculum (e.g., Eisner, 1985). The hidden curriculum is also frequently referred to as the "implicit" or "enacted" curriculum (e.g., Aoki, 1988; Jackson, 1968) and reveals how the official curriculum is developed and interpreted as the educator and participants interact in the educational setting (Connelly & Clandinin, 1988). In contrast to the "explicit" curriculum (i.e., the intended course of study), the hidden curriculum represents that which is not openly intended for students to learn but may be learned or is learned as a consequence of instruction.

Critique of Family Life Education Practice

Assumptions about program implementation in family life education appear to reflect the fidelity perspective, and these assumptions are evident in both program design and evaluation. For example, some family life programs are intentionally designed to ensure fidelity. These programs generally are carefully "scripted" and standardized and require specific training for the educators using them. Sexual abuse prevention programs for young children and some parent education programs are frequently developed in this way (e.g., see Harman & Brim, 1980; Repucci & Herman, 1991). According to some writers, programs are "scripted" to ensure the credibility of these programs and to reduce the potential for the attitudes and beliefs of the educator to alter the intent of the program (e.g., Harman & Brim, 1980).

Many less "scripted" family life education curriculum documents also suggest an assumption of fidelity in implementation. This concern for fidelity is evident in carefully worded, specific goals and objectives for a sequential series of classes or sessions. Instructors are frequently provided with detailed guidelines and strategies for using certain teaching techniques and resource materials, for posing specific discussion questions, and for assessing program outcomes (e.g., see Hoopes et al., 1984, for examples of such programs).

The assumption of fidelity is also apparent in program evaluation practices in family life education, as most evaluations focus on the attainment of prespecified educational objectives and emphasize the measurement of outcomes in relation to these. Although most discussions of program evaluation in family life education acknowledge the potential influence of external factors on program outcomes, many evaluation procedures embody the assumption that the program is a "treatment" or "intervention" to be used or implemented as intended and for which there should be at least some predictable outcomes. (Some program evaluations reflecting this perspective include Jorgensen, 1991; Miller & Dyk, 1991; Powell & Jorgensen, 1985.)

The findings of some recent studies of family life education programs have raised questions about this predominant assumption of fidelity. For example, Thomas (1990) studied the curriculum beliefs and practices of six family life educators and found that, although all were using the same family life education program, the program was interpreted differently in each classroom. These interpretations were influenced by the characteristics of their educational settings (such as the gender composition of the classes) as well as by the teachers' personal beliefs about family life education. Not only did each teacher make different decisions about what content to emphasize and what concepts to include or to exclude as they implemented the family life program, but each teacher also articulated a unique conception of the central purpose of family life education that appeared to substantially shape classroom practices.

Studies on the actual use of family life programs have provided insight into a "hidden" family life curriculum. Friesen et al. (1988) found that, although the family life education curriculum document explicitly stressed the importance of providing program participants with accurate information about human sexuality and sexually transmitted diseases, in the classrooms studied, considerable inaccurate, incomplete, and misleading information was presented. Similarly, Thomas (1992) reported that, although both males and females were enrolled in the same family life education course, in each of six classrooms studied, the curriculum in use was characterized by a "female orientation," in which female experiences and discourse predominated. This orientation occurred despite the fact that the curriculum document was explicitly coeducational and was intended to educate both males and females for their current and future family roles.

These findings not only challenge the fidelity perspective of implementation but also raise questions about program outcomes and the extent to which these are actually related to the program as it was developed and intended. While family life education programs are presumably developed because it is believed that they will effect some specific and identifiable change, research on program implementation in general suggests that program evaluation strategies in family life education may need to take into account the potential alteration of programs in use and the impact of such alteration on intended outcomes.

EVALUATION OF PROGRAMS

Program evaluation is primarily concerned with determining the quality, effectiveness, or worth of a program. Program evaluations are conducted to assess the impact of a program or the results of instruction, facilitate decision making about current and future programming, expedite policy formation, or improve existing materials or programs (Worthen & Sanders, 1987). These evaluation purposes highlight a distinction between formative evaluation (i.e., to assist in program improvement or revision) and summative evaluation (i.e., to assess the overall success or effectiveness of a particular program). (See Scriven, 1967.) Although there is some potential overlap between these two general purposes of program evaluation, the relative emphasis on one or the other implies certain evaluation goals and strategies as well as the eventual or potential uses of the evaluation findings (Miller & Seller, 1990; Worthen & Sanders, 1987).

Program evaluations may be generally classified as those using primarily quantitative methods (such as surveys and experiments), those using qualitative methods (such as observations, interviews, and case studies), or those using a combination of the two approaches.[1]

Program Evaluation in Family Life Education

Program evaluation in family life education has generally been quite limited (Darling, 1987; Small, 1990). Those program evaluations that have been conducted reflected a concern with summative evaluation or the measurement and assessment of program outcomes (see, for example, Jacobs, 1988; Small, 1990). This emphasis in program evaluation appears to be based on the assumption that family life education has a positive influence on program participants, and most evaluation efforts have been directed toward determining whether changes in knowledge, attitudes, and occasionally behavior have occurred (Arcus, 1986). These summative evaluations have generally used quantitative methods, particularly surveys and experiments (Darling, 1987; Weiss & Jacobs, 1988).

Insights From Educational Research and Theory

Since the late 1960s, writing and research about program evaluation has expanded rapidly (Worthen, 1991). Of particular relevance to this chapter is the work on methods for conducting program evaluations and on issues related to the conceptualization of evaluation studies.

The relative utility of quantitative and qualitative methods in program evaluations has been the focus of considerable debate in the educational literature (Lynch, 1983; Worthen, 1991). The selection of methods in program evaluation is, however, ultimately dependent upon the kinds of questions to be addressed by the evaluation and will influence the choice of evaluation criteria and the selection of data sources (Borich, 1983; Cronbach, 1982). For example, Patton (1990) suggested that qualitative methods are potentially useful for "capturing differences among people and programs" and for learning about "the extent to which a program was actually implemented" (pp. 104-105). Thus qualitative methods may be effectively (although not exclusively) used in formative evaluation to address questions about how programs are perceived and experienced and to identify potential links between participants' perceptions and experiences and program outcomes. Quantitative methods are most useful in determining program outcomes and program effectiveness, and they facilitate the collection of vast quantities of data that can be used to compare outcomes.

The evaluation methods, however, are only one facet of an evaluation study. All program evaluations encompass assumptions about the nature and purpose of evaluation as well as implied views of the criterion of worth (i.e., what should be evaluated) and of what constitutes a program (House, 1983; Werner, 1978). These assumptions shape the conceptualization of evaluation studies, influence the type of evaluation activities conducted, and contribute to the diversity of evaluation approaches (see Worthen & Sanders, 1987).

The assumptions underlying various approaches to program evaluation have been described as evaluation perspectives. While the literature includes several such perspectives, those identified by Aoki (1986) are used here to illustrate how differing assumptions about evaluation ultimately provide access to and facilitate understanding of different aspects of programs.

Aoki (1986) identified three perspectives of program evaluation: technical, situational, and critical. The technical perspective suggests a view of programs as plans for instruction, in which means have been developed to achieve prespecified ends. In this perspective, evaluation is primarily concerned with measuring the extent to which program objectives have been attained, and judgments of worth emphasize how well goals and objectives have been achieved. The situational perspective views programs as inseparable from the context into which they are introduced. Programs are therefore considered to be interpreted differently depending on how participants experience them. Thus program evaluation is concerned with discovering the perceptions and viewpoints of program participants, and the worth of a program is based on its relevance for participants. The critical perspective of program evaluation centers on the assumptions, beliefs, and values that underlie programs, and evaluation concerns are directed at making these explicit. Judgments about the worth of a program are therefore made in relation to perceptions of the value of its aims and purposes. Aoki suggested that ideally all three perspectives should be considered in program evaluations.

One additional point concerning program evaluations warrants discussion. Most program evaluations are ultimately conducted to serve the interests of particular audiences and therefore may be characterized as a "political activity" (Cronbach et al., 1980). Indeed, Worthen (1991) described program evaluation as "inextricably bound with public policy formation and all of the political forces involved in that process" (p. 406). Program evaluators must therefore consider that there may be some unarticulated evaluation purposes and that the findings may be used in ways that are not always readily apparent. As Straton (1977) indicated, important questions for program evaluators include the extent to which political and programmatic issues or motives underlie any program evaluation and the extent to which evaluation studies are used to legitimize policymaking.

Critique of Family Life Education Practice

Despite widespread concern about the impact of family life education, most program evaluation efforts to date are narrow in scope, limited in methodology, and confined to a concern with measuring program outcomes in relation to program objectives.[2] Few evaluations in family life education have been conducted for formative purposes, that is, to understand how participants experience and respond to a program in use, how these perceptions and experiences might be related to potential outcomes, or how the program might be improved or revised. The focus in family life education on the summative purposes of evaluation ignores the actual educational experiences of learners in family life programs and fails to identify variables apart from the program itself that might ultimately influence behavior.

There is some evidence, however, that family life education is beginning to consider alternative evaluation approaches. Recently, for example, Jacobs (1988) proposed an approach for evaluating family programs that included both formative and summative purposes or components. This "five-tiered approach" was based on the assumption that, as programs are used, they develop and mature and that evaluation efforts may become more precise if evaluation is conducted sequentially over time. The approach is therefore developmental in nature, and specific evaluation strategies are identified at different points in the program's development. At first glance, this evaluation model appears to have some potential not only for addressing the lack of concern for programs in use but also for considering program impact over time, an issue not attended to in family life education (Arcus, 1986; Hey & Neubeck, 1990).

A potential limitation of Jacobs's model, however, is that it seemingly reflects a concern for fidelity of program implementation, with formative evaluation strategies intended to facilitate and ensure fidelity. While there is evidence of concern for understanding how the program operates, the focus of this concern is "how well the objectives appear to be implemented" (Small, 1990, p. 133). Similarly, while the model does account for the possibility that, over time, program participants may actually shape the nature of the program in ways that have significant implications for eventual program outcomes, the emphasis appears to be on evidence of program impact rather than on the modifications that occurred, the reasons for modification, and the implications of these for subsequent program design and development.

When considered in relation to Aoki's (1986) three evaluation perspectives, evaluation studies in family life education suggest the predominance of a technical perspective. As noted earlier, most program evaluations in family life education have measured program outcomes and the extent to which specific objectives have been realized. While these concerns are particularly significant with respect to cost-effectiveness, accountability, and funding, important insights into both program design and program impact would be gained if multiple perspectives were employed when undertaking program evaluations. If, for example, a critical perspective is employed in evaluation, there is opportunity to reflect on the appropriateness of program goals, whether they are educationally justifiable and whether it is reasonable to expect that they might be achieved. Program evaluators might thus avoid what Bruess and Greenberg (1988) called a potential "evaluation trap." According to these authors, limiting program evaluation to examining the achievement of objectives without examining the objectives themselves may present a distorted picture of the program. They suggested that some objectives may be "shortsighted . . . [and] relate to changes in some specific behavior and ignore other outcomes of the program . . . [or] . . . it may be unrealistic to expect certain objectives to be achieved given the financial resources, time allocation, and personnel." To evaluate a program in terms of such objectives would lead to the erroneous conclusion that the program is ineffective when, in fact, "the problem would be the objectives and the evaluation, not the program" (p. 302).

Perhaps the limited attention to program evaluation in family life education stems from political issues. As Small (1990) suggested, it may be that in family life education funding for programs and evaluation are closely linked; policymakers demand not only financial accountability but also verification of program effectiveness. The extent to which such demands have contributed not only to the relatively few family life education program evaluations but also to the almost exclusive reliance on a single approach to evaluation warrants careful consideration, however. If program evaluation is confined to summative purposes and quantitative methods, it is perhaps not surprising that researchers have learned relatively little about the effectiveness of family life education.

SUMMARY AND CONCLUSIONS

In this chapter, the current practices in family life education program development, implementation, and evaluation have been reviewed and critically analyzed in relation to educational theory and research on these educational processes. This analysis revealed that, in the past, program practices in family life education have been conducted from a limited perspective, with little attention to the potential contributions of educational theory and research. Indeed, program practices in family life education to date have been largely unquestioned. This may be due in part to the somewhat reactive role that family life education has historically played in providing programs in response to community needs. The immediacy with which these programs were developed and implemented perhaps provided little opportunity for such critical reflection. Consequently, many issues related to family life programs remain unaddressed.

Although the processes of program development, implementation, and evaluation have been discussed separately in this chapter, these processes are not unrelated and mutually exclusive events but are interactive and reciprocal. The approach taken to program development, for example, comprises certain assumptions about how the program will be implemented or used, which in turn has implications for program evaluation. For example, a program designed in a carefully "scripted" fashion, with specific directions for program users, implies an expectation that the program will be implemented as intended by the developer. Evaluation then focuses on the extent to which there is congruence between program objectives and program outcomes.

At the same time, the way in which the concept of program is interpreted will influence how the processes of development, implementation, and evaluation are conceptualized and approached. For example, when curriculum is regarded as a plan, program documents tend to be prescriptive and content focused. When the experiential dimension of curriculum is considered (i.e., consideration of the context into which a program is introduced), documents tend to be less prescriptive and provide opportunities for interpretation and adaptation by program users. Similarly, it is more likely that fidelity will be either expected or assumed during implementation when curriculum is considered to be a plan; when curriculum is viewed as an experience, varying degrees of adaptation will be assumed. Finally, evaluation concerns will likely emphasize the measurement of outcomes in relation to prespecified objectives when curriculum is limited to the notion of a plan. Alternatively, if curriculum is viewed as experience, evaluation might also emphasize understanding the influences on program outcomes.

Current program practices in family life education indicate that much of the work in this field has been based on a view of "curriculum as plan." Family life education has tended to adhere to traditional views of program design, in which education is narrowly conceived as behavior change and in which program design has been dominated by the Tylerian model. Similarly, the literature of family life education reflects a narrow view of program implementation, in which the introduction or adoption of family life programs has been of paramount concern. Assumptions about how family life programs will be used suggest a concern for adoption of the program as intended by the developer, and very little attention has been given to examining how family life programs are actually used or interpreted in practice.

Finally, program evaluation in family life education has reflected a generally one-sided approach that indicates a concern with the measurement of the achievement of prespecified objectives. Consequently, evaluation questions have tended to be narrow in focus and, for the most part, evaluation methods have been limited to surveys and experiments. The predominance of this narrow view of program has limited the possibilities for all three processes and suggests the need in family life education to expand the traditional understanding of curriculum as plan to encompass curriculum as experience.

Several important challenges for family life education emerge from the preceding analysis. First, program developers must look beyond the conception of programs as plans for instruction. As noted previously, programs are ultimately also experiences, and those who design programs need to take into account the potential for multiple interpretations of their planned intentions. As well, developers must consider the assumptions that are implicit in the decisions they make with respect to program design, for these assumptions embody particular valued educational ends. Program developers therefore must raise questions about the valued ends that are implied by the program objectives and by the selection and organization of knowledge or content. What valued ends, for example, are implied by an emphasis on the transmission of facts and information or on the acquisition of specific skills and behaviors? How are these implicit valued educational ends related to the goals and purposes of the field of family life education?

Second, consideration of how family life programs are actually used in practice is required. Attention to this aspect of program implementation might yield important information about how to design programs more effectively and whether program objectives and content are relevant to program participants' lives. While most family life programs are presumably designed to address the needs of individuals and families, what is known about the extent to which such programs are actually meeting these needs?

Third, the focus of evaluation studies in family life education must be expanded. In particular, the use of multiple methods in program evaluations and a reconceptualization of evaluation studies in general are essential. Greater attention must be devoted to assessing the actual as well as the intended program outcomes. What information does a pre- and posttest reveal about what program participants actually learned? While evaluators may discover that an objective was not achieved, what does this finding indicate about how the program might be altered or about whether the objective itself was worthwhile or realistic in the first place? Evaluators must also carefully consider whose interests evaluation studies ultimately serve. To what extent have the possibilities for program evaluations been constrained because of expectations and requirements related to funding for programs? To what extent have such requirements precluded longitudinal studies of the impact of family life education?

Finally, the professional preparation of family life educators must include comprehensive instruction in the processes of program development, implementation, and evaluation. This instruction should go beyond teaching educators the technical skills for generating program goals and objectives and identifying learning activities and be expanded to include the multiple views of programs, their "experiential" quality, and the diversity of strategies for evaluation.

None of the above, however, can be accomplished without careful examination of unquestioned practices, and perhaps this presents the most serious challenge for family life education. As it is likely that the demand for family life education programs will increase during the twenty-first century (Hey & Neubeck, 1990), it is crucial that this work begin immediately.

NOTES

1. While there are limitations inherent in the quantitative-qualitative dichotomy, the distinction is useful for the purposes of discussion (e.g., Borich, 1983). (See Cronbach, 1982; Jacobs, 1988; Worthen & Sanders, 1987, for elaboration of specific approaches to program evaluation.)

2. Reviews of evaluation studies in various specializations in family life education such as marriage preparation, sexuality education, and parent education are reported in the relevant chapters in Volume 2 of the *Handbook of Family Life Education*.

REFERENCES

Allen, A. A., & King, K. F. (1970). Family relations courses in high schools in the United States. *Journal of Home Economics, 62*(1), 19-22.

Aoki, T. (1986). Interests, knowledge and evaluation: Alternative approaches to curriculum evaluation. *Journal of Curriculum Theorizing, 6*(4), 27-44.

Aoki, T. (1988). Toward a dialectic between the conceptual world and the lived world: Transcending instrumentalism in curriculum orientation. In W. Pinar (Ed.), *Contemporary curriculum discourses* (pp. 402-416). Scottsdale, AZ: Gorsuch Scarisbrick.

Arcus, M. E. (1986). Should family life education be required for high school students? An examination of the issues. *Family Relations, 35,* 347-356.

Ben-Peretz, M. (1990). *The teacher-curriculum encounter: Freeing teachers from the tyranny of texts.* Albany: State University of New York Press.

Berman, P. (1981). Educational change: An implementation paradigm. In R. Lehming & M. Kane (Eds.), *Improving schools: Using what we know* (pp. 253-289). Beverly Hills, CA: Sage.

Bloom, B. S. (Ed.). (1956). *Taxonomy of educational objectives: Handbook I. Cognitive domain.* New York: David McKay.

Borich, G. D. (1983). Evaluation models: A question of purpose not terminology. *Educational Evaluation and Policy Analysis, 5*(1), 61-63.

Bruess, C. C., & Greenberg, J. S. (1988). *Sexuality education: Theory and practice* (2nd ed.). New York: Macmillan.

Cheung, K. C., & Taylor, R. (1991). Towards a humanistic/constructivist model of science learning. *Journal of Curriculum Studies, 23*(1), 21-40.

Connelly, F. M., & Clandinin, D. J. (1988). *Teachers as curriculum planners: Narratives of experience.* Toronto, Ontario: OISE Press.

Coombs, J. R., & Daniels, L. B. (1991). Philosophical inquiry: Conceptual analysis. In E. C. Short (Ed.), *Forms of curriculum inquiry* (pp. 27-41). New York: State University of New York Press.

Cronbach, L. J. (1982). *Designing evaluations of educational and social programs.* San Francisco: Jossey-Bass.

Cronbach, L. J., Ambron, S., Dornbusch, S., Hess, R., Hornik, R., Phillips, D., Walker, D., & Weiner, S. (1980). *Toward reform of program evaluation: Aims, methods and institutional arrangements.* San Francisco: Jossey-Bass.

Cuban, L. (1979). Determinants of curriculum change and stability, 1870-1970. In J. Schaffarzick & G. Sykes (Eds.), *Value conflicts and curriculum issues* (pp. 141-198). Berkeley, CA: McCutchan.

Darling, C. A. (1987). Family life education. In M. B. Sussman & S. K. Steinmetz (Eds.), *Handbook of marriage and the family* (pp. 815-833). New York: Plenum.

Driver, R., & Oldham, V. (1986). A constructivist approach to curriculum development in science. *Studies in Science Education, 13*, 105-122.

Egan, K. (1979). *Educational development*. New York: Oxford University Press.

Eisner, E. (1985). *The educational imagination: On the design and evaluation of educational programs* (2nd ed.). New York: Macmillan.

Fisher, B. L., & Kerckhoff, R. K. (1981). Family life education: Generating cohesion out of chaos. *Family Relations, 30*, 505-509.

Friesen, J. D., Arcus, M. E., Fisher, D., Thomas, J., & Young, R. (1988). *A field-based investigation of the British Columbia family life program*. Victoria: British Columbia Ministry of Education.

Fullan, M. (1982). *The meaning of educational change*. Toronto, Ontario: OISE Press.

Fullan, M. (1991). *The new meaning of educational change*. Toronto, Ontario: OISE Press.

Fullan, M., & Pomfret, A. (1977). Research on curriculum and instruction implementation. *Review of Educational Research, 47*(1), 335-397.

Gay, G. (1991). Curriculum development. In A. Lewy (Ed.), *The international encyclopedia of curriculum* (pp. 293-302). Oxford: Pergamon.

Gross, P. (1984). *On family life education: For family life educators* (2nd ed.). Montreal: Concordia University, Centre for Human Relations and Community Studies.

Guerney, B., & Guerney, L. F. (1981). Family life education as intervention. *Family Relations, 30*, 591-598.

Hamm, C. (1989). *Philosophical issues in education: An introduction*. Philadelphia: Falmer.

Harman, D., & Brim, O. G. (1980). *Learning to be parents: Principles, programs and methods*. Beverly Hills, CA: Sage.

Hennon, C. B., & Arcus, M. E. (1993). Life-span family life education. In T. H. Brubaker (Ed.), *Family relations: Challenges for the future* (pp. 181-210). Newbury Park, CA: Sage.

Hey, R., & Neubeck, G. (1990). Family life education. In D. H. Olson & M. K. Hanson (Eds.), *2001: Preparing families for the future* (pp. 8-9). St. Paul, MN: National Council on Family Relations.

Hoopes, M. H., Fisher, B. L., & Barlow, S. H. (1984). *Structured family facilitation programs: Enrichment, education, and treatment*. Rockville, MD: Royal Tunbridge Wells.

House, E. R. (1983). Assumptions underlying evaluation models. In G. Madaus, M. S. Scriven, & D. L. Stufflebeam (Eds.), *Evaluation models: Viewpoints on educational and human service evaluation* (pp. 48-64). Boston, MA: Kluwer-Nijhoff.

Jackson, P. W. (1968). *Life in classrooms*. New York: Holt, Rinehart & Winston.

Jackson, P. W. (1992). Conceptions of curriculum and curriculum specialists. In P. W. Jackson (Ed.), *Handbook of research on curriculum* (pp. 3-40). Washington, DC: American Educational Research Association.

Jacobs, F. H. (1988). The five-tiered approach to evaluation: Context and implementation. In H. B. Weiss & F. H. Jacobs (Eds.), *Evaluating family programs* (pp. 37-68). New York: Aldine De Gruyter.

Jorgensen, S. R. (1991). Project Taking Charge: An evaluation of an adolescent pregnancy prevention program. *Family Relations, 40*, 373-380.

Kerckhoff, R. K. (1964). Family life education in North America. In H. T. Christensen (Ed.), *Handbook of marriage and the family* (pp. 881-911). Chicago: Rand McNally.

Kliebard, H. M. (1977). The Tyler rationale. In A. A. Bellack & H. M. Kliebard (Eds.), *Curriculum and evaluation* (pp. 56-67). Berkeley, CA: McCutchan.

Krathwol, D. R., Bloom, B. S., & Masia, B. D. (1964). *Taxonomy of educational objectives: Handbook II. Affective domain*. New York: David McKay.

Levin, E. (1975). Development of a family life education program in a community social service agency. *The Family Coordinator, 24,* 343-349.

Lynch, K. B. (1983). Qualitative and quantitative evaluation: Two terms in search of meaning. *Educational Evaluation and Policy Analysis, 5*(4), 461-464.

Macdonald, J. B., & Wolfson, B. J. (1970). A case against behavioral objectives. *The Elementary School Journal, 71*(3), 119-128.

Mace, D. (1981). The long, long trail from information-giving to behavioral change. *Family Relations, 30,* 599-606.

Mertens, C. E. (1991, November). *Insuring quality family life education programs and experiences: The role of certification.* Paper presented at the annual meeting of the National Council of Family Relations, Denver, CO.

Miller, B. C., & Dyk, P. H. (1991). Community of Caring effects on adolescent mothers: A program evaluation case study. *Family Relations, 40,* 386-395.

Miller, J. P., & Seller, W. (1990). *Curriculum perspectives and practice.* New York: Longman.

Moss, J. J., & Elbert, M. (1987, November). *The affective domain in family life education.* Paper presented at the annual meeting of the National Council on Family Relations, Atlanta, GA.

Muraskin, L. D. (1986). Implementing family life education: A study of sex education in New Jersey school districts. *Family Life Educator, 4*(31), 25-27.

National Commission on Family Life Education. (1968). Family life education programs: Principles, plans, procedures: A framework for family life educators. *The Family Coordinator, 17,* 211-214.

National Council on Family Relations. (1984). *Standards and criteria for the certification of family life educators, college/university curriculum guidelines, and content guidelines for family life education: A framework for planning programs over the life span.* Minneapolis, MN: Author.

Patton, M. Q. (1990). *Qualitative evaluation and research methods* (2nd ed.). Newbury Park, CA: Sage.

Peters, R. S. (1967). *The concept of education.* London: Routledge & Kegan Paul.

Phillips, D. D., & Soltis, J. F. (1985). *Perspectives on learning.* New York: Teachers College Press.

Posner, G. J. (1988). Models of curriculum planning. In L. E. Byer & M. W. Apple (Eds.), *The curriculum: Problems, politics and possibilities* (pp. 77-97). New York: State University of New York Press.

Posner, G. J., & Rudnitsky, A. N. (1986). *Course design: A guide to curriculum development for teachers* (3rd ed.). White Plains, NY: Longman.

Powell, L. H., & Jorgensen, S. R. (1985). Evaluation of a church-based sexuality education program for adolescents. *Family Relations, 34,* 475-482.

Repucci, N. D., & Herman, J. (1991). Sexuality education and child abuse prevention programs in schools. In G. Grant (Ed.), *Review of research in education* (Vol. 17, pp. 127-166). Washington, DC: American Educational Research Association.

Schubert, W. H. (1984). *Curriculum books: The first eighty years.* New York: University Press of America.

Scriven, M. (1967). The methodology of evaluation. In R. W. Tyler, R. M. Gagne, & M. Scriven (Eds.), *Perspectives of curriculum evaluation* (pp. 39-83). Chicago: Rand McNally.

Sheek, G. W. (1984). *A nation for families.* Washington, DC: National Academy for Families and Center for the Family, American Home Economics Association.

Small, S. A. (1990). Some issues regarding the evaluation of family life education programs. *Family Relations, 39,* 132-135.

Smith, W. M., Jr. (1968). Family life education—Who needs it? *The Family Coordinator, 17,* 55-61.

Stern, E. E. (1969). Family life education: Some rationales and contents. *The Family Coordinator, 18,* 39-43.

Straton, R. G. (1977). Ethical issues in evaluating educational programs. *Studies in Educational Evaluation, 3*(1), 57-66.

Tanner, D., & Tanner, L. (1980). *Curriculum development* (2nd ed.). New York: Macmillan.

Thomas, J. (1988, November). *Theoretical perspectives of curriculum in family life education: Implications for practice.* Paper presented at the annual meeting of the National Council on Family Relations, Philadelphia.

Thomas, J. (1990). *Conceptions of curriculum and classroom practice: An ethnographic study of family life education teachers.* Unpublished doctoral dissertation, University of British Columbia.

Thomas, J. (1992). Two worlds of curriculum: The case of family life education. In L. B. Peterat & E. Vaines (Eds.), *Lives and plans: Signs for transforming practice.* Peoria, IL: Glencoe.

Thomas, J., & Arcus, M. (1992). Family life education: An analysis of the concept. *Family Relations, 41,* 3-8.

Tyler, R. W. (1949). *Basic principles of curriculum and instruction.* Chicago: University of Chicago Press.

Wagman, E., & Cooper, L. (1981). *Family life education: Teacher training manual.* Santa Cruz, CA: Network.

Walker, D. F., & Soltis, J. (1986). *Curriculum and aims.* New York: Teachers College Press.

Weiss, H. B., & Jacobs, F. H. (1988). *Evaluating family programs.* New York: Aldine De Gruyter.

Werner, W. (1978). Evaluation: Sense-making of school programs. In T. Aoki (Ed.), *Curriculum evaluation in a new key* (pp. 5-24). Vancouver: University of British Columbia, Centre for the Study of Curriculum and Instruction.

Werner, W., & Aoki, T. (1979). *Programs for people: Introducing program development, implementation, and evaluation.* Vancouver: University of British Columbia, Centre for the Study of Curriculum and Instruction.

Worthen, B. R. (1991). Program evaluation. In A. Lewy (Ed.), *The international encyclopedia of curriculum* (pp. 401-406). Oxford: Pergamon.

Worthen, B. R., & Sanders, J. R. (1987). *Educational evaluation: Alternative approaches and practical guidelines.* New York: Longman.

Wright, L., & L'Abate, L. (1977). Four approaches to family facilitation: Some issues and implications. *The Family Coordinator, 26,* 176-181.

Zaccone, P. R. (1986). The New Jersey mandate and Essex County: A study. *Family Life Educator, 4*(3), 23-25.

Zais, R. S. (1976). *Curriculum: Principles and foundations.* New York: Crowell.

6

Gender Issues in Family Life Education

A Feminist Perspective

Margaret M. Bubolz
Patrick C. McKenry

DURING THE PAST DECADE, gender issues have emerged as a critical matter in family life education. The purpose of this chapter is to provide a brief historical perspective on these issues and to discuss gendered meanings of behaviors and roles of males and females in relation to content, goals, and delivery of family life education. Basic assumptions and premises that underlie the examination of gender issues will be followed by an overview of contemporary women's and men's movements and selected areas of the new scholarship on gender. The chapter concludes with implications for curricula and delivery of family life education.

HISTORICAL PERSPECTIVE

Historically, the majority of family life education programs have been offered through home economics with the students and teachers primarily females (Baker & Darcy, 1970; Kerckhoff, Habig, & *The Family Coordinator* Family Life Education Panel, 1976; Mason, 1974; McBride & McBride, 1990; Somerville, 1971). In her 1971 decade review of family life and sex education, Somerville pointed out some of the problems associated with this situation. While the focus of home economics since its beginnings has been on the family, emphasis on family relations, particularly as a part of secondary education programs, was not perceived to be as great as that given to foods and nutrition, clothing, textiles, and furnishings. Home economics teachers were often considered inadequately prepared to teach family relations and the field was seen as female centered with content oriented toward the traditional roles of women in the home and family. An image of "conventionality or indeed of prudery in relation to home economics teachers" (Somerville, 1971, p. 15) was assumed to preclude their effectiveness to teach sex education. A similar view was held regarding the predominance of single females at the elementary school level (Malfetti & Rubin, 1968).

Identification of community family life programs with home economics or with women contributed further to the perception of family life and parent education as a female province. For example, family life education offered through the Cooperative Extension Services of the land-grant colleges typically has been a part of home economics programs. Program delivery has varied by states but prior to the 1970s and 1980s, and to some extent today, adult extension home economics programs are largely carried out through women's groups, often called "homemakers' clubs." Parent education was usually perceived as mother education conducted through women's groups such as "child study clubs." (For further information concerning the evolution of family life education, see Chapter 2.)

Following the nationwide expansion of family life and sex education in the 1960s, much attention was given to preparation and criteria for family life and sex educators (Carrera, 1971; Committee on Educational Standards and Certification for Family Life Educators, 1970; Fohlin, 1971; Malfetti & Rubin, 1968). Emphasis was placed on academic preparation and personal qualities such as emotional stability, good judgment, wholesome family life, and "experiences which have provided him with a realistic understanding of life" (Kirkendall, 1950, p. 181). While little attention was given to gender, it was stated that men and women, married or single, were equally successful in sex education with mixed or sex segregated students and also that age, sex, and marital status were unimportant (Carrera, 1971).

Gender, however, loomed larger in an influential article by Kerckhoff, Hancock, and *The Family Coordinator* Family Life Education Panel titled "The Family Life Educator of the Future" (1971). Of interest, this exemplary teacher was always referred to as a male. The article asked: "What kind of person will he be? What professional preparation will he have?

What will his job be like?" It was in this period that several surveys of family life education reported that family life education in secondary schools was primarily conducted through home economics; most of the teachers were women; and girls outnumbered boys more than 2 to 1 (Mason, 1974). Use of the masculine pronoun might be assumed to indicate that the panel felt that more males should be involved. Indeed, one panelist was quoted: "He will be a person who is successful in his own personal relationships. Marriage should not be required, certainly, but the field needs a smaller percentage of never-married women" (Kerckhoff et al., 1971, p. 317). Another panelist asserted that this view perpetuated the myth that a woman without a man was incomplete. Evidently, the stereotype of the "old maid schoolteacher" still persisted, although Mason (1974) reported that in a Kentucky survey only one fifth of the family life teachers were single.

Since the 1960s, there has been some increase in the number of males receiving undergraduate degrees in home economics, with a larger increase in those receiving doctoral degrees, many of whom are in family life or child development (Harper, 1981). Family life courses and programs at the collegiate level have increased, and relatively large numbers of males now teach family life courses at the college level. At secondary and elementary levels, family life, sex, and parent education courses are offered under a variety of auspices such as health education, biology, social studies, or as integrated programs as well as in home economics. There are some male teachers and greater numbers of boys in home economics and family life classes. At the community level, marriage enrichment and communication training programs for parents and children and marital partners have been widely promoted for both sexes through religious and other organizations. All of these developments might be presumed to help dissipate the perception of family life education as primarily education for women and girls taught by females.

There is, however, very little definitive knowledge about current participation patterns, perceptions, and practices related to gender in the delivery or content of family life education. A review of *Family Relations/The Family Coordinator*, the primary journal for family life education, over the past 25 years indicates that until recently very few studies or articles addressed gender issues. In a special issue of *Family Relations* (Moss & Brasher, 1981), devoted entirely to family life education, virtually no explicit attention was given to this subject. The only mention of gender issues concerned the need to evaluate educational materials for sex bias (Griggs, 1981). In an overview of trends, issues, and concerns in family life education in the late 1980s (Darling, 1987), the need for integration of males and females of all ages in family life education was endorsed, but gender issues were not identified as a major concern in the field.

As family life education is a very broad field, encompassing sex education, parent education, and marriage education, it is not possible to review how all of these specializations have dealt with gender issues. A primary purpose of this chapter is to outline some of the most critical current issues around gender that have a bearing on family life education in a comprehensive sense.

BASIC ASSUMPTIONS AND PREMISES

In this chapter, gender is used to mean the socially constructed concepts of feminine and masculine that typically accompany the sexual biological categories of females and males. A gender model perspective focuses on perceived differences between the sexes (J. Scott, 1986) reflected in the division of labor and roles, power relationships, personality, behavioral attributes, and self-concepts that are assigned on the basis of sex (Ferree, 1990). The use of this perspective assumes an interdisciplinary biosocial model in which biological and social-cultural factors have jointly contributed to human development and behavior (Filsinger, 1988; Troost, 1988). Physiological and hormonal variations between males and females and their complementary roles in reproduction are biological sex differences. Contemporary research has also suggested that there may be variations in aggression and brain structure between the sexes (Gladue, 1988; Rossi, 1984). Gender, on the other hand, is socially and culturally constructed rather than a biological given. An assumption of this chapter is that there are similarities in potential and in capacities between the sexes and in the roles they can play. At this time in history, however, gender as a social construction has tended to emphasize "maleness and femaleness as oppositional categories with unequal social value" (Ferree, 1990, p. 868).

The authors of this chapter take the position that values and goals of egalitarianism, justice, self-determination, and responsibility must be paramount and should underlie female/male relationships, roles, behavior, development, and opportunities. These values should not only influence what is taught in family life education, but they should also influence decisions regarding how, by whom, and for whom family life education is conducted. Greater flexibility in gender roles and efforts to reduce or eliminate gender stratification can have societal as well as familial and personal benefits for children and adults of both sexes

(Losh-Hesselbart, 1987). These include a more optimal balance of paid work and family activities, better use of talent, employment advantages for many classes of workers, as well as higher levels of social, psychological, or physical well-being. There will likely be resistance to some role changes (Goode, 1982) and, during this period of changes in gender behavior and roles, there will be a backlash to feminism (Ebeling, 1990; Faludi, 1991), stress, confusion, and social disorganization. There can be no turning back, however, and increasing inclusion of gender issues in family life education will help to move society in the direction of greater equality and justice between and for the sexes.

The above premises and values are consistent with tenets of contemporary feminism, and in this respect the authors of this chapter come from a feminist position. In their view, these premises and assumptions represent a more just and humane position that will help to enhance the quality of life of all individuals and families as they relate to each other and with systems in their environment over the life cycle.

WOMEN'S AND MEN'S MOVEMENTS

In the past 20 years, gender-based political forces have emerged to promote these aforementioned goals and values and thereby have challenged traditional conceptualizations of family, human development, and relationships between men and women. Feminism, beginning as a political movement, has led to the emergence of a new scholarship on women with a sensitivity to the politics of gender. A smaller, less developed men's movement also has developed in response to feminism in an attempt to interpret what changing gender roles and feminism mean for modern man.

Feminism and the Family

The resurgence of the women's movement since the 1960s has been accompanied by a growing literature by feminist scholars. This literature is often referred to as the "new scholarship on women" (Komarovsky, 1988) or the feminist perspective on human development and relationships (e.g., Ferree, 1990). Feminist writers have contended that the concerns of women have been overlooked, misrepresented, or even trivialized by previous authors who have perceived men and the male role as dominant and superior in society (Komarovksy, 1988; Scanzoni, Polonko, Teachman, & Thompson, 1989). This movement challenges much of the content of family life education curricula that are often based on traditional, outdated models of male and female role behaviors. This literature also compels family life educators to assess their own level of gender awareness, to deal with the politics of gender in their instruction, and to construct environments conducive to the analysis and critique of traditional gender roles.

Although the ideology may vary somewhat, feminism has basically claimed that ours is a gender-stratified society that has subordinated women's interests to those of men. The primary goal of feminism is to create a society in which gender will become a far less significant basis for allocating social tasks, prestige, and power. A feminist perspective on families stands in contrast to traditional notions of family as most fully articulated by the structural-functional perspective (see Parsons, 1951), wherein a differentiation of instrumental (male) and expressive (female) roles within the family was perceived as congruent with functional prerequisites of our social system.

Feminist scholars (e.g., Ferree, 1990; Scanzoni et al., 1989; Thorne & Yalom, 1982) have challenged the ideology of a monolithic, singular family as implied by structural-functionalism; they have resisted the belief that any specific family arrangement is natural, biological, or functional in a timeless way. Feminists have also argued that the related ideology of heterosexuality, marriage, and pronatalism places a burden on those in other life-styles, such as lesbians and gay men, the unmarried, and those without children.

Similarly, feminists have rejected the structural-functional notion that a unitary family interest as represented by husbands and fathers permeates conventional models of family. Feminist research recognizes the diverging and sometimes conflicting interests of family members (Ferree, 1990).

Feminists thus have concluded that much of the existing family science literature is seriously biased. Because the ideas of struggle, conflict, difference, and economics are inconsistent with the romantic ideals of traditional family life, feminists have asserted that there has not been sufficient attention to power or equity issues in marriage or to the legitimacy of alternatives to the traditional family.

The implications of this evolving paradigm are many and profound. In general, feminism argues for attention to (a) equity and justice in status and power in relationships and responsibility for self and others; (b) the importance of the sociohistorical cultural context in understanding the dynamic and ever changing nature of the family and problems of families and individuals; (c) recognition and legitimation of a diversity of family forms; (d) acknowledgment of the historical construction of the connections between families, households, and the economy and the centrality of issues related to paid and unpaid work; (e) the importance of economic self-sufficiency for women and families; (f) acknowledgment of individual differences in family experiences; and (g) the potential rewards of androgynous gender roles for all family members. Later in this chapter, these issues will be examined in relation to the content and delivery of family life education.

Men's Movements

While for some men the feminist movement has prompted a retreat to traditional constructions of gender and engendered resistance (Goode, 1982), for others it has inspired a serious reevaluation of traditional perspectives. An increasingly visible group of men has argued that the economic, legal, social, and political rewards that patriarchy has conferred upon them in the twentieth century have come at too high a personal and individual cost. This "men's movement" is actually an amalgam of groups with varied purposes and contrasting styles.

Male feminists constitute the predominant force in the men's movement. Male feminists offer support for the social, political, and economic struggles of women while viewing the traditional male sex role as pathological (Shiffman, 1987). Through men's studies on college campuses and a variety of formal and informal efforts, this group seeks more androgynous role behaviors for men, especially a more expressive male role within the family.

Another position within the men's movement is termed the *masculinist position* or the *men's rights movement*. This group views sexism as an injustice affecting men as much as women but historically caused and/or perpetuated by women as well as by men. The masculinist agenda seems to focus mostly on changes in laws and practices in divorce settlements, child custody, insurance charges, and the male-only draft registration.

An emerging third group within the overarching men's movement is termed the *mythopoetic* (Bly, 1990; Keen, 1991; Lee, 1989). This group maintains that, as Western society has become increasingly industrialized and urbanized, men have become disconnected from their male identities and emotions. It is the purpose of this movement to help men shed their victim self-image by helping them to reclaim power over their lives. This movement focuses on the use of mythic retreats and other experiential activities to facilitate an emotional return to primitive masculinity. Masculinity is reframed beyond the traditional male role, however, to include full emotional expression.

These three men's groups represent some diversity of opinion, but they have many common objectives, somewhat similar to those of feminists, including gender equity in relationships; analysis of what masculinity means in light of recent societal changes; the promotion of healthier, more androgynous gender role behavior, including greater emotional expressiveness; and recognition of diversity in family forms. Although the men's movements often are supportive of feminist issues and more general issues related to gender equity, the essence of the movement is not political but more of self-analysis and reflection. Compared with the feminist movement, the men's movements represent a very small part of either the scholarship or the advocacy regarding families. Yet these movements do represent the first attempts by men to seriously challenge traditional role behaviors and, unlike feminism per se, offer men positive alternatives to patriarchal roles.

ISSUES IN THE NEW SCHOLARSHIP

During the past two decades, the new feminist scholarship has questioned traditional positivist-empirical views of science, theory, and research and has advocated a political, emancipatory role for knowledge in the direction of societal change (Osmund, 1987; Sprey, 1988; L. Thompson, 1992; P. J. Thompson, 1989). Previously held assumptions and beliefs about the family, human development, and masculine and feminine personality have been vigorously challenged. Stereotypical thinking about male and female traits, such as masculine self-sufficiency and feminine dependency, has been widely condemned and countered by the fact that there is remarkable variability in many traits within genders as compared with mean differences between genders.

One stream of research and theory has explored potential gender differences in men's and women's development that are rooted in child rearing and other experiences that help perpetuate traditional gender roles (e.g., Miller, 1986). Because gender roles are largely reproduced from one generation to the next in the family, it is important to examine this stream of scholarship in family life education.[1]

Included in this stream are works by Chodorow (1973, 1978, 1979) in which she theorized why child care and child rearing continued to be primarily women's responsibility. She asserted that early identification by daughters with the mother led to a greater capability for empathy, caring, and sensitivity on the part of girls. For boys, the salience of difference from the mother and females was important and helped develop notions that individualism and separateness are desirable and necessary for fulfillment. Ruddick (1982) proposed that everyday practices of mothering led to virtues of humility, resilient cheerfulness, a high value on obedience, and attentive love. Because women have been the primary caregivers, these capacities are more fully developed in women. To foster positive qualities of caring and to bring about change that would be beneficial to families, individuals, and society, these scholars advocated sharing by men and women in all aspects of child care and treating boys and girls in the same way in child rearing.

Rossi (1977, 1981), however, coming from a biosocial perspective, contended that innate factors in the infant such as sucking and grasping and reciprocal factors in the mother to relate intensely to the child have the potential for heightened maternal investment in the child. At least in the early months of life, this surpasses the potential for investment by men in fatherhood. Parent and family life education for both boys and girls can help them to "parent," but residues of greater maternal than paternal attachment may endure into later stages of parent-child relations.[2]

Issues of morality and moral development are critical in family life education. As typically practiced, family life is a central arena for moral dilemmas and has been described as unjust to both women and children (Moller Okin, 1989). Gilligan (1977, 1982), among others, expanded Kohlberg's (1976, 1981) assumption that the moral domain was covered by the concept of justice based on individual rights. Gilligan (1988) asserted that the concept of care was equally important. Justice and care can abide in both males and females, but males more often use the justice/individual rights approach and females the care/connection approach. Females more often than males use both approaches. Moral conflicts occur in families all the time, creating dilemmas in which the two coordinates of justice and care must both be considered.

Differences in women's and men's ways of knowing and communicating have been another active area of the new scholarship with relevance to family life education. Belenky, Clinchy, Goldberger, and Tarule (1986) maintained that women's patterns of discourse involve listening, refraining from speaking out, questioning, and subjectivity. These have been undervalued by the dominant intellectual ethos of objectivity and positivist knowledge. Tannen (1990) asserted that men and women have equally valid but different conversational styles. For men, conversations are negotiations while for women they are means for confirmation, support, and consensus. Discourse between the sexes becomes asymmetrical and leads to misjudgments, frustration, and lack of understanding. Pearson, Turner, and Todd-Mancillas (1991) reported that women tend to listen more and exhibit greater empathy. Studies have shown that men talk more than women, interrupt more often, and are more likely to fail to respond to topics initiated by women (Stewart, Stewart, Friedley, & Cooper, 1990).

Another stream of the new scholarship has emphasized androgyny. This was originally viewed very favorably (Bem, 1978) and parents and others were urged to work toward androgyny in child rearing (DeFrain, 1979; Osofsky & Osofsky, 1972). The concept is now being questioned, however. The notion that there are feminine and masculine ways of behaving that both sexes can and should acquire has been alleged to subvert efforts to degenderize behavior (Walsh, 1987). Bem (1983) proposed that the child's knowledge of cultural messages about gender should be retarded by emphasizing basic biological correlates of sex, anatomy, and reproduction to strengthen the belief that sex is to be defined only on these bases rather than treating cultural correlates of sex as definitional.

Summary of Issues Arising From the New Scholarship

Issues embedded in the new scholarship that are of special relevance to family life education are summarized in these questions: (a) Are there discernible differences between the genders in personality and characteristics such as ways of knowing, moral reasoning, communication, and other behaviors? (b) Are there differences within genders in which some females are more like some males, and vice versa? (c) If there are differences, does it matter if they are products of innate differences or early experiences and socialization or are the interaction of innate and social-cultural variables? (d) If differences exist, regardless of their genesis, is equality of treatment and valuation of the sexes possible? (e) What are the consequences for child rearing, human development, and societal well-being of the acknowledgment or suppression of gender differences or similarities? (f) To what extent can males and females be socialized and nurtured in similar ways so that exaggerated traditional masculine and feminine traits are no longer relevant? (g) Should androgyny continue to be a goal of child rearing and adult behavior? (h) What are the consequences for children and adults if parenting is mainly the responsibility of either males or females or is carried out by both sexes? (i) How can the needs and rights of men, women, and children and the inherent conflicts between individual rights and obligations and those of the society be reconciled? (j) What are the political and ideological assumptions that influence the research questions, theoretical explanations, and educational practices that are proposed?

Discussion of these issues should undergird decisions and practices related not only to the content but also to the delivery, context, recipients, and teachers of family life education. It is important to point out that potential gender differences should be seen as relative tendencies, not hard and fast differences that apply to all members of either sex or to individuals. It is also important to emphasize that research and theory that focus on possible gender differences should not be used in family life education to support traditional sex stereotypes or to assume the superiority of either sex.

IMPLICATIONS FOR FAMILY LIFE EDUCATION

Recent gender role changes, feminism, the emergence of feminist scholarship, and the men's movements yield numerous implications for family life education. These gender role perspectives most directly affect the content areas of sexuality, dating and relationship development, parenthood and child rearing, work and family life, family transitions, and family crises. Within each of these content areas, alternative perspectives to be addressed and issues of importance to various gender-oriented political movements and related conceptualizations of family are presented.

Sexuality

Most family life education curricula begin with some background information on the development of males and females for intimate relationships. Too often, however, this introductory material is essentially reproductive and hygiene education with a strong emphasis on biology (Kirkendall, 1984). Feminists have considered biology as secondary to culture and history and have encouraged greater focus on the social forces that explain gender and the development of gender roles. Thus it would seem important to present the development of sexuality in the context of what Spanier (1980) refers to as "sexualization" or Gagnon (1977) terms "sexual scripting," that is, emphasizing social influences. Feminists and other scholars have claimed that biological perspectives on sexuality often have been interpreted to exaggerate gender differences and minimize similarities in desire and functioning.

Support for maintaining this traditional perspective is derived from the extant literature, which continues to support traditional gender roles, presenting women as socialized for a subordinate role generally and certainly with regard to sexuality. Feminist writers have long suggested that from a feminist perspective, as a part of women's oppression, women have been socialized into silence about sexuality. As a result, the knowledge of women's sexuality is infused with myths, such as that women have less sexual desire. Because of men's control and negative socialization, women often deny their sexuality, learn not to be sexual, do not initiate sex, manipulate sexual relations, and confuse sexual relations and intimacy. Also, consistent with the Judeo-Christian tradition, heterosexuality within the context of marriage is viewed as the only normal expression of sexual intimacy.

Many within the women's movement have equated the drive for sexual equality with gender equality. This is often expressed by women advocating control of their own bodies, including abortion rights, legitimate choice concerning sex and reproduction, and the legitimacy of an array of household and sexual arrangements. Consistent with the feminist agenda, such control is meant to empower women.

Thus the new scholarship on women and related attempts to facilitate equity in relationships suggest that, in the area of sexuality, family life educators should be aware of their own biases and defuse the many myths regarding both male and female sexual development. Emphasis should be given to gender similarities as well as differences, the importance of clear and open communication as a basis for intimacy, the needs and rights of both sexes for sexual fulfillment, and the legitimacy of variant sexual relationships.

In terms of men per se, the new scholarship related to feminist thought would argue for a more multifaceted male sexual role. For example, LoPicolo (1983) and Zelbergeld (1981) concluded that the rather high rates of male dysfunction in our society are related to narrow gender role definitions that dictate sexual aggressiveness, performance, and ultimate responsibility for their partner's sexual satisfaction. A more androgynous role would allow men to be less mechanistic in their sexual approach, to more fully receive as well as give sexual pleasure, and to appreciate female sexuality.

Dating, Mate Selection, and Relationship Development

As in the case of sexuality, social scientists' traditional conceptualization of dating and mate selection have been challenged by feminist thought, concerns for gender equity, and changing gender roles. The traditional developmental progression of young adult heterosexual dating culminating in mate selection and lifelong marriage now competes with a diversity of alternative patterns of relationship development (and dissolution) that reflect the changing status of women and the functionality of more androgynous gender roles.

Family life educators should note that an increasing number of adults are spending a greater part of their lives unmarried by delaying marriage, never marrying, or divorcing and not remarrying (Teachman, Polonko, & Scanzoni, 1987). This trend away from marriage is related to other changes for women: women's greater economic independence, higher levels of education, desire for greater autonomy in relationships, and the view of some women that the patriarchal marital institution is oppressive to women. For men, such changes in the lives of women challenge their privileged position, result in role ambiguity, and place greater responsibility on men for their own emotional well-being.

Traditionally, sex has been equated with marriage for women. Many women today, however, are entering the historically male world of premarital sex. Recent research has indicated a gender role convergence not only in premarital but also extramarital and postmarital behaviors (Hunt, 1974; Macklin, 1987; Nass, Libby, & Fisher, 1984). Sexuality is increasingly being redefined by women in terms of personal autonomy and nonexploitive relationships. To a lesser extent, men also are opting for alternatives to traditional marriage as they realize the restraints of the traditional male role. Because women's traditional roles have been devalued, women increasingly have moved into these and other traditionally male roles and behaviors. Feminism, however, would suggest the intrinsic value of traditional female roles and a pedagogy that respects these alternatives (see Tetreault, 1986; P. J. Thompson, 1986).

Men and women who are moving away from long-term heterosexual monogamous marriage are meeting intimacy needs through a variety of life-styles, including cohabitation, serial marriage or conjugal succession, gay/lesbian relationships, or merely as singles with varying levels of commitment to others. Similarly, marriage and childbearing are increasingly disassociated. These changing life-styles suggest to educators the affirmation of alternative life-styles and that greater attention be given to responsible sexuality and the changing meaning of commitment.

The traditional dating experience and corresponding relationship development have changed markedly for men and women largely as a response by women who have developed strong commitments to their own occupational and economic achievement. Because of women's lower pay, occupational segregation, lack of support for families in the work force, and male reluctance to share family responsibilities, however, women have been forced to minimize costs to societally valued achievement by engaging in temporary and/or informal unions rather than marrying for security. Dating for many women has thus taken on a life course perspective as they move in and out of relationships in response to career and individual development. Similarly, women also are experiencing a number of intimate relationships both over the life course as well as simultaneously. The idea of more than one partner has traditionally been viewed as deviant for women yet acceptable for men.

These multiple relationships for women are not necessarily sexual and meet needs not normally met in traditional monogamous relationships.

A primary implication of women's greater career/economic investment is that men and women will continually have to negotiate and renegotiate the nature of their relationship. The issue of domination is central to a feminist perspective. Men are assumed to resist women's growing economic independence with struggle and conflict as a result. Because of society's romantic conceptualizations of relationship development, couples have not been taught how to communicate effectively, deal with power issues, and handle conflict (Scanzoni et al., 1989).

Romantic love has been inextricably linked to relationship development and sex, in particular for women. Romantic love is viewed by feminists as the basis of women's oppression, however, because love between the sexes is complicated by an unequal balance of power. Romantic love is thought to cloak male domination, dictating that women must be submissive and that relationships be nonconflictual. Feminists have noted that sex has become theoretically and practically of greater significance than the legal marital ritual itself for women. Feminists view love as following the establishment of equity in a relationship; thus love would necessarily follow sex instead of preceding it as in the traditional sense. Commitment from a feminist perspective is defined as an obligation to continued negotiation, not to lifelong love and marriage. Thus bargaining and other related communication skills loom as important skills to be developed.

Feminist scholarship in the area of premarital relationships, as in the area of marital relationships generally, has focused to a great extent on male use of violence as the ultimate form of male control of women's sexuality. While date violence is contradictory to notions of romantic love, about 80% of women report having experienced sexual aggression on a date (Polonko, 1990). Society's discomfort with this phenomenon has resulted in its trivialization or in blaming the victim. In their focus on prevention and the development of healthy relationships, family life educators have the responsibility of increasing awareness of the prevalence and seriousness of this problem and the underlying dynamics of such behaviors.

Parenthood and Child Rearing

Issues involving gender role socialization have been raised in previous sections. Here the gender issues surrounding having children and care of young children will be briefly discussed.

One of the most enduring cultural images has been that a woman's identity was inextricably bound to motherhood; without children, a woman was considered incomplete and inferior (Thompson & Walker, 1989). A married woman who was suspected of being childless by choice was considered selfish or immature and violating her obligations; however, unmarried woman with children were generally condemned and scorned. Similar views regarding men have not been strongly held. The major image of father has been that of breadwinner who is minimally involved in childbearing and child rearing.

With increased economic opportunities for women and the need for women's participation in the labor force, the availability of effective contraception, legalized abortion, costs of raising children, and acceptance of alternative family life-styles, having children has become optional for both women and men. Estimates of the percentages who may remain child free during their lifetimes range from 5% of all adults to between 20% and 25% of the baby-boom cohort (Seccombe, 1991). Pros and cons of parenthood are issues for both sexes and are central to feminists and women's rights advocates. These issues permeate debates around access to and control over contraception, abortion rights, rights of pregnant women to engage in behavior potentially harmful to the fetus, child support, women's career tracks, unmarried parenthood, parenthood and child rearing by lesbians and gays, surrogate parenting, and biosocial innovations (Edwards, 1991). A central issue is that of conflict over whose rights and responsibilities shall have precedence.

"Should You Stay Home With Your Baby?" was the title of a widely discussed 1981 article by Burton White, a well-known child advocate.[3] White asserted that most children would be developmentally advantaged if they were solely cared for by parents and other family members as opposed to having substitute care. He cited the significance of the mother-infant bond in emotional development and asserted that, other things being equal, an infant's parents, because of their greater love for, social-emotional investment in, and commitment to the child, were more likely than other people to meet the child's developmental needs.

On the other side of the infant care debate, research in the 1970s that focused on children in high-quality, university-based child care centers found little reason for concern with regard to socioemotional development in terms of bonding between child and mother (Belsky & Steinberg, 1978). More recent studies that focused on children receiving nonparental care on a routine basis in their first year outside the context of the university centers intensified the debate, however. Belsky (1990) reported that children in any of a variety of child care arrangements for 20 or more hours per week, beginning in the first year of life, were at elevated risk of being insecure in attachment to their mothers at 12 or 18 months and more disobedient and aggressive at ages 3 to 8 years. Belsky and Eggebeen (1991) reported that children with early and extensive maternal employment were significantly more compliant than age-mates without such experience. These findings stimulated much reaction and critique (McCartney & Rosenthal, 1991; Scarr, 1991; Vandell, 1991), illustrating the complexity as well as the political nature of the debate. Timing and extent of mother's employment, quality of care, supportive marital and family relations, socioeconomic resources, and degree of occupational and other stressors in the parents' lives are important confounding factors involved in the outcomes for children of the care they receive. The critical question becomes this: What combination of parental/family and extrafamilial care is needed to provide the nurturance and support that children and families need?

Within this question, several gender issues emerge. If a choice is possible, should the mother or father or both stay home to care for a child? Is there an innate potential for mothers to relate more intensely to infants that exceeds the potential of fathers? Are men denied a significant role with their children by traditional child care arrangements? What about the guilt that is alleged to accompany a woman's decision to use nonparental infant care? Is a "mommy track" of interrupted career development a reasonable option for women? Is a "father track" a viable alternative for men?

Issues surrounding children have crucial implications for the community and society; they are not just private family matters or issues for individual men and women. For example, whose responsibility is it to pay for food, housing, medical services, and care of children or provide parental leave and other supports so that one or both parents can stay home to care for young children? If children are not well cared for, what are the consequences for society? Family life education should include discussion and debate about these issues.

Work and Family Life

Work, paid and unpaid, is a central arena for gender issues in family life. From a feminist perspective, both wage work and housework or family work are examples of gendered labor. They disclose "a set of culturally and historically specific tasks that convey social meanings about masculinity and femininity, and therefore about power" (Ferree, 1990, p. 872). Wage work and the provider role have traditionally been equated with masculinity and housework and family and child care with femininity. Men's wage work and career paths have traditionally been built on a structure of family support, which is mainly seen as women's responsibility. The growing numbers of women who work for wages might be helping to bring about changes in gendered perceptions of wage work. There have not, however, been concomitant changes in perceptions of family work. Thompson and Walker (1989) reported that, no matter how the division of labor is measured, wives continue to do about 2 to 3 times as much family work as their husbands. While some men are doing more household work and child care (Pleck, 1985), the widespread entry of women into paid employment has not led to significant changes in men's family work (Coltrane & Ishii-Kuntz, 1992).

In addition to the fact that women provide a larger quantity than men, family work traditionally assigned to women differs from men's in what is done, when it is done, the circumstances in which it is done, and how it is experienced (Thompson & Walker, 1989). Women's family work is described as a more focal part of their psychological functioning, but family work is not considered men's real work.

Rudd and McKenry (1982) reported that employed married mothers can feel overloaded but still see husbands and children as supportive because of having low expectations for help with family work. Research has not reported a clear connection between division of family labor and husbands' marital and personal well-being, but it has shown a positive link between fair division of family work and wives' marital and personal well-being. Some women are reluctant to push for a more equitable division of family work because it may lead to fighting with loved ones. Getting other family members to do household tasks may be seen as nagging. Wives also complain about the quality of husband's household work and thus prefer to do it themselves. Some are reluctant to give up control over the one domain in which they have power and receive self-esteem.

Matters of power, inequity, and caring are embedded in the above discussion, constituting reasons that household work remains one of the most controversial domains for gender issues in family life. Gender issues with respect to paid work are also pervasive and have profound implications for family life. For example, who should stay home to care for him or her when a child (or parent) is sick? Whose career is the most important? Can dual careers be successfully combined with parenthood? Who should control the income of husbands or wives? How is income to be allocated? Who sets the priorities? Family life education must address these issues.

Family Transitions

Changing gender roles, the men's movements, and the new scholarship on women call into question the traditional developmental schema that have been used to describe and explain family development

throughout the life cycle. Traditional life-cycle approaches have emphasized structure as opposed to process, stability as opposed to change
(Scanzoni et al., 1989). Approaches that emphasize change, role flexibility, life-style options, and equity would seem more appropriate given
societal changes in recent years. New developmental conceptualizations
must be developed that acknowledge the reality of family living today
by moving away from the patriarchal ideal. With high rates of divorce
and the acceptance of family variations, it no longer can be assumed that
traditional marriage for a lifetime is a realistic goal.

The concept of conjugal succession per se has brought about changes
in family imagery and family relationships (Furstenberg & Spanier,
1984). There are few theoretical trajectories, however, that assume that
life course experiences for women or men involve moving in and out of
relationships as they pursue career goals. Scanzoni and colleagues
(1989) have developed a model of individual/family development that
incorporates notions of nonsexual exclusivity, along with gender equity,
role flexibility, and life-style options. The emphasis is on role flexibility
from a social exchange perspective; that is, it is assumed that men and
women continually seek to negotiate changes in behaviors that may be
more favorable as opposed to following static traditional role assignments. Thus sexual exclusivity is negotiated for specific time periods.

Feminists recognize this element of conflict as inherent in all intimate
relationships that should be recognized and openly dealt with in contrast to romantic views of love that fail to acknowledge individual
differences and conflict in intimate relationships (Scanzoni et al., 1989).
To enable students to deal with such negotiations, family life educators
must concentrate on facilitating communication and critical assessment
skills, exploding romantic myths, and creating an environment where
both males and females can gain competence and confidence to deal
with each other as equals (K. P. Scott, 1986).

The traditional family developmental/life-cycle approaches to understanding family changes in behavior over time are based on the
presence or absence of children, their biological aging, and the aging of
adults. In the role flexibility/life-style option model, children would no
longer be the basis for family life-cycle stage demarcation because they
are no longer synonymous with definitions of family and are often
linked to oppression of women. Even with children, research evidence
indicates that life course trajectories are no longer unidirectional, hierarchical, sequenced in time, cumulative, and irreversible. Individuals
beyond adolescence undergo myriad different changes. Thus the concept of family stages itself may have lost any real relevance. The individual is seen as the source of action—an active participant, in motion,

continually changing. Rapid changes in society have dramatically altered social roles and typical life course or developmental models to the point that discontinuity is a reality that should be recognized and accepted. Thus traditional conceptions of predictable life-cycle progressions are increasingly untenable (Scanzoni et al., 1989).

Family Crises, Conflict, and Violence

Traditional family life education programs devote some attention to what is usually termed *family crises* or *problems*, though ordinarily as an addendum outside the context of "normal" family development. These often include life events that many feminists and other gender role scholars would term other *transitions*, such as divorce or remarriage. Likewise, many crises facing women, such as violence, male domination, and economic disenfranchisement, are minimized in the traditional literature.

In spite of many crisis elements, divorce is increasingly being viewed by feminists as well as social scientists in general as a normative transition instead of a crisis—merely another indication that permanence in intimate relationships no longer prevails (Price & McKenry, 1988). Divorce can be seen as an intrinsic part of a cultural system that values individual discretion and emotional gratification. Scanzoni and colleagues (1989) have concluded that divorce has become almost institutionalized and represents no great departure from normal marital practice.

Traditional conceptualizations of the family have tended directly or indirectly to blame women economically for divorce as they are perceived as primarily responsible for the socioemotional well-being of the family. Feminists have responded that most negative outcomes of divorce are economic in nature (Polonko, 1990) and that these economic problems are not the result of divorce per se but the structural economic dependence of women, the absence of full-time participation of women in the labor force, the occupational segregation of women, and a wage system that assumes that a male will be head of the household. On the other hand, there is an assumption fostered by social scientists as well as public policymakers that, because of men's preoccupation with instrumental endeavors and a lack of commitment to relationships, they too should be blamed for divorce by being disconnected from their children.

Consistent with the trend toward viewing divorce as a transition, divorce research is increasingly indicating positive as well as negative effects for all family members—even though researchers seldom hypothesize that such effects exist. More specifically, many women have benefited emotionally from separation and subsequently have experienced more complete identity development and emotional growth, whereas many men have expressed satisfaction with the opportunity of taking on a more nontraditional role with their children (McKenry & Price, in press; Price & McKenry, 1989).

Family life education students, male and female, must be made aware of the vulnerability of women who are not economically independent and the politics of divorce that economically penalizes women and minimizes men's emotional contact with their children. As Brown and Paolucci (1979) asserted, students must be freed from underlying assumptions and beliefs that surround their view of families so as to critically assess their lives.

Similarly, feminist thought would suggest that remarriage should no longer be considered either a crisis or a benefit, especially in terms of women—instead, merely as a transition in life-style that may be beneficial for some and not for others. Remarriage has traditionally been viewed as necessarily good for women as a way to get them "back on track." Yet, women often trade autonomy for economic security. Feminists have noted that women with more economic resources are less likely to marry and that remarriage is related to high stress, wife battering, and reduction of father support and contact (Polonko, 1990). Remarriage may also be problematic for women and men because of society's failure to accept stepfamily structures as able to meet the same functions as traditional first marriages (Cherlin, 1981). Remarriage is perhaps best viewed as any other alternative structure, that is, of potential value and benefit to the extent that it is characterized by equity and meets the individual needs of its members. Feminist theory suggests that conceptualizations of both divorce and remarriage be broadened to include dissolutions and developments of nonlegal unions, such as cohabitation, gay or lesbian relationships, and unmarried partners.

In terms of stress and crisis generally, the feminist position is that family scientists have failed to examine the so-called seamier aspects of family that would challenge our sentimental view of family (Polonko, 1990). Somerville (1972) stated that a strong traditional bias among family life educators exists that often leaves them socially and emotionally unprepared to deal with these issues. Thus there are numerous problems facing millions of families for which there are few data to guide appropriate interventions, such as alcoholism and drug addiction, child abuse, and poverty.

Feminist scholarship has been directed toward recognition of the high degree of struggle, dissension, and disenchantment, along with crucial value and behavioral differences between men and women, that characterize most families and with which most families must cope. Feminists predict that this conflict will escalate as gender roles continue to change and contradict even more traditional assumptions regarding family role behavior. The most extreme form of such conflict is manifest in family violence, a topic that has received much feminist attention in recent years.

Violence is sometimes broadly defined by feminists to go beyond physical cruelty and include situations that occur whenever one group controls the life chances, environment, actions, and perceptions of another group in their own interests as men often do in regard to women (Lengerman & Wallace, 1985). Most attention has been focused on emotional and physical cruelty, however. The feminist perspective is that abuse is essentially the result of inequity. That is, because women are valued sexually and not economically, they tend to be objectified, thus placing them at risk for abuse. Although the men's movements are characteristically sympathetic with this position, feminists would suggest greater attention be given to the male perpetrator and the origin of this abusive pattern. They would encourage greater recognition of (a) the greater levels of male aggressiveness and (b) the fact that many of these men were abused themselves as children by men as well as women.

GENDER ISSUES IN THE DELIVERY OF FAMILY LIFE EDUCATION

Allen (1988) has pointed out that the content and delivery or context of family life education are interdependent and equally important. In considering gender issues, the component parts must be viewed as a complex system of interrelationships. Gender issues relative to content are relevant also for delivery of family life education, including perceptions, sponsorship or auspices, students, selection and training of teachers, and pedagogy of family life education. Because there is little conclusive contemporary research on these matters, however, the intent here is to raise issues that call for serious attention and study by family life educators.

Perceptions and Auspices

How is family life education perceived by boys and girls and men and women? Do perceptions differ by the auspices through which such education is provided? For example, are programs offered through or labeled home economics perceived differently from those called family life, family science, family ecology, life skills, health, human development, or social studies? How do perceptions differ at various levels of education? What variables help explain differences in perceptions? Program auspices for family life education have implications for power and control. In times of diminishing resources at all levels of education, the issue of who conducts and controls family life education becomes a political one. Are power and control related to the gender traditionally associated with the discipline through which family life education programs are offered?

Students and Recipients

Assuming that family life education is useful for both, should it be required for both boys and girls? Many courses have been electives, especially for boys (Arcus, 1986). What benefits are there to having both sexes in the same classroom? Are there times when separate classes or discussions by males and females are advantageous? Some early proponents of women's studies advocated courses designed not only by and about women but for women (Cebik, 1975). They argued that all-female classes would provide the climate for fuller exploration of women's experiences. The typical classroom environment is reported to favor masculine patterns of assertive speech, impersonal and abstract styles, and competitive interchanges that inhibit women's full participation (Allen, 1988). With respect to home economics, proposals for segregated classrooms and programs bear reexamination. The field has been criticized as being too female oriented and helping to perpetuate traditional social roles, male domination, and structures of inequality. The profession has worked toward involving more males as teachers and students. The potential positive as well as negative impacts of its traditionally all-female classes and emphasis on women's roles in the family need to be examined. Feminism stresses the importance of male and female students learning from each other in an atmosphere that fosters fairness and mutual respect (K. P. Scott, 1986).

Teachers

What difference, if any, does it make if family life educators are males or females? Do men and women bring different perspectives and experiences to bear in their teaching? Thomas (1992) reported findings from an ethnographic study of female home economics teachers that provides insight into these issues. She found that teachers made extensive use of stories and personal experiences. Teachers' experiences permeated classroom discourse, influenced content, and were a central theme in presentation of content. When certain life events had not been experienced, such as having a child, there was an expressed lack of confidence in teaching this material. Although there were male students in all but one of the settings, concerns, content, and interactions reflected a predominantly female orientation. Boys were not ignored but the "male voice" was subordinate and males were hesitant to engage in dialogue about the male perspective on gender issues. Instances of gender bias toward undermining males were observed.

This study raises critical issues related to the impact of experience, gender orientation, role modeling, potential sex biases, and professional preparation of the teacher on the content and conduct of family life education. Female instructors may find that they will need to encourage male participation and accept the reality of the male experience. The value of such strategies as team teaching by a male and female or bringing in teachers of the opposite sex as guest speakers needs to be investigated.

Pedagogy

Gender issues in the pedagogy of family life education revolve around such questions as these: Are there feminist and nonfeminist or masculine pedagogies? If so, what are the implications for family life education? What are the outcomes of using methods and materials designated as feminist or otherwise? What is the interaction between pedagogical methods, gender of the teacher, and gender of the students?

Allen (1988) proposed that there is a feminist pedagogy and describes three selected qualities of feminist teaching with suggestions for implementing them in family studies: recognizing and respecting diversity, cooperative/interactive teaching and learning, and consciously creating an atmosphere of equality. The feminist perspective as outlined by Allen is designed to empower students, assist them in making their own life-style decisions, and provide them with communication skills to effectively negotiate relationships. She encouraged the use of participatory learning strategies such as self-disclosure and valuing the personal experiences of students and the teacher. Also suggested was use of multiple perspectives and viewpoints in materials, especially the missing voices of female authors. She pointed out that teachers need to be aware of how their classroom behaviors may communicate different expectations for men and women. These include such behaviors as ignoring and interrupting women students, calling directly on men but not on women, and responding more extensively to men's comments than women's (Good, Sikes, & Brophy, 1973; Hall & Sandler, 1982).

Walker, Kees Martin, and Thompson (1988) reinforced Allen's themes and added these additional principles: recognition of the cultural context of individuals and families, being sensitive to the responsiveness of the vulnerable, priority of client's perspectives of problems and solutions, and empowerment of clients. Family life educators need to ask: How and to what extent can feminist principles be incorporated into the pedagogy of family life education? What are the consequences of using feminist principles? What are the outcomes of their use?

Sexism in written and audiovisual teaching materials is another gender issue that has been widely explored in recent years with much effort made to eliminate sexist language and gender stereotypes. Family life education materials are certainly in need of continuous scrutiny in this regard (Griggs, 1981). Hutton (1976) reported reinforcement of sex stereotypes in junior high school home economics texts and DeFrain (1977) concluded that the vast majority of child-rearing guides implicitly or explicitly endorsed traditional roles of father as dominant breadwinner and mother as nurturant caretaker.[4]

CONCLUSIONS AND IMPLICATIONS

Given that gender role change represents perhaps the most fundamental and controversial change in family life in this century, this chapter has reviewed, from a feminist perspective, current theoretical perspectives on gender as these relate to families. This chapter has also discussed gender issues in terms of specific components of family life education, including content and delivery.

While not every professional can embrace all the implications of the scholarship represented here, it is assumed that the values of egalitarianism, justice, choice, and self-determination in female-male relationships, behavior, and development are important to the profession of family life education. Furthermore, regardless of one's professional training or personal values, there are certain realities that must be acknowledged in preparing students for family living today. Current demographic trends and research findings as well as feminist and other gender perspectives challenge all family life educators to reexamine traditional conceptualizations of "the family" that no longer serve its members well. Current demographic trends clearly reveal the increasing economic independence of women as measured by their work roles, status as heads of households, and increasing economic equity. Also, research suggests the dysfunctional nature of aspects of traditional gender roles today; for example, such role behaviors have been related to family violence, child abuse, the feminization of poverty or the "new poor," and barriers to intimacy. The emergence and acceptance of alternative family forms would suggest that family form/structure is increasingly viewed as secondary to the substance/process that facilitates individual well-being. Family life educators should realize that our literature on families is incomplete and biased with traditional gender role assumptions that are no longer valid for the majority.

In addition to the recognition of gender role change and the limitations of traditional gender role assumptions, family life educators must also deal with a dynamic, ever changing conceptualization of family. While conjugal succession may not describe the majority of intimate relationships now or in the future, intimate relationships at the very least will be characterized by continual restructuring and renegotiation. These changes in family living over the life course suggest the importance of teaching about change, coping, communication, and negotiation.

Education of women for traditional family roles must be accompanied by education for economic independence and thus empowerment. Women who are not self-sufficient have been judged to be both economically and emotionally at risk. Likewise, men will continue to pursue narrow, emotionally barren roles and contribute to women's oppression if they are not exposed to alternatives. More opportunities for education and support for men to facilitate greater involvement in child rearing and other family work are needed.

Feminism has evoked both negative and positive responses from men. The loosely organized male-focused groups that make up the men's movements represent a small minority of men who are constructively dealing with these gender issues and their challenges to traditional definitions of masculinity. These men are assessing the benefits that may accrue to them by adopting more androgynous characteristics and humanitarian values and seeking more of an expressive function in their family relations. Family life educators can facilitate men's awareness of these options, which might result in their greater family satisfaction.

Because this chapter was primarily concerned with the theoretical underpinnings of gender and their implications for family life education content, it has not focused in great depth on pedagogy, characteristics of teachers and students, curriculum, and materials. As mentioned earlier, feminists do indicate that pedagogy is as important as content, and feminist models of instruction are emerging, such as in Allen (1988).[5] The incorporation of this content into existing curricula presents many challenges similar to the difficulties encountered in the treatment of any material that is new and controversial. Educators will be required to be innovative in their approaches because there are so few guidelines and materials available; in general, the family life education literature has not dealt with the implications of changing gender roles and feminist theory. In fact, much of what is available to teachers suffers from the same gender bias that educators will be attempting to overcome. Certainly, the introduction of gender issues into family life curricula will require use of less didactic forms of instruction and will demand that instructors acquire new teaching techniques, such as critical reasoning, as well as new content. Instructors will be required to become comfortable with greater subjectivity and allow students more responsibility for their own learning. Finally, at a time when certain political forces threaten the very existence of family life education programs and already limit the content in many districts, educators will have to work closely with communities in the development and implementation of these programs.

This chapter has endorsed a paradigm for change in social structures, norms, and beliefs that deny full equality and participation for the sexes. The authors envision a future in which family issues will no longer be seen mainly as women's issues but one in which men and women will both carry responsibility for maintenance, nurturing, caring, and support of families and their members. Family life education can contribute to this change. The challenge is large but is filled with possibilities to contribute to a higher quality of family life and increased individual and societal well-being.

NOTES

1. There is a large and growing body of research and theory on gender. In this chapter, examples of works are cited that have been especially productive in generating gender issues salient to family life education. It is not the purpose of this chapter to do a thorough review of the works cited or of the debates surrounding the issues raised. Readers are advised to keep abreast of the current literature related to gender and family life education.

2. A biosocial view is not without critics. Fausto-Sterling (1985) concluded that there was little support for suggesting that innate biological differences between men and women result in differences in thinking, feeling, and behaving that limit and define gender abilities.

3. The title does not indicate that it is women who are being addressed, but the first sentence makes this clear. At that time, to have directed this question to men probably would have been considered absurd. Perhaps it would still be.

4. Gender issues in family life education are not limited to America. A recent news article ("Japanese Schoolbooks," 1992) reported that roles of the father and mother at home depicted in Japanese elementary home economics textbooks are changing from the traditional, stereotyped Japanese division of roles by sexes.

5, For additional feminist resources of interest to family life educators, see: Thompson, L. (1988). Feminist resources for applied family studies. *Family Relations, 37*, 99-104.

REFERENCES

Allen, K. R. (1988). Integrating a feminist perspective into family studies courses. *Family Relations, 37*, 29-35.

Arcus, M. (1986). Should family life education be required for high school students? An examination of the issues. *Family Relations, 35*, 347-356.

Baker, L. G., & Darcy, J. (1970). Survey of family life and sex education programs in Washington secondary schools and development of guidelines for statewide coordinated programs. *The Family Coordinator, 19*, 223-228.

Belenky, M. F., Clinchy, B. M., Goldberger, N. R., & Tarule, J. M. (1986). *Women's ways of knowing*. New York: Basic Books.

Belsky, J. (1990). Parental and nonparental child care and children's socioemotional development: A decade in review. *Journal of Marriage and the Family, 52*, 885-903.

Belsky, J., & Eggebeen, D. (1991). Early and extensive maternal employment and young children's socioemotional development: Children of the national longitudinal survey of youth. *Journal of Marriage and the Family, 53*, 1083-1098.

Belsky, J., & Steinberg, L. D. (1978). The effects of day care: A critical review. *Child Development, 49*, 929-949.

Bem, S. (1978). Probing the promise of androgyny. In J. Sherman & F. Denmark (Eds.), *The psychology of women: Future directions in research*. New York: Psychological Dimensions.

Bem, S. (1983). Gender schema theory and its implications for child development: Raising gender-schematic children in a gender-schematic society. *Signs: Journal of Women in Culture and Society, 8*(4), 598-616.

Bly, R. (1990). *Iron John: A book about men*. Reading, MA: Addison-Wesley.

Brown, M., & Paolucci, B. (1979). *Home economics: A definition*. Washington, DC: American Home Economics Association.

Carrera, M. A. (1971). Preparation of a sex educator: A historical overview. *The Family Coordinator, 20*, 99-108.

Cebik, L. B. (1975). Women's studies and home economics. *Journal of Home Economics, 67*, 27-30.

Cherlin, A. (1981). *Marriage, divorce, remarriage*. Cambridge, MA: Harvard University Press.

Chodorow, N. (1973). Family structure and feminine personality. In M. Z. Rosaldo & L. Lamphere (Eds.), *Women, culture & society* (pp. 43-66). Stanford, CA: Stanford University Press.

Chodorow, N. (1978). *The reproduction of mothering: Psychoanalysis and the sociology of gender*. Berkeley: University of California Press.

Chodorow, N. (1979). Feminism and difference: Gender, relation and difference in psychoanalytic perspective. *Socialist Review, 46*, 42-64.

Coltrane, S., & Ishii-Kuntz, M. (1992). Men's housework: A life course perspective. *Journal of Marriage and the Family, 54*, 43-57.

Committee on Educational Standards and Certification for Family Life Educators. (1970). Family life and sex education: Proposed criteria for teacher education. *The Family Coordinator, 19*, 183-185.

Darling, C. A. (1987). Family life education. In M. A. Sussman & S. K. Steinmetz (Eds.), *Handbook of marriage and the family* (pp. 815-833). New York: Plenum.

DeFrain, J. D. (1977). Sexism in parenting manuals. *The Family Coordinator, 26,* 245-251.

DeFrain, J. (1979). Androgynous parents tell who they are and what they need. *The Family Coordinator, 28,* 237-244.

Ebeling, K. (1990, November 19). The failure of feminism. *Newsweek,* p. 9.

Edwards, J. N. (1991). New conceptions: Biosocial innovations and the family. *Journal of Marriage and the Family, 53,* 349-360.

Faludi, S. (1991). *Backlash.* New York: Crown.

Fausto-Sterling, A. (1985). *Myths of gender biological theories about women and men.* New York: Basic Books.

Ferree, M. M. (1990). Beyond separate spheres: Feminism and family research. *Journal of Marriage and the Family, 52,* 866-884.

Filsinger, E. E. (1988). Biology reexamined, the quest for answers. In E. E. Filsinger (Ed.), *Biosocial perspectives on the family* (pp. 9-38). Newbury Park, CA: Sage.

Fohlin, M. B. (1971). Selection and training of teachers for life education programs. *The Family Coordinator, 20,* 231-242.

Furstenberg, F. F., Jr., & Spanier, G. B. (1984). The risk of dissolution in remarriage: An examination of Cherlin's hypothesis of incomplete institutionalization. *Family Relations, 33,* 433-441.

Gagnon, J. H. (1977). *Sexualities.* Glenview, IL: Scott, Foresman.

Gilligan, C. (1977). In a different voice: Women's conception of self and morality. *Harvard Educational Review, 47*(4), 481-517.

Gilligan, C. (1982). *In a different voice: Psychological theory and women's development.* Cambridge, MA: Harvard University Press.

Gilligan, C. (1988). Adolescent development reconsidered. In C. Gilligan, J. Ward, & S. Taylor (Eds.), *Mapping the moral domain: A contribution of women's thinking to psychology and education* (pp. vi-xxxix). Cambridge, MA: Harvard University Press.

Gladue, B. A. (1988). Biological influences upon the development of sexual orientation. In E. E. Filsinger (Ed.), *Biosocial perspectives on the family* (pp. 61-92). Newbury Park, CA: Sage.

Good, T., Sikes, J., & Brophy, J. (1973). Effect of teacher sex and student sex on classroom interaction. *Journal of Educational Psychology, 65,* 74-87.

Goode, W. (1982). Why men resist. In B. Thorne & M. Yalom (Eds.), *Rethinking the family* (pp. 131-150). New York: Longman.

Griggs, M. B. (1981). Criteria for the evaluation of family life education materials. *Family Relations, 30,* 549-556.

Hall, R. M., & Sandler, B. R. (1982). *The classroom climate: A chilly one for women?* Washington, DC: Association of American Colleges. (Available from Project on the Status and Education of Women, Association of American Colleges, 1818 R Street NW, Washington, DC, 20009)

Harper, L. J. (1981). Home economics in higher education: Status and trends 1980. *Journal of Home Economics, 73,* 14-18.

Hunt, M. (1974). *Sexual behavior in the 1970s.* New York: Dell.

Hutton, S. S. (1976). Sex role illustrations in junior high school home economics textbooks. *Journal of Home Economics, 68,* 27-30.

Japanese schoolbooks bend gender stereotypes. (1992, February 17). *Detroit Free Press,* p. E-1.

Keen, S. (1991). *Fire in the belly: On being a man.* New York: Bantam.

Kerckhoff, R. K., Habig, M., & *The Family Coordinator* Family Life Education Panel. (1976). Parent education as provided by secondary schools. *The Family Coordinator, 25,* 127-130.

Kerckhoff, R. K., Hancock, T. W., & *The Family Coordinator* Family Life Education Panel. (1971). The family life educator of the future. *The Family Coordinator, 20*, 315-325.

Kirkendall, L. A. (1950). *Sex education as human relations.* Sweet Springs, MO: Inor.

Kirkendall, L. A. (1984). The journey toward SIECUS: A personal odyssey. *SIECUS Report, 12*, 1-4.

Kohlberg, L. (1976). Moral stages and moralization: The cognitive-developmental approach. In T. Lickona (Ed.), *Moral development and behavior: Theory, research and social issues.* New York: Holt, Rinehart & Winston.

Kohlberg, L. (1981). *The philosophy of moral development.* San Francisco: Harper & Row.

Komarovsky, M. (1988). The new feminist scholarship: Some precursors and polemics. *Journal of Marriage and the Family, 50*, 585-593.

Lee, J. (1989). *Fly boy: Healing the wounded man.* Deerfield Beach, FL: Health Communications.

Lengerman, P. M., & Wallace, R. A. (1985). *Gender in America: Social control and social change.* Englewood Cliffs, NJ: Prentice-Hall.

LoPicolo, J. (1983). The prevention of sexual problems in men. In G. S. Albee & H. Leitenberg (Eds.), *Promoting sexual responsibility and preventing sexual problems.* Hanover, NH: University Press of New England.

Losh-Hesselbart, S. (1987). Development of gender roles. In M. B. Sussman & S. K. Steinmetz (Eds.), *Handbook of marriage and the family* (pp. 535-564). New York: Plenum.

Macklin, E. D. (1987). Nontraditional family forms. In M. Sussman & S. Steinmetz (Eds.), *Handbook of marriage and the family* (pp. 317-354). New York: Plenum.

Malfetti, J. L., & Rubin, A. M. (1968). Sex education: Who is teaching the teachers? *The Family Coordinator, 17*, 110-118.

Mason, R. L. (1974). Family life education in the high schools of Kentucky. *The Family Coordinator, 23*, 197-201.

McBride, B. A., & McBride, R. J. (1990). The changing role of father: Some implications for educators. *Journal of Home Economics, 82*, 6-10.

McCartney, K., & Rosenthal, S. (1991). Maternal employment should be studied within social ecologies. *Journal of Marriage and the Family, 53*, 1103-1107.

McKenry, P. C., & Price, S. J. (in press). Alternatives for support after divorce: A review of the literature. *Journal of Divorce and Remarriage.*

Miller, J. B. (1986). *Toward a new psychology of women* (2nd ed.). Boston: Beacon.

Moller Okin, S. (1989). *Justice, gender, and the family.* New York: Basic Books.

Moss, J. J., & Brasher, R. (Eds.). (1981). Family life education [Special issue]. *Family Relations, 30*(4).

Nass, G., Libby, R., & Fisher, M. (1984). *Sexual choices.* Monterey, CA: Wadsworth.

Osmund, M. W. (1987). Radical-critical theories. In M. B. Sussman & S. K. Steinmetz (Eds.), *Handbook of marriage and the family* (pp. 103-124). New York: Plenum.

Osofsky, J. D., & Osofsky, H. J. (1972). Androgyny as a life style. *The Family Coordinator, 21*, 411-418.

Parsons, T. (1951). *The social system.* Glencoe, IL: Free Press.

Pearson, J. C., Turner, L. H., & Todd-Mancillas, W. (1991). *Gender and communication* (2nd ed.). Dubuque, IA: William C Brown.

Pleck, J. (1985). *Working wives/working husbands.* Beverly Hills, CA: Sage.

Polonko, K. (1990, November). *Implications of feminist scholarship for the study of families and children.* Paper presented at the annual meeting of the National Council on Family Relations, Seattle, WA.

Price, S. J., & McKenry, P. C. (1988). *Divorce.* Newbury Park, CA: Sage.

Price, S. J., & McKenry, P. C. (1989). Current trends and issues in divorce. *Family Science Review, 2*, 313-348.

Rossi, A. (1977). A biosocial perspective on parenting. *Daedalus, 106*(2), 1-31.

Rossi, A. (1981). On the reproduction of mothering: A methodological debate. *Signs: Journal of Women in Culture and Society, 6*(3), 492-500.

Rossi, A. (1984). Gender and parenthood. *American Sociological Review, 49*, 1-19.

Rudd, N. M., & McKenry, P. C. (1982, June). *Social psychological and economic indicators of family satisfaction with the dual-work role.* Paper presented at the annual meeting of the American Home Economics Association, Cincinnati, OH.

Ruddick, S. (1982). Maternal thinking. In B. Thorne & M. Yalom (Eds.), *Rethinking the family* (pp. 76-94). New York: Longman.

Scanzoni, J., Polonko, K., Teachman, J., & Thompson, L. (1989). *The sexual bond: Rethinking families and close relationships.* Newbury Park, CA: Sage.

Scarr, S. (1991). On comparing apples and oranges and making inferences about bananas. *Journal of Marriage and the Family, 53*, 1099-1100.

Scott, J. (1986). Gender: A useful category of historical analysis. *American Historical Review, 91*, 1053-1075.

Scott, K. P. (1986). Learning sex-equitable social skills. *Theory into Practice, 25*, 243-249.

Seccombe, K. (1991). Assessing the costs and benefits of children: Gender comparisons among childfree husbands and wives. *Journal of Marriage and the Family, 52*, 191-202.

Shiffman, M. (1987). The men's movement: An exploratory empirical investigation. In M. S. Kimmel (Ed.), *Changing men: New directions in research on men and masculinity* (pp. 295-314). Newbury Park, CA: Sage.

Somerville, R. M. (1971). Family life and sex education in the turbulent sixties. *Journal of Marriage and the Family, 33*, 11-35.

Somerville, R. M. (1972). *Introduction to family life education.* Englewood Cliffs, NJ: Prentice-Hall.

Spanier, G. B. (1980). Sexualization and premarital and sexual behavior. *The Family Coordinator, 24*, 33-41.

Sprey, J. (1988). Current theorizing on the family: An appraisal. *Journal of Marriage and the Family, 50*, 875-890.

Stewart, L. P., Stewart, A. D., Friedley, S. A., & Cooper, P. J. (1990). *Communication between the sexes* (2nd ed.). Scottsdale, AZ: Gorsuch Scarisbrick.

Tannen, D. (1990). *You just don't understand: Women and men in conversation.* New York: William Morrow.

Teachman, J. D., Polonko, K. A., & Scanzoni, J. (1987). Demography of the family. In M. S. Sussman & S. K. Steinmetz (Eds.), *Handbook of marriage and the family.* New York: Plenum.

Tetreault, M. K. (1986). The journey from male-defined to gender-balanced education. *Theory into Practice, 25*, 227-234.

Thomas, J. (1992). Two worlds of curriculum: The case of family life education. In L. B. Peterat & E. Vaines (Eds.), *Lives and plans: Signs for transforming practice.* Alexandria, VA: American Home Economics Association.

Thompson, L. (1988). Feminist resources for applied family studies. *Family Relations, 37*, 99-104.

Thompson, L. (1992). Feminist methodology for family studies. *Journal of Marriage and the Family, 54*, 3-18.

Thompson, L., & Walker, A. J. (1989). Gender in families: Women and men in marriage, work, and parenthood. *Journal of Marriage and the Family, 51*, 845-872.

Thompson, P. J. (1986). Beyond gender: Equity issues for home economics education. *Theory into Practice, 25*, 277-283.

Thompson, P. J. (1989). The Hestian paradigm: Theory construction for home economics. In F. H. Hultgren & D. L. Coomer (Eds.), *Alternative modes of inquiry in home economics research* (pp. 95-116). Alexandria, VA: American Home Economics Association.

Thorne, B., & Yalom, M. (1982). *Rethinking the family: Some feminist questions.* New York: Longman.

Troost, K. M. (1988). Sociobiology and the family: Promise versus product. In E. E. Filsinger (Ed.), *Biosocial perspectives on the family* (pp. 188-205). Newbury Park, CA: Sage.

Vandell, D. L. (1991). Belsky and Eggebeen's analysis of the NLSY: Meaningful results or statistical illusions? *Journal of Marriage and the Family, 53*, 1100-1103.

Walker, A. J., Kees Martin, S. S., & Thompson, L. (1988). Feminist programs for families. *Family Relations, 37*, 17-22.

Walsh, M. R. (1987). Is androgyny a solution? In M. R. Walsh (Ed.), *The psychology of women: Ongoing debates* (pp. 203-205). New Haven, CT: Yale University Press.

White, B. (1981). Should you stay home with your baby? *Young Children, 37*(1), 11-17.

Zelbergeld, B. (1981). *Male sexuality.* New York: Bantam.

7

Ethnicity and Diversity in Family Life Education

Gladys J. Hildreth
Alan I. Sugawara

ETHNICITY IS AN IMPORTANT ISSUE in the study of the family. Many studies have shown that there are cultural variations in the various domains of family development from the time that a baby is born to the death of older family members (Feagin, 1984). Most if not all cultures have established norms regarding dating, marriage, parenting, money, education, death, and related topics. As well, it has been noted that, although all babies are essentially the same despite differences in climate and in history, a competent mother will be competent within her own culture (Kissen, 1991).

Families are a major vehicle for the transmission of cultural values and traditions from one generation to another and for the socialization of children for living within the society at large (Saracho & Spodek, 1983). In relatively homogeneous societies, the transmission of these values and traditions appears to have occurred with relative ease. As people migrate, however, interactions between peoples with various linguistic and cultural heritages have become more commonplace and the transmission of family values and traditions has become more difficult. Such difficulties are inevitable when family values and traditions come into conflict with those of the larger, more diverse cultural environment (Jim & Suen, 1990).

It is clear that the world no longer consists of isolated homogeneous societies (Banks, 1979). People with different linguistic and cultural heritages may live within the same communities or within relatively close proximity to each other (Saracho & Spodek, 1983). In Europe, for example, there are multicultural areas in the Alsace-Lorraine regions of France and Germany, in the Sudetenland of Czechoslovakia, and in the Basque region of France and Spain (Saracho & Spodek, 1983). In North America, multicultural areas were present long before the settlement of the first Europeans (John, 1988; Saracho & Spodek, 1983). Multilingualism and multiculturalism therefore are contemporary facts of life.

Multilingualism and multiculturalism as facts of life have important implications for family life education. Historically, many family life education programs appear to have emphasized uniformity rather than diversity; that is, they have focused almost exclusively on the norms and practices of the dominant culture. Among other things, this has made it difficult for many participants to maintain their own culture at the same time that they participate in the broader culture. At the current time, however, if family life education is to accomplish its goal of strengthening and enriching individual and family well-being, then family life educators can no longer overlook the implications of cultural diversity in the development and provision of programs to support and empower all families.

This chapter will briefly describe some of the critical issues faced by families in culturally diverse societies, and attention will be drawn to implications of these issues for family life education. Several models for dealing with intergroup relationships will be described and evaluated for their relevance to family life education. As well, suggestions regarding important dimensions in designing appropriate programs for individuals and families in a culturally diverse society will be discussed.

At the onset, it should be noted that scholars have disagreed on the definition of such terms as *culture, ethnicity*, and their derivatives. For the purpose of this chapter, *culture* is used as a general term to describe the totality of values, beliefs, and behaviors common to a large group of people. This may include the sharing of characteristics such as language, feelings, ideas, thinking patterns, modes of acting, physical attributes, communication styles, and material artifacts. As such, it can be said that all are part of one "human culture" or part of several different cultures, that is, the American culture, Canadian culture, Japanese culture, Mexican culture, Indian culture, and so on.

Cultures, however, are not static entities but change over time as they interact with one another and with the environment. The terms *multicultural, multilingual,* and *cultural diversity* therefore are used to describe the condition of a wide range of differences that exist among and within these cultural groups relative to the characteristics that define them. Multicultural education then focuses upon an approach to education that takes seriously the common characteristics that exist among different cultural groups, the unique qualities that make them distinct as a result of their cultural pasts, and the new cultural characteristics that emerge as a result of the interactions that occur between them.

Ethnicity, however, is a much more specific term used to focus on the degree to which a group of people share a sense of group identification, whether through kinship, a shared linguistic commonality, values, attitudes, or modes of thinking, feeling, and behaving. There may be a variety of ethnic groups within a culture, such as African Americans, Chinese Canadians, and Hispanos.

FAMILY ISSUES AND CONFLICTS

To develop relevant programs in culturally diverse societies, family life educators must be cognizant of the issues faced by families in these societies. Jim and Suen (1990), for example, have cited several current issues facing Chinese immigrant families living in Canada: (a) the portrayal of the plight of Vietnamese refugees by mass media sensationalism, reinforcing negative public opinion of refugees; (b) affluent immigrants who do not devote ample time to parenting, thus causing family breakdown; (c) school problems related to dropouts, truancy, fighting, poor performance, or nonparticipation of their children; (d) criminal activities related to theft, assaults, gangs, and prostitution; and (e) racial tensions brought on by the clash of cultural values that threaten the majority population, uncertain or confused about the pending influx of Asian immigrants.

Other ethnic and racial groups also face a number of issues and conflicts. For example, in the United States, African American unemployment rates, poverty rates, and single-parent, female-headed households are still higher than those of the American majority. Furthermore, recent cuts in federal funding of programs in job training and education, as well as lack of support for affirmative action and civil rights programs, have led many African American leaders to feel that they still have not been dealt with fairly by society.

Mexican Americans are the largest Spanish-speaking group and, next to African Americans, are the single largest minority group in the United States. They have a high birthrate compared with other ethnic and racial groups (Banks, 1988), and although life has improved for some Mexican American families, they still face many problems related to income, education, and other socioeconomic conditions. Dinnerstein and Reimers (1988) have reported that the majority of the Spanish-speaking people in the United States find themselves near the bottom of the socioeconomic ladder. According to Banks (1988), Mexican American families face an important challenge in increasing the educational status of their youth to make them more employable.

Although a number of classification schemes have been used to summarize these issues, the scheme developed by Jim and Suen (1990) to understand the transitions and cultural conflicts experienced by Chinese parents and teenagers in Canada appears useful. Their classification scheme included issues associated with (a) migrants and their expectations, (b) conflicts and transitions, (c) dual cultural dilemmas, and (d) bicultural (intergenerational) conflicts.

Migrants and Their Expectations

Despite the fact that groups of people with similar ethnic backgrounds have migrated to similar geographic areas, their common cultural heritage does not ensure that they are a totally homogeneous group of people (Banks, 1979; Chan, Takanishi, & Kitano, 1975; Jim & Suen, 1990; M. K. Kitano, 1983; Laosa, 1977; Saracho & Hancock, 1983). Even among individuals from the same ethnic background, there is some cultural variability. Several examples illustrate the complexity of this point. Native Americans, for example, represent a large number of tribes with different linguistic and cultural heritages (John, 1988; H. H. L. Kitano, 1991). There is no one kind of Indian, no one tribe, no one Indian nation. Likewise, not all Asians living within a particular geographic area can be described as Chinese, and not all Chinese come from mainland China. Some may be locally born, while others may have come from Taiwan, Hong Kong, South America, or Southeast Asia (Jim & Suen, 1990).

Furthermore, not all Mexican Americans refer to themselves by the same name (Saracho & Hancock, 1983). Those of Mexican descent living in northern New Mexico and southern Colorado call themselves Spanish Americans, while others call themselves Latin Americans, Chicanos, Hispanos, Spanish speaking, La Raza, and Americans of Mexican descent (Ramirez & Castaneda, 1974). As well, Vietnamese immigrants cannot be considered to be the same (M. K. Kitano, 1983). Some come from rural or urban areas, others from intellectual or illiterate families, and still others are war refugees or are immigrants through free choice. Understanding these important cultural distinctions helps to provide insight into the diverse backgrounds from which people come and from which their expectations have evolved (Jim & Suen, 1990).

More generally, while many people may have migrated to a particular geographic region as a result of free choice (in search of better jobs or an improved quality of life), the migrations of still others may have been forced or impelled (because of environmental/ecological changes in their homelands, civil and international wars, differences in political and religious ideology, and oppressive economic conditions; Lee, 1966; McKee, 1985; Peterson, 1958; Ravenstein, 1885, 1889; Schermerhorn, 1970). These different migration experiences may result in the development of different expectations in the new environment. At least some of these will be relevant to family life education.

Conflicts and Transitions

Entering a new cultural environment and learning to adjust to a new set of values and traditions may be exciting to some, but it may take its toll on others (Jim & Suen, 1990). As ethnic values clash with the values of the new environment, a wide range of emotions may be experienced (anger, hatred, frustration, hostility, confusion, and fear), and these are likely to manifest into a variety of behaviors (struggle, discrimination, violence, withdrawal, denial, depression, illness, isolation). In such circumstances, identities need to be reestablished, values reexamined, old customs abandoned or retained, practices learned and unlearned, new relationships forged, challenging opportunities confronted, risks taken, and fears conquered, so that positive growth within a new cultural environment can take place (Jim & Suen, 1990). Because of their understanding and skills in working with families over the life span, family life educators are well qualified to help families make these cultural transitions.

Dual Cultural Dilemmas

As migrants settle within the new cultural environment, contrasting features of their traditional culture and those of the new cultural environment are gradually experienced. Some of these experiences have to do with contrasting cultural features associated with the nature of the family, interpersonal relationships, values and beliefs, cultural taboos, marriage practices, disciplinary style, rights and privileges, and politics (Jim & Suen, 1990).

Several examples illustrate these potential dilemmas. The traditional Chinese family has been described as extended, multigenerational, patriarchal, authoritarian, and responsible for its individual members for life (Jim & Suen, 1990), but in Canada families are generally nuclear, immediate, egalitarian, and responsible for their children until legal age. Among some traditional Hawaiian and Indian families (Gallimore, Boggs, & Jordan, 1974; H. H. L. Kitano, 1991; Wax, 1971), values such as interdependence, cooperation, and shared family functioning are often emphasized, while the U.S. culture stresses such values as independence, competition, and individual achievement (Gallimore et al., 1974). In the traditional Japanese culture, people are frequently described as emotionally restrained, moralistic regarding sex, and with marriages sometimes arranged or approved by their families (Jim & Suen, 1990; M. K. Kitano, 1983; Sue, 1973). In Canada and the United States, however, people are generally verbally expressive, receive sex education in the schools, and perceive marriage as a private, personal decision. Traditional Mexican, Japanese, Korean, and Vietnamese cultures accord respect and authority to the elders (Jim & Suen, 1990; H. H. L. Kitano, 1973; M. K. Kitano, 1983; Pitler, 1977; Ramirez & Castaneda, 1974; Saracho & Hancock, 1983; Sue, 1973), while in Canada and the United States the cultural emphasis is on youth. Finally, African Americans are said to be relational rather than analytical in their cognitive style (Akbar, 1975; Cohen, 1971; Hale, 1983; Hillard, 1976; Young, 1970). They tend to view things in their entirety rather than in isolated parts, prefer inferential rather than deductive/inductive reasoning, focus on people and their activities rather than objects, and identify the uniqueness of things rather than their commonalities, and they are affective rather than objective in their responses. All of these contrasting cultural features pose real challenges for family life educators as they seek to help families in culturally diverse societies.

Bicultural (Intergenerational) Conflicts

Once settled within a new cultural environment, migrants gradually establish their own families and encounter issues related to differing methods of child rearing (Jim & Suen, 1990). These bicultural conflicts emerge as a result of the different values and beliefs held by parents and their children, particularly during the adolescent years. These bicultural, intergenerational conflicts occur in such areas as family relationships, socialization experiences, education, and employment.

Conflicts Regarding Family Relationships

Bicultural conflicts related to family relationships include issues surrounding the expression of love, the role of family members, traditions and cultural values, parenting styles, obedience, communication, and problem solving. For example, among some Chinese Canadian parents, there is a relative absence of verbal and physical affection (Jim & Suen, 1990), but having lived in a more expressive Canadian culture, their adolescents may become confused about the lack of empathy they receive from their parents. In some Japanese American families, mothers are viewed as loving wives, submissive and nurturing, while their adolescent daughters may be attempting to break away from such gender role stereotypes so as to pursue careers of their own (Jim & Suen, 1990; M. K. Kitano, 1983). Some Hawaiian, Native American, and Mexican American parents may emphasize family ties, cooperation, and interdependence, while their adolescents desire the independence, individuality, and freedom experienced in the larger society (Gallimore et al., 1974; Gulick, 1960; M. K. Kitano, 1983; Ramirez & Castaneda, 1974; Saracho & Hancock, 1983). In addition, Japanese American children are often expected to show obedience and deference to their parents and are admonished to keep their problems internal to the family (e.g., a face-saving device), but adolescents often test parental limits, resent following orders, and may seek the help of friends or a counselor to deal with family problems (Kitano, 1973; M. K. Kitano, 1983). Helping families to deal with these bicultural, intergenerational family conflicts is well within the domain of family life education.

Conflicts Regarding Socialization

Parents and adolescents may also experience conflicts on such matters as identity, dating and peers, social skills, food, and fears (Jim & Suen, 1990). African American parents may wish their children to emulate their own cultural values and to adopt role models associated with their own cultural heritages, yet these cultural values and models find limited display in the mainstream of society (Hale, 1983). Some Chinese Canadian parents may believe it is not appropriate for their adolescents to date at a young age; however, pressures from peers may lead adolescents to rebel against such parental restrictions (Jim & Suen, 1990). While Japanese American parents may wish their children to develop social skills that maintain proper relationships with members of their own cultural group, adolescents may find it both necessary and essential to develop skills in cross-cultural interaction to achieve some success in the larger society (M. K. Kitano, 1983). Korean parents may prefer to eat foods associated with their own culture, but their adolescents may prefer fast-food restaurants where peer social interaction and fun take place (Jim & Suen, 1990). Finally, fears related to such things as interracial marriages may occur among Chinese parents, yet their adolescents, because of their association with individuals from a wide range of cultural backgrounds, may find such fears obsolete (Jim & Suen, 1990). Helping families with these issues, too, lies well within the domain of family life education.

Conflicts Regarding Education

Another set of issues is related to education, including conflicts between parents and adolescents regarding expectations, future goals, relationships between home and school, educational processes, practices, and alternative programs (Jim & Suen, 1990). Among Mexican American and Hawaiian parents, family ties and commitment are viewed as very important values (Gallimore et al., 1974; M. K. Kitano, 1983; Ramirez & Castaneda, 1974; Saracho & Hancock, 1983). Education proves useful by contributing to family well-being, and being socially educated is more important than being academically educated. When their children enter the public schools, however, they are often confronted with a value system having different goals, leading to feelings of frustration, lack of confidence in school situations, and underachievement.

On the other hand, Chinese parents in Canada and the United States frequently have very high expectations for their children's academic achievement (Jim & Suen, 1990; M. K. Kitano, 1983). These expectations place pressures on adolescents to perform at levels that are sometimes unrealistic. If such expectations are not met, ridicule may be experienced, leading to low self-esteem, resentment, and at times a rejection of this cultural value. Furthermore, some Chinese Canadian parents perceive that their children's education should be goal oriented, a means of securing financial success as a result of years of persistent study (Jim & Suen, 1990). Their adolescents, however, are influenced by a society in which instant gratification and peer pressures are present, so that oftentimes easy gratification of goals, reinforced by peer pressure, is pursued.

African American parents are said to raise their children in social networks of physical closeness, acceptance, and care (Ebsen, 1973; Gitter, Black, & Mostofsky, 1972; Hale, 1983; Newmeyer, 1970; Young, 1970). Such early socialization experiences may have an impact on their children, making them more people oriented, affective, and proficient in nonverbal communication. Add to these African American children's motoric precocity and high energy levels, then one can understand how the school system, with its emphasis on objects, verbal communication, deductive/inductive reasoning, and low movement activities, is at odds with the African American child (Boykin, 1977; Guttentag, 1972; Guttentag & Ross, 1972; Hale, 1983; Morgan, 1976).

Conflicts Regarding Employment

Finally, there are a number of conflicts associated with employment. These may include conflicts between parents and adolescents over the work ethic, salaries, skills, occupation/profession, expectations, and unemployment (Jim & Suen, 1990). Among traditional Japanese American parents, unspoken loyalty is often given in return for long-term employment (M. K. Kitano, 1983) and there is a perception that one should start from the bottom of the job ladder before moving up. Furthermore, verbal agreements between employers and employees frequently have been used as acceptable contracts. Today's adolescents, however, can expect good pay for good work, enter jobs at various levels with proper training, and sign job-related legal agreements. Unemployment was once viewed as a sign of failure, disgrace, and stigma, but now some see welfare as a right or as an opportunity to start a new career or get job training (Jim & Suen, 1990).

In the past, among families from a variety of cultural groups, many businesses were family owned, and one entered the system through family ties and connections. Today, adolescents are confronted with corporate structures in which jobs and promotions are often based on skill, seniority, and performance. It should be noted, however, that among some ethnic groups, such as African Americans, years of discrimination forbade them from exercising their civil rights (Dinnerstein & Reimers, 1988). Parents experiencing these conditions were limited in their expectations and opportunities for entering into the mainstream of American economic life. Today, however, equal opportunity and affirmative action programs, though threatened at times, have allowed their children the opportunity to enter the world of employment through recognition of their equal opportunity and civil rights (Jim & Suen, 1990). In other ethnic groups, however, such as Hawaiians and Native Americans, whose cultural values have centered upon family interdependence, cooperation, and sharing, entrance into the world of work where individual achievement and competition predominate has not been easy (Gallimore et al., 1974; John, 1988; H. H. L. Kitano, 1991; M. K. Kitano, 1983). To participate in the mainstream of economic life, many of these adolescents have had to struggle with ways to develop their skills, attitudes, and expectations without necessarily abandoning their cultural heritages.

MODELS OF INTERGROUP RELATIONS

Several models of intergroup relations have been used by educators to help individuals and families deal with issues associated with cultural diversity. These models include (a) assimilation, (b) amalgamation, (c) cultural pluralism, and (d) ethnogenesis.

Assimilation Theory

Assimilation theory espouses as its end goal the conformity of an ethnic minority group to the majority or dominant culture (Appleton, 1983; Feagin, 1984; McLemore, 1983; Parillo, 1990). It asserts that over time different ethnic minority groups will gradually become like the dominant culture, until, finally, all would merge into one common culture patterned after the dominant group. Characteristics of the dominant group are viewed as superior and desirable, while those of the minority group are considered abnormal, inferior, and undesirable (McLemore, 1983). This process is called "acculturation" and occurs on at least two levels: (a) behavioral/cultural (e.g., modes of behavior associated with the dominant culture) and (b) structural (e.g., organizations, institutions, and general civic life of the dominant culture; Gordon, 1964).

Assimilation theory as an educational strategy in dealing with cultural diversity has been evident in a number of societies. For example, often what is taught in the public schools, regardless of children's cultural backgrounds, suggests that the dominant cultural values are being transmitted as the common cultural values (Banks, 1979). The values of various ethnic minority groups may not be taken seriously in the educational process and ultimately may be ignored. While human beings enjoy a common human culture, whether such a common culture can be identified as the dominant culture is certainly open to question. Furthermore, whether a dominant culture's characteristics are superior to those of a minority culture cannot be truly substantiated. In addition, it seems unlikely even within the most minority of cultures that people will totally relinquish all of their cultural characteristics for those of another culture. Such cultural characteristics are too deeply ingrained within individual personalities. This may be one of the reasons that, even after generations have passed, ethnic groups have continued to maintain their distinctiveness from other cultural groups. Yet, through interaction with other cultural groups, these ethnic groups have changed, and new cultural characteristics have emerged. The assimilationist educator has no way of dealing with such emergent cultural characteristics. As a basis for developing strategies for family life education programs in a culturally diverse society, therefore, this approach is highly ethnocentric, limiting, and restrictive and is bound to promote prejudice and schisms among various cultural groups.

Amalgamation Theory

Amalgamation theory espouses as its end goal the development of a new cultural group resulting from a synthesis of previously existing groups through the blending of their biological and/or cultural differences (Appleton, 1983; Parillo, 1990). Called the "melting pot theory," this approach, like the assimilation approach, embraces the concept of the disappearance of minority group cultures but adds to it the disappearance of the dominant culture as well (McLemore, 1983). What emerges is a unique new cultural group harboring contributions from all cultural groups present.

This theory was popular for a time because it moved beyond describing people in terms of their past ethnic heritages and centered on the unique characteristics that emerge as a result of the interaction between various groups. Evidence in support of this approach, however, is marginal at best. Some examples include the intermarriages that occur between people of different nationalities, races, and, to a lesser degree, religions in Hawaii and instances where cultures have borrowed ideas, behaviors, and values from each other, such as the Spanish architectural influences in the southwest United States, the inclusion of foods from a wide variety of ethnic groups in diets, recreational activities, and holiday celebrations (Appleton, 1983).

Beyond these examples, however, evidence for amalgamation is quite sparse. A number of possible reasons can be given for the limitations of this approach as a basis for developing strategies for use by family life educators in helping individuals and families live within a culturally diverse society (Appleton, 1983; Banks, 1988). For one thing, amalgamation requires that both the dominant and the minority cultures be willing to forgo their own cultural heritages in exchange for a new and emerging one. Minority groups continue to flourish throughout the world, however, and many continue to struggle for equality under the power of dominant cultural groups. In fact, what has happened to this approach is a reinterpretation of the concept of "melting pot" to mean "dominant cultural conformity" or the remaking of groups of people into the dominant cultural mode (Herberg, 1960). Therefore, while this approach clearly recognizes the emergence of unique cultural characteristics that occurs as a result of interactions between peoples from various cultural groups, it fails to recognize that there are both common as well as distinct past cultural characteristics among all cultural groups. Furthermore, the tendency by some to reinterpret the emerging unique cultural group as "dominant cultural conformity" is misleading and does not accurately reflect the nature of our current culturally diverse societies.

Cultural Pluralism

Cultural pluralism as an explicit theory of ethnic diversity can be traced to the writings of Kallen (1915). He objected to the notion that ethnic groups should give up their distinct cultures to become American and he believed that, although all Americans should master the American culture and participate on an equal footing in occupational, educational, and political life, they should also have the freedom to decide how much of their cultural heritage they wish to retain.

While the idea of cultural pluralism is a simple one, the goal of the theory from which this concept emerges is not as clearly delineated or as easy to describe as those of the "Anglo-conformity" or "melting pot" ideologies. Much of this confusion arises because different pluralists have advocated different degrees of separation between various cultural groups (McLemore, 1983).

At the current time, scholars have distinguished between two different types of cultural pluralism: classical cultural pluralism and modified cultural pluralism (Appleton, 1983). In classical cultural pluralism, diverse groups of people live together in peaceful coexistence as common members of society, with each group maintaining its own cultural distinctiveness and identity. With the passage of time, however, and with more interactions between the groups, these groups may adopt common political values, share language, exchange ideas, and thus decrease the cultural distance between them.

In spite of its effectiveness in describing important features of ethnic groups in the United States, however, modified cultural pluralism still fails to capture certain aspects of change among different ethnic groups (Appleton, 1983; Banks, 1988). These groups change and develop in directions that cannot be solely explained on the basis of characteristics inherited from their ethnic past or those that develop through interactions with other groups to form a common culture.

Ethnogenesis

According to this approach to cultural diversity (Greeley, 1974), ethnic groups are viewed as dynamic, flexible mechanisms that grow and change but still have integrity as ethnic groups that is not necessarily threatened by such change. When different migrant groups come into contact with each other, there already exists between them various common characteristics. These common characteristics are part of the original cultural system of each group and are diagrammed in Figure 7.1. This initial degree of similarity among different migrant groups varies, with some groups having more common characteristics and others having less. For example, among European groups that emigrated to America, many shared a broad Western cultural heritage. Most Irish, for instance, spoke English and were aware of the English political system when they arrived in America. Individuals who emigrated from Southeast Asia, however, did not share such linguistic and cultural characteristics. Whichever the case, these common characteristics influence the dynamics that develop between the groups over time.

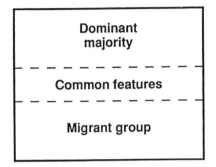

Figure 7.1. Original Cultural System
SOURCE: Adapted from *Cultural Pluralism in Education: Theoretical Foundations* by Nicholas Appleton. Copyright © 1983. Reprinted with permission from Longman Publishing Group.

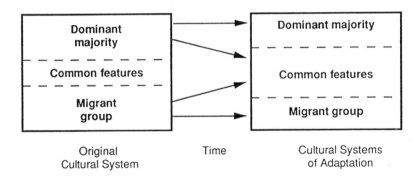

Figure 7.2. Modified Group Identity
SOURCE: Adapted from *Cultural Pluralism in Education: Theoretical Foundations* by Nicholas Appleton. Copyright © 1983. Reprinted with permission from Longman Publishing Group.

With continued group interaction, acculturation and other experiences in the larger society lead to the growth of a common culture between them. Migrant groups become more like the dominant culture, and the dominant culture becomes somewhat like the migrant group. Certain migrant characteristics may persist along with the growth of the common culture, however, leading to a modified group identity. This process of group identity development was previously described as "modified cultural pluralism" and is diagrammed in Figure 7.2.

It should be indicated, however, that, although this process of adaptation can bring diverse groups together to build a common culture, it can also work in the other direction. Under the impact of a dominant

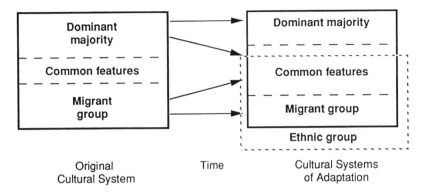

Figure 7.3. Ethnic Group Development

SOURCE: Adapted from *Cultural Pluralism in Education: Theoretical Foundations* by Nicholas Appleton. Copyright © 1983. Reprinted with permission from Longman Publishing Group.

culture, some migrant traits become more rather than less distinct. What emerges, then, is an ethnic group that has a combination of traits that make them both similar to and different than the common culture and their migrant past. The growth of this ethnic group beyond the characteristics of the dominant culture and its original migrant group is diagrammed in Figure 7.3 and illustrated by the dotted line.

From the perspective of ethnogenesis, therefore, an ethnic group can move back toward the original cultural system as well as expand to new horizons. At times, an ethnic group can reassert and rediscover aspects of its own cultural heritage previously lost to acculturation. Ethnogenesis thus is not unidirectional but multidirectional in nature. Ethnic groups have undergone a variety of changes over past generations. In many respects, they have assimilated into the mainstream of society yet still remain unique politically, culturally, and residentially. They are not the same as they were in the past but nevertheless are viable and in some respects more unique than in the past. The Navaho Indians of North America, for example, are not the same people they were 50 or 100 years ago. They are distinctly Navahos, but in different ways, some of which are traditional Navaho, some of which are influenced by the society at large, and some of which have emerged as a result of the interaction between their past cultural heritage and the society at large. Such a process continues on through time, exemplifying the dynamic evolutionary nature of ethnogenesis, which characterizes all ethnic groups.

As a foundation for developing strategies for use in family life education programs, ethnogenesis provides a more comprehensive approach than assimilation, amalgamation, or cultural pluralism. It does so by viewing ethnic groups as dynamic, flexible entities (a) often sharing and developing a common culture between them, (b) at times seeking to maintain and enhance their unique cultural heritages, and (c) continuously evolving into the unique ethnic groups they are today and will be in the future. It is these three aspects of the ethnogenesis process that family life educators must consider in designing programs focused on helping individuals and families within a culturally diverse society.

DESIGNING CULTURALLY RELEVANT FAMILY LIFE EDUCATION PROGRAMS

Program development and evaluation specialists have identified at least four dimensions that must be considered in designing culturally relevant programs (Morris, 1983; Ramsey, Vold, & Williams, 1989). These include (a) understanding the needs, expectations, and strengths of the families for whom the program is to be designed; (b) developing goals and objectives that match these family needs, expectations, and strengths; (c) designing and implementing appropriate programs; and (d) evaluating the effectiveness of the program. (Readers should refer to Chapter 5 in this volume for a more extensive discussion of program development, implementation, and evaluation.)

Needs, Expectations, and Strengths

Families from different cultural backgrounds manifest different needs, expectations, and strengths that must be considered in designing relevant and appropriate programs. Failure to consider these characteristics is bound to lead to programs that are meaningless and ineffective. A newly arrived family from Vietnam, for example, may be socially isolated, economically poor, and unaware of the resources available to help them survive in a new cultural environment (M. K. Kitano, 1983). After years of cultural decimation, many Native Americans are more than ever committed to the revitalization of their cultural heritages and have special needs related to this goal (John, 1988). Among Japanese Americans, the gradual disappearance of their ethnic group resources (e.g., organizations, community credit system) has led many to now depend upon the larger community for a variety of social and economic services (H. H. L. Kitano, 1991). Knowledge of these and other needs of different cultural groups will be vital to the development of relevant family life education programs.

In addition to these needs, the different expectations that may characterize various cultural groups must also be taken into account. For example, Chinese Canadian parents are said to have high expectations for their children to achieve academically (Jim & Suen, 1990) while Mexican American families are likely to emphasize the value of family ties and the importance of being socially rather than academically educated (Saracho & Hancock, 1983). Furthermore, many African Americans, having finally had their civil rights recognized, are eager to actively participate in the larger society as significant contributing members whether through their own resources, equal opportunity, or affirmative action programs. These and other expectations that characterize various cultural groups need to be incorporated into family life education programs if they are to have meaning for individuals and families within these groups.

Recognizing the strengths of these families can also be useful in designing appropriate family life education programs. Use of these strengths in program development and implementation can motivate families to take responsibility for resolving their own problems and meeting their own needs, thus empowering them to live meaningfully and effectively within the society at large. For example, capitalizing on the importance of close family ties among Hawaiian families can lead to more active participation on the part of their parents in the public school education of their children (M. K. Kitano, 1983). In addition, the achievement of Japanese Americans in many professions such as law, medicine, education, and pharmacology can be used as an asset in meeting the needs of people within a community (H. H. L. Kitano, 1991). Employing individual and family role models from various cultural backgrounds can help to communicate the important messages regarding available services provided by family life education programs. When designing family life education programs, it is important not to overlook the strengths that families from different cultural groups bring to these programs.

A note of caution must be introduced regarding the manner in which one understands the needs, expectations, and strengths of various cultural groups in designing programs. During the 1960s, the cultural deficit or compensatory model was used to design education programs for children and families from different cultural groups. This model emphasized the need to intervene in the lives of individuals and families so that remediation of previously low achievement could occur. Such an approach not only undermined the strength that characterizes various cultural groups but also robbed them of their dignity as a people. More recently, the concept of cultural difference has been emphasized. This approach makes no value judgment about the relative "goodness" of each cultural group, and there is no intervention into the life of such a cultural group for the purpose of remediation and molding. Instead, all cultural groups are valued for their uniqueness, so that programs change to meet the needs of individuals and families rather than vice versa. As a result, the dignity, integrity, and diversity of all cultural groups are preserved. Family life education programs that are sensitive to the diverse needs, expectations, and strengths of various cultural groups and are flexible enough to adjust their programs to meet this diversity are more likely to achieve success in aiding individuals to live meaningfully and effectively in a diverse society.

Goals and Objectives

The goals and objectives of a program should match as closely as possible the needs, expectations, and strengths of the families for which the program is designed. If such a match does not occur, the program is not likely to be meaningful or effective.

For example, the fact that newly arrived Vietnamese families may not be knowledgeable about the resources available to help them in adjusting to the new cultural environment suggests that goals and objectives surrounding learning how to access these resources would be worthwhile. For Chinese Canadian parents, appropriate goals and objectives may be related to the concerns and problems that arise from their high expectations for their children's academic achievement. Because of their strong emphasis on family interdependence, the involvement of Hawaiian families in the education of their children may be an important goal.

Several educators have attempted to classify various goals and objectives for multicultural education programs (Grant & Sleeter, 1989; Ramsey et al., 1989; J. Williams, 1979). The classification schemes of Grant and Sleeter (1989) are the most developed. They include four approaches to program design, organized according to their overall goals: (a) the *teaching the culturally different approach,* which focuses on adapting the usual program procedures to meet the needs and facilitate the development of culturally different individuals and families that do not benefit from the standard approach; (b) the *single group approach,* which focuses on the specific needs of individuals and families from single cultural groups; (c) the *human relations approach,* which focuses on the development of intergroup relations among individuals and families through self-understanding and understanding of others with the purpose of diminishing racial and cultural discrimination; and (d) the *social reconstructionist approach*, which focuses on empowering individuals and families of all cultural groups to change aspects of the deep structures of society that foster unequal relationships between people.

In reality, the above categories are not mutually exclusive. In working with families from diverse cultural backgrounds, all of these goals may apply. For example, families from one cultural group may have children experiencing adjustment problems in school. For these children, the goals related to "teaching the culturally different" may be appropriate. Another family may have to confront relationship problems with their neighbors, so that goals of the "human relations approach" may be more relevant. As well, another family may be struggling with obtaining the needed service that is not currently available in the community, so that the "social reconstructionist approach" may be more appropriate. An examination of the various approaches espoused by Grant and Sleeter (1989), however, does suggest a gradual movement away from dealing with the needs of specific cultural groups separately to approaches that involve the active participation of many cultural groups together. For example, in the "teaching the culturally different" and "single group" approaches, only one cultural group may be involved. In the "human relations," "multicultural education," and "social reconstructionist" approaches, however, the achievement of goals and objectives would most likely occur if a variety of cultural groups were actively involved in interaction. Family life educators must ensure not only that the goals and objectives of a program match the needs, expectations, and strengths of the families for which it was designed but also, on a broader level, that these goals reflect the most appropriate approach to multicultural education.

Designing and Implementing Programs

Morris (1983) identified at least three elements to be considered in designing and implementing effective multicultural family life education programs: (a) an educator's sensitivity to and knowledge of cultural diversity; (b) selection of appropriate curriculum activities, teaching procedures, and instructional materials; and (c) knowledge of available human resources.

Sensitivity to and Knowledge of Cultural Diversity

Family life educators play a crucial role in designing and implementing programs for culturally diverse societies, and the success of these programs, to a large extent, depends upon the sensitivity and knowledge of these educators about cultural diversity.

Being sensitive to cultural diversity requires family life educators to be positive in their attitudes and behaviors toward various cultural groups (Morris, 1983). Members of various cultural groups are quite aware of the sincerity and insincerity of educators in their attitudes and behaviors toward culturally different groups. These attitudes and behaviors, expressed verbally or nonverbally, are often used by members of different cultural groups to judge the worth various educators place on cultural diversity. For example, if a Japanese American child offers a family life educator some "sushi" for lunch, and the educator grunts and withdraws, saying, "Ugh! I don't like Japanese food. It all tastes so rancid!" such verbal and nonverbal behaviors may communicate to the child that being Japanese is unacceptable and bad. Likewise, if a family life educator consistently ignores the language style of Mexican Americans, this may be interpreted as a rejection, thus impeding the learning process. It is often through the acceptance of the language styles of a culturally different individual that the process of education begins.

In addition to sensitivity to cultural diversity, obtaining accurate information about cultural groups is also crucial for family life educators. Family life education programs based on myths and stereotypes about different cultural groups are bound to end in failure. To obtain accurate information about various cultural groups, select informational materials carefully to ensure quality and representation of various viewpoints (Morris, 1983). For information regarding a social and historical perspective on the development of various cultural groups in America, see Dinnerstein and Reimers (1988), Dinnerstein, Nichols, and Reimers (1990), and Mindel, Habenstein, and Wright (1988). More practical books on multicultural education in children's classrooms may also be useful to family life educators, including works by Banks (1987, 1988), Grant (1977), Grant and Sleeter (1989), Hernandez (1989), and Tiedt and Tiedt (1990). At the current time, publications on multicultural family life education are sparse, but the concepts in these books can easily be applied to family life education programs.

In addition to obtaining information about different cultural groups through the written word, personal interactions with members of culturally diverse groups are also helpful in expanding an educator's awareness of differences in experiences and viewpoints (Morris, 1983). For example, informal and formal discussions with colleagues, parents, friends, and various resource people who are sensitive to and have knowledge of different cultural groups can be instrumental in clarifying understandings and misinterpretations (Morris, 1983), and public lectures presented by individuals from various cultural groups who can provide greater insight into the nature of cultural diversity are also helpful.

Activities, Procedures, and Materials

Banks (1979) has identified four models to be used in classifying curriculum activities. These models are somewhat reminiscent of those previously described in the discussion of the models used by educators in helping families deal with issues associated with cultural diversity and Grant and Sleeter's (1989) ideas regarding program designs around which goals and objectives can be organized. Banks's models include (a) the Dominant Culture Model, with curriculum activities solely associated with the dominant culture; (b) the Ethnic Additive Model, where curriculum activities associated with several cultural groups are presented separately and added to the first model; (c) the Multiethnic Model, consisting of curriculum activities focused on various ethnic groups from their own historical and social perspectives; and (d) the Ethnonational Model, with curriculum activities taken from a multinational perspective.

A critical examination of these models indicates that the Dominant Culture Model is educationally inappropriate for multicultural family life education programs, because it consists of curriculum activities solely associated with the needs and concerns of the dominant culture and may therefore reinforce negative perceptions of cultural diversity. The Ethnic Additive Model has curriculum activities associated with different cultural groups, but they are used as distinct and separate units and thus do not fully reflect or appreciate the dynamic nature of cultural diversity. Both the Multiethnic and the Ethnonational models, however, appear to be appropriate for designing family life education programs in a culturally diverse society, because they give full consideration to the needs and concerns of all ethnic groups, recognizing their common cultural needs, needs that arise from their ethnic pasts, and needs that emerge as a result of the interaction between various cultural groups.

The selection of teaching procedures is also an important consideration in multicultural family life education programs. Different procedures may be more adaptable or suitable for different cultures. According to Hernandez (1989), teaching procedures can be classified into three general categories: (a) competitive, involving the use of procedures that emphasize the attainment of individual goals by constantly comparing the performance of an individual with those of others; (b) cooperative, involving the use of procedures that emphasize the attainment of group goals through the active participation of individuals together in developing an enterprise; and (c) individualistic, involving the use of procedures that emphasizes the attainment of individual goals, independent of others, based on an individual's own unique pattern and rate of development. For families with cultural heritages close to the dominant American culture, for example, competitive procedures may lead to successful attainment of goals. For families with values centered upon interdependence and cooperation, however, such procedures may not be as efficacious. The efficacy of various teaching approaches therefore may vary depending upon the cultural backgrounds from which individuals and families come.

Gonzales-Mena (1992) has suggested several ways in which family life educators might help individuals and families resolve their dual cultural and bicultural conflicts. These include (a) resolution through understanding and negotiation (e.g., both parties see the other's perspective and both compromise), (b) resolution through educator education (e.g., educator comes to see the family's perspective and the educator changes), (c) resolution through family education (e.g., family comes to see the educator's perspective and the family changes), and (d) conflict management with no resolution (e.g., each party has a view of the other's perspective and each is sensitive and respectful but is unable to change because of differing values and beliefs). Family life educators should be aware that all of these scenarios are possible when helping families deal with their dual cultural and bicultural dilemmas. We hope, however, that sensitivity and respect for the values and beliefs of all parties involved in the conflict are protected, so that such conflict does not continue uncontained or escalate.

Instructional materials are an important aspect of any family life education program. To date, few materials have been developed specifically for multicultural family life education programs. Many that have been developed for children's classrooms can, however, be adapted for use by family life educators (Banks, 1974; Dunfee, 1976; Morris, 1983; Ramsey et al., 1989). In addition to evaluating specific instructional materials (books, stories, props, posters) for their educational value, age appropriateness, usability, and technical quality, these materials should be evaluated for their multicultural content by observing whether they include representations of various cultural groups, provide accurate and reliable information about these cultures, present diversity as a positive fact of life, and appreciate the current life-styles and historical contributions of various cultural groups (Morris, 1983). For information concerning guidelines for evaluating multicultural instructional materials, see Banks (1974, 1979, 1987, 1988), Dunfee (1976), and Ramsey et al. (1989) as well as various organizations, journals, books, and magazines addressing ethnicity, diversity, and multicultural education.

Human Resources

In multicultural programs, the use of human resources from within the community (e.g., school professionals, parents, individuals from medicine, law, social services, government, business, and philanthropic organizations as well as concerned citizens) can bring special cultural knowledge and experience to family life education programs. Involvement of these individuals will require collaboration, however, and this collaboration develops as a result of sensitivity, knowledge, planning, organizing, sharing, caring, and commitment (Morris, 1983).

It would be difficult if not impossible to update multiethnic family life education curricula with the same speed that immigration is occurring throughout the world. Thus ongoing attention needs to be given to the formulation of new directions in programs to more adequately address the educational, social, and economic needs of all ethnic groups in a particular community.

Sedlacek (1983) has identified several variables that may contribute to achievement and success. While these variables are not limited to use with minority students, they do offer a framework for helping students to overcome the belief that minority children possess low status and have little self-esteem.

A positive self-concept in minority children appears to be related to success with later life experiences, and many studies have indicated that minority students with a strong self-concept are more successful than children with lower self-concept. Henderson (1979) has stated that minority students who feel abused, neglected, or rejected tend to abuse, neglect, and reject other people. Family life educators can play a very important role in the development of a positive self-concept in minority children by using examples from the students' cultural background in a positive fashion and by not expecting the students to provide the information simply because they are members of that particular minority group.

How well minority students participate in school and in other life situations may also depend on how well they understand and cope with racism. There appears to be no set of guidelines to assist people to effectively cope with racism. It is usually through everyday experiences of trial and error that these lessons are learned. Nonetheless, it is important for students to be prepared to deal with racism in a positive fashion whenever it occurs. Family life educators can assist students to develop effective behaviors that will not allow the effects of racism to serve as obstacles to their success.

Efforts to eradicate prejudice and discrimination have grown in the last 15 years (Glazer & Ueda, 1982). Traditional methods for teaching people how to deal with prejudice have not been totally effective, however. These methods have included archaic and crystallized social work concepts such as the need for cooperation, nonduplication of services, assimilation, and acceptance. These practices are based on the philosophy that humans are basically good and will do the right thing if told what to do (Florez, 1977). Programs in family life education appear to have followed a similar pattern. New and different methods need to be created to deal with the multitude of injuries that persons can experience when different cultures are brought together.

According to Sedlacek (1983), successful minority students are able to engage in effective self-appraisal. They are aware of their deficiencies and are willing to engage in self-improvement techniques to overcome shortcomings. For example, often minority students will not verbalize their experiences or ask questions in a class that is designed for discussion. This may be a result of feelings of shyness, feelings that one's contributions are unimportant, or language problems. Family life education should provide opportunities to encourage minority students to identify areas for personal development and to develop strategies to help overcome difficulties.

Evaluation

There are two major types of evaluation procedures used by family life educators in assessing the effectiveness of their multicultural programs: (a) formative evaluation and (b) summative evaluation (L. R. Williams, 1989). Formative evaluations are assessments that are used throughout program implementation to gain feedback about the ongoing functioning of various aspects of the multicultural program. Summative evaluations are those that determine the effects of the entire multicultural program on individuals and families enrolled in the program. Because these procedures are more fully discussed in Chapter 5 of this volume, they will not be further elaborated here. It should be noted, however, that the results of these evaluations may lend power and persuasiveness to the adoption of a particular multicultural approach to family life education because of its demonstrated efficacy (L. R. Williams, 1989).

SUMMARY

One of the primary goals of family life education is to support and empower individuals and families to live meaningfully and effectively in the society at large. This involves active participation in the larger society, with a dignity, respect, and acceptance that allows all individuals and families to make significant contributions to and receive benefits from others in a manner that strengthens and enhances their individual and family well-being. Because individuals and families in society come from culturally diverse backgrounds, family life education programs must not overlook such cultural diversity. Failure to incorporate cultural diversity will interfere with the achievement of the goals of the field.

This chapter has explored some of the critical issues that family life educators must address in designing family life education programs for individuals and families living within a culturally diverse society. These issues included those associated with migrants and their expectations, conflicts and transitions, dual cultural dilemmas, and bicultural (intergenerational) conflicts. In addition, various models of intergroup relations (assimilation, amalgamation, cultural pluralism, ethnogenesis) were explored for general strategies that could be used to deal with these critical issues. A critical examination indicated that ethnogenesis, with its emphasis on common cultural characteristics, unique cultural pasts, and emergent cultural characteristics, provided the best theoretical framework from which strategies for more comprehensive family life education programs should be developed. Finally, important programmatic dimensions in designing family life education programs for a culturally diverse society were discussed. These included understanding the needs, expectations, and strengths of the families for whom the program is to be designed; developing goals and objectives that match these family needs, expectations, and strengths; designing and implementing programs, taking into consideration an educator's sensitivity to and knowledge of cultural diversity; selection of curriculum activities, teaching procedures, instructional materials, and human resources; and evaluating the effectiveness of the program.

Although this chapter does not address all of the issues, strategies, and suggestions that may arise when educators design family life education programs for a culturally diverse society, it is hoped that the ideas presented herein may assist family life educators in designing programs that will help the individuals and families of all cultural groups participate equally in the mainstream of society, appreciate and respect their own unique cultural heritages and those of others, and achieve their fullest potential as they evolve over time, making significant and meaningful contributions to the society at large.

REFERENCES

Akbar, N. (1975). *Learning styles of the Afro-American child.* Paper presented at the annual meeting of the National Black Child Development Institute, San Francisco.

Appleton, N. (1983). *Cultural pluralism in education: Theoretical foundations.* New York: Longman.

Banks, J. A. (1974). Ecaluating and selecting ethnic studies materials. *Educational Leadership, 31,* 593-596.

Banks, J. A. (1979). *Teaching strategies for ethnic studies* (2nd ed.). Boston: Allyn & Bacon.

Banks, J. A. (1987). *Teaching strategies for ethnic studies* (4th ed.). Boston: Allyn & Bacon.

Banks, J. A. (1988). *Multiethnic education: Theory and practice* (2nd ed.). Boston: Allyn & Bacon.

Boykin, A. W. (1977). Experimental psychology from a black perspective: Issues and examples. In W. Cross (Ed.), *Final report from the Third Conference on Empirical Research in Black Psychology.* Washington, DC: National Institute on Education.

Chan, K. A., Takanishi, R., & Kitano, M. K. (1975). *An inquiry into Asian American preschool children and families in Los Angeles.* Los Angeles: University of California. (ERIC Document Reproduction Service No. ED 117 251)

Cohen, R. (1971). The influence of conceptual rule-sets on measures of learning ability. In American Anthropological Association (Eds.), *Race and intelligence.* New York: American Anthropological Association.

Dinnerstein, L., Nichols, R. I., & Reimers, D. M. (1990). *Natives and strangers.* New York: Oxford University Press.

Dinnerstein, L., & Reimers, D. B. (1988). *Ethnic Americans* (3rd ed.). New York: Harper & Row.

Dunfee, M. (1976). Curriculum materials for celebrating the bicentennial. *Educational Leadership, 33,* 267-272.

Ebsen, A. (1973). The care syndrome: A resource for counseling in Africa. *Journal of Negro Education, 42,* 205-211.

Feagin, J. R. (1984). *Racial and ethnic relations* (2nd ed.). Englewood Cliffs, NJ: Prentice-Hall.

Florez, J. (1977). Chicanos and coalitions as a force change. In R. Rothman (Ed.), *Issues in race and ethnic relations* (pp. 228-235). Itasca, IL: F. E. Peacock Publishers.

Gallimore, R., Boggs, J. W., & Jordan, C. (1974). *Culture, behavior and education: A study of Hawaiian Americans.* Beverly Hills, CA: Sage.

Gitter, A. G., Black, G. H., & Mostofsky, D. I. (1972). Race and sex in perception of emotion. *Journal of Social Issues, 28,* 63-78.

Glazer, N., & Ueda, R. (1982). Efforts against prejudice. In T. F. Pettigrew, G. M. Fredrickson, D. T. Knobel, & R. Ueda (Eds.), *Prejudice* (pp. 88-124). Cambridge, MA: Harvard University Press.

Gonzales-Mena, J. (1992). Taking a culturally sensitive approach in infant-toddler programs. *Young Children, 47,* 4-9.

Gordon, M. M. (1964). *Assimilation in American life.* New York: Oxford University Press.

Grant, C. A. (1977). *Multicultural education: Commitments, issues and application.* Washington, DC: Association for Supervision and Curriculum Development.

Grant, C. A., & Sleeter, C. E. (1989). *Turning on learning: Five approaches for multicultural teaching.* Columbus, OH: Charles E. Merrill.

Greeley, M. (1974). *Human nature, class and ethnicity.* New York: John Wiley.

Gulick, J. (1960). *Cherokee at the crossroads.* Chapel Hill: University of North Carolina, Institute of Research on Social Science.

Guttentag, M. (1972). Negro-white differences in children's movement. *Perceptual and Motor Skills, 35,* 435-436.

Guttentag, M., & Ross, S. (1972). Movement responses in simple concept learning. *American Journal of Orthopsychiatry, 42,* 657-665.

Hale, J. (1983). Black children: Their roots, culture, and learning styles. In O. N. Saracho & B. Spodek (Eds.), *Understanding the multicultural experience in early childhood education.* Washington, DC: NAEYC.

Henderson, G. (1979). *Understanding and counseling ethnic minorities.* Springfield, IL: Charles C Thomas.

Herberg, W. (1960). *Protestant-Catholic-Jew.* Garden City, NY: Doubleday.

Hernandez, H. (1989). *Multicultural education: A teacher's guide to content and process.* Columbus, OH: Charles E. Merrill.

Hilliard, A. (1976). *Alternatives to IQ testing: An approach to identification of gifted minority children.* Los Angeles: California State Department of Education.

Jim, E., & Suen, P. (1990). *Chinese parents and teenagers in Canada: Transitions and conflicts.* Vancouver, B. C.: Canadian Mental Health Association.

John, R. (1988). The Native American family. In C. H. Mindel, R. W. Habenstein, & R. W. Wright, Jr. (Eds.), *Ethnic families in America* (3rd ed.). New York: Elsevier.

Kallen, H. (1915, February). Democracy vs. the melting pot. *The Nation,* pp. 190-194, 217-220.

Kissen, W. (1991). Commentary: Dynamics of enculturatic. In M. C. Formstein (Ed.), *Cultural approaches to parenting* (pp. 185-193). Hillside, NJ: Lawrence Erlbaum.

Kitano, H. H. L. (1973). Japanese American mental illness. In S. Sue & N. Wagner (Eds.), *Asian Americans: Psychological perspectives.* Ben Lomond, CA: Science and Behavior Books.

Kitano, H. H. L. (1991). *Race relations* (4th ed.). Englewood Cliffs, NJ: Prentice-Hall.

Kitano, M. K. (1983). Early education for Asian American children. In O. N. Saracho & B. Spodek (Eds.), *Understanding the multicultural experience of early childhood education.* Washington, DC: NAEYC.

Laosa, L. M. (1977). Socialization, education and continuity: The implications of the sociocultural context. *Young Children, 32,* 21-27.

Lee, E. S. (1966). A theory of migration. *Demography, 3,* 45-57.

McKee, J. O. (1985). *Ethnicity in contemporary America: A geographical appraisal.* Dubuque, IA: Kendall-Hunt.

McLemore, S. D. (1983). *Racial and ethnic relations in America* (2nd ed.). Boston: Allyn & Bacon.

Mindel, C. H., Habenstein, R. W., & Wright, R., Jr. (1988). *Ethnic families in America: Patterns and variations* (3rd ed.). New York: Elsevier.

Morgan, H. (1976). Neonatal precocity and the black experience. *Negro Educational Review, 27,* 129-134.

Morris, J. B. (1983). Classroom methods and materials. In O. N. Saracho & B. Spodek (Eds.), *Understanding the multicultural experience in early childhood education.* Washington, DC: NAEYC.

Newmeyer, J. A. (1970). *Creativity and nonverbal communication in adolescent white and black children.* Cambridge, MA: Harvard University Press.

Parillo, V. N. (1990). *Strangers to these shores* (3rd ed.). Cambridge, MA: Harvard University Press.

Peterson, W. (1958). A general typology of migration. *American Sociological Review, 23,* 256-265.

Pitler, B. (1977). Chicago's Korean American community. *Integrated Education, 88,* 44-47.

Ramirez, M., II, & Castaneda, A. (1974). *Cultural democracy, biocognitive development, and education*. New York: Academic Press.

Ramsey, P. C., Vold, E. B., & Williams, L. R. (1989). *Multicultural education: A source book*. New York: Garland.

Ravenstein, E. G. (1885). The laws of migration. *Journal of the Royal Statistical Society, 48*, 167-227.

Ravenstein, E. G. (1889). The laws of migration. *Journal of the Royal Statistical Society, 48*, 241-301.

Saracho, O. N., & Hancock, F. M. (1983). Mexican American culture. In O. N. Saracho & B. Spodek (Eds.), *Understanding the multicultural experience of early childhood education*. Washington, DC: NAEYC.

Saracho, O. N., & Spodek, B. (1983). *Understanding the multicultural experience of early childhood education*. Washington, DC: NAEYC.

Schermerhorn, R. A. (1970). *Comparative ethnic relations*. New York: Random House.

Sedlacek, W. E. (1983). Teaching minority students. In J. H. Cones, J. Nonnan, & D. Janha (Eds.), *Teaching minority students* (pp. 39-50). San Francisco: Jossey-Bass.

Sue, D. W. (1973). Ethnic identity: The impact of two cultures on the psychological development of Asians in America. In S. Sue & N. Wagner (Eds.), *Asian Americans: Psychological perspectives*. Ben Lomond, CA: Science and Behavior Books.

Tiedt, P. L., & Tiedt, I. M. (1990). *Multicultural teaching* (3rd ed.). Boston: Allyn & Bacon.

Wax, M. (1971). *American Indians*. Englewood Cliffs, NJ: Prentice-Hall.

Williams, J. (1979). Perspectives on the multicultural curriculum. *Social Science Teacher, 8*, 245-256.

Williams, L. R. (1989). *Multicultural education: A source book*. New York: Garland.

Young, V. H. (1970). Family and childhood in a southern Georgia community. *American Anthropologist, 72*, 269-288.

8

Religious and Theological Issues in Family Life Education

Jo Lynn Cunningham
Letha Dawson Scanzoni

WHEN ROBERT COLES (1990) conducted research among the Hopi children of New Mexico and Arizona, he found himself at an impasse. For 6 months, he had been visiting a school to interview the children about their religious beliefs and practices, but response had been so limited that he was ready to abandon the entire project. One day, a Hopi mother told him to expect a worsening of the situation. At first offended by her comments, he decided to hear her out. The woman told Coles that these Native American children considered their spiritual lives private matters totally bound up with their homes and families, an existence that to them was far removed from school. When they entered the school building, their spiritual consciousness was suspended temporarily so they could do the arithmetic, reading, and writing expected of them there. Spiritual discussions were inappropriate in this setting. The woman went on to say that the children felt the personal questions forced them to act "silent and sullen and stupid" (p. 24), making them feel even less inclined to cooperate with the researcher. When Coles took her advice and visited the children in their homes, they gradually opened up. They shared their deepest beliefs about their prayers to ancestors and to the vast sky, their profound reverence for nature, their attachment to the land, their sacred commitment to care for it, and their thoughts on peace and harmony between the earth and its peoples. Their attendance in schools based on white cultural values seemed detached from the world they treasured—a world in which spirituality was paramount, with beliefs and customs passed on by grandparents and parents. The separation of their religious and familial heritage was inconceivable. Home and religion belonged together and could not be discussed without a recognition of this connection.

This religion-family connection also was evident in earlier times. For example, "the Greek word *oikos*, which often is translated as home, actually encompassed not only the people of the family but also its land (an important symbol of lineage), work (production), and altar (representing religious rituals and values)" (Summers & Cunningham, 1989, p. 327). Only more recently has the *oikos* become differentiated, separating religion, family, and other social institutions (e.g., education) that also had been a function of the *oikos* (Everett & Everett, 1985).

THE FAMILY LIFE EDUCATION AND RELIGION CONNECTION

In conceptualizing the fields of family studies, religion/theology, and education as separate domains, it must be recognized that the three fields actually overlap, with each intersection representing integrative areas of study and application (family life education, religious education, and the study of families and religion). The unique focus of this chapter is the intersection of *all three areas* (see Figure 8.1). Thus it is based on information from the basic (or "primary") areas of family studies, religion/theology, and education and also on the intersecting (or "secondary") areas of family life education, religious education, and the study of families and religion. In keeping with this perspective, attention is directed to the reciprocal relationships between and among these areas, relationships that are viewed as systemic rather than as linear, one-way, or causal in nature.

The central concepts representing the domain of this chapter are defined in relatively broad ways. *Religion* is viewed as including both general belief systems and formal religious institutions and as encompassing both theological and broader spiritual perspectives. This broad definition encompasses many varieties of religious expression. *Family life* also is considered in broad terms, including not only marriage and parenting but also such topics as values, gender roles, and interpersonal relationships. *Education* is defined broadly as well, reflecting a theoretical/philosophical position in which education is seen as a subset of the development of an individual or group. Education thus includes a variety of implicit as well as explicit, conscious as well as unconscious, and intentional as well as unintentional interventions. Among such

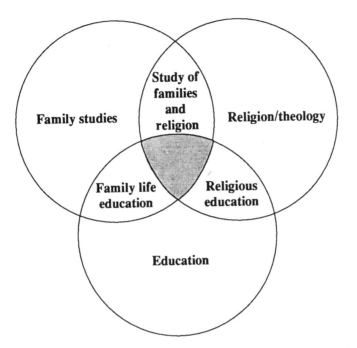

Figure 8.1. Religious and Theological Issues in Family Life Education: Conceptual Model of Contributing Bodies of Knowledge

interventions are *formal* educational programs, organized and presented in a systematic manner to a designated audience, as well as *informal* programs and various other experiences (for example, recreation or worship), counseling or therapy, and even advocacy (which may be seen as education at the systemic or institutional level).

Influences Between Families and Religion

Because theological perspectives are part of the general philosophical approach or worldview of an individual or a culture, such perspectives cannot be ignored by family life educators. Religious viewpoints have a significant but often unexamined influence on the assumptions with which various family life education topics are approached and discussed. In Judaism, for example, religious faith and practices are inextricably linked to everyday family living. Jewish scripture and tradition have emphasized religious observances within the home—remembering the weekly Sabbath with a special meal and lighting of the candles, gathering family members together to participate in the Pass-over seder, celebrating Hanukkah, observing a kosher kitchen, and other home-centered expressions of faith in God and solidarity with the larger family, the Jewish people. According to Lamm (1980), the family is viewed as "the primary source of blessing for humankind" (p. 127), for it is in a family that children can learn trust, compassion, uncondi-tional love, moral teachings, how to celebrate and express joy, and how to live with and relate to two or three generations.

The interconnectedness of religion and family also is evident among Hindu immigrants to the United States. R. B. Williams (1987) stated that "because of the importance of home shrines and family rituals in Hindu-ism, Hindus can participate fully in the ceremonies of their religion while only rarely going to temples or official meetings" (p. 248). He called the "family Hinduism" characteristic of these immigrants to America "the most important element in transmitting religious beliefs and practices" (p. 248).

As Thornton (1985) has emphasized, "Religious institutions and values had significant effects on family life in societies of the past and are important factors in family structure and relationships today" (p. 381). Concurrently, "changes in family life have had substantial effects on the religious doctrines, teachings, and programs of religious institutions; . . . the varying responses of the churches to these family changes have modified the influence of religion in the lives of individuals and their families" (pp. 381-382).

D'Antonio (1985) has called attention to the tensions felt by Ameri-can Roman Catholics as the processes of modernization, rationalization, and the quest for personal autonomy influence family behavior and thereby challenge church pronouncements and authority. The life expe-riences of parishioners cause them to question or personally repudiate many of the church's established teachings on family issues, thus pres-suring the church hierarchy to respond with an openness to change. At the same time, within both the laity and the clergy/hierarchy, a strong countermovement has resisted any deviation from tradition.

After an extensive overview of journals published in the 1980s in the fields of family studies, religion, sociology, psychology, and therapy, D. Thomas and Cornwall (1990) concluded that, although increasing attention is being given to the study of religion and the family, the focus has been almost entirely on the impact of religious beliefs, practices, and affiliations on family life. Only limited attention has been directed toward the impact of families on religion. Garrett (1989) pointed out that the positive role of religion and family as reinforcing and maintaining basic societal values has been given more heed than has the failure to adapt constructively to contemporary family challenges. Examples are

the increasing problems of families among the under-class, the rising proportion of children in poverty, the enduring conflict between the norms/behavior
patterns legitimated by the youth peer culture and parents, the strains generated by dual-wage earner families, the difficulties of sustaining a companionate relationship in marriage, the pervasive eroticism of contemporary
American culture, the problems associated with reconstituted families, the
failure of American society to embrace a nonsexist social order, and a host of
other issues. (p. 106)

Family life educators face family challenges similar to those of the
religious institutions.

Families Serving Religion or Religion Serving Families?

Even within the same faith perspective, the relationship between
families and religious institutions depends in part on the perceived
purpose or primary role of each. This relationship is quite different, for
example, if the primary role of a religious institution is seen as winning
converts to the faith or if it is seen as providing support for individuals
in their personal and spiritual development. Similarly, it is different if
the primary role of the family is seen as procreation and socialization of
children or if it is seen as the nurturance of all members and the
facilitation of their individual development.

Browning and Browning (1991) and Vos (1991) presented a view of
the family as existing to serve the mission of the church. Thus the major
task of families is seen as raising children for the kingdom of God.

In contrast, a perspective that might be described as church/religion
serving the family has been presented by Hauerwas (1985), who suggested that the primary educational role for religious institutions is
character building. According to Hauerwas, fidelity is the underpinning
of character, which in turn provides a solid foundation for the love and
faithfulness necessary for solid marriage and family relationships.

A third relationship between church and family was presented by
Bender (1982), who suggested that both institutions serve essentially the
same mission and thus that a family perspective needs to be included in
all ministry. A similar reciprocal model also was presented by Thompson (1989), who emphasized that "the family is intrinsically formative
spiritually" and also that "various spiritual practices may realistically
support the health and growth of the family within its larger communities" (p. 11). From this standpoint, family life education and religious
education might be assumed to be mutually reinforcing at the very least,
if not parallel or integrated and, in some cases, perhaps virtually indis-
tinguishable.

RELIGIOUS DIMENSIONS OF FAMILY LIFE EDUCATION

Abbott, Berry, and Meredith (1990) stated that the cradle-to-grave involvement in religion of many individuals calls for serious attention on the part of family professionals. By overlooking this reality, "some of our family theories and therapeutic interventions have limited relevance and impact on those whose family paradigm is constructed with religious beliefs and values" (p. 447). They urged that family life curricula include discussions of the religious dimensions of family situations, relationships, and decision making. Furthermore, if therapists and family life educators are going to respect and work within the value systems of clients and students, they cannot afford to overlook the religiosity factor.

Overlapping Goals and Common Concepts in Religion and Family Life Education

A general goal often claimed by both religion and family life education is that of helping people develop toward human wholeness, both individually and in their corporate relationships. Both family life education and religion emphasize respect and consideration of others, the importance of self-understanding and self-esteem, good communication skills among family members, and taking responsibility for one's actions.

Human Development

In examining human development across the life span, researchers have given attention to such questions as faith development, religious education, moral development, and religiosity. Identity development has been examined in terms of the potentially interrelated dimensions of religion, family, and community (Koteskey, Walker, & Johnson, 1990).

Included in the developmental perspective have been efforts to uncover children's religious concepts, such as their perceptions of God (Coles, 1990), and adolescents' and young adults' incorporation of religion into their worldview, their decisions about nonmarital sexual activity (Thornton & Camburn, 1989; Udry, 1988), their use of alcohol and other drugs (Perkins, 1985), and their degree of religious identification and participation and how this carries over into adult life (Cornwall, 1988; Hoge, Petrillo, & Smith, 1982; Stott, 1988). Religion as a factor in mate selection was an early part of the sociological literature and thus became a fairly standard component of family life education programs dealing with choosing a marriage partner. Probably stemming from this area as well as a practical problem-focused approach was the attention given to "mixed marriages" (those between members of different religious groups).

Some families are concerned about declines in religious participation as adolescents strive for independence. Other families may experience stress because their adolescent or young adult has become involved with a different religious group or cult. As noted by Sirkin (1990), the underlying family problem in such cases may stem more from a clash of values between parents and child than from a specific belief system. Such families may need help in understanding developmental processes such as individuation. At the same time, family life education efforts may be directed toward reducing the vulnerability of youth to the psychological seduction of coercive cults. Thus some educators have encouraged the study of cults as a way of helping students to learn and evaluate systems of thought (Majka, 1986).

Young adulthood is considered particularly important from the standpoints both of religion and of family life education because what happens at this stage can have significant consequences for the rest of life. Parks (1986) emphasized that this is the stage at which maturity brings renunciation of conventional, authority-bound forms of understanding so that they can be replaced with a personally constructed form of knowledge and trust uniquely developed and acknowledged as one's own. Parks challenged educational and religious institutions to assist young adults in meeting this challenge.

Applying a developmental perspective to an examination of the role of religion in the lives of individuals and families has yielded useful information for family life educators. For example, involvement in religious institutions and stage of the family life cycle have been shown to be related. Although some cohort effects have been suggested, even the "baby-boomer" generation has increased formal religious involvement after moving into the parenting stage (Roozen, McKinney, & Thompson, 1990). Personality theories, studies of adult development, and data from gerontological research have been used as the basis for examining the religious education needs of adults. Increasing emphasis is being placed on the aid required by this population in facing issues of continuity and change in their lives (Kollar, 1986). Johnson and Mullins (1989) have called for more research on the role of religion in the lives of elderly persons. They noted that "the limited research that has been done provides little support for or against the popular notion that people generally become more religious as they get older" and that "those who are already religious may find their beliefs and personal religious practices becoming more important, especially the belief in life after death, even though they may have to curtail their organizational or social involvements due to declining health or physical mobility" (p. 3).

Death education typically has included consideration of the religious dimension, a perspective that has been influenced by the work of Kubler-Ross (1969). Attention to the association between religion and attitudes toward death has not been limited to the elderly. For example, much research in recent years has been concentrated on adolescent bereavement and the role of religion in the reactions of young people to the death of a parent, a sibling, or a friend or to their own impending death (Balk, 1991; O'Brien, Goodenow, & Espin, 1991).

Ethics, Values, and Moral Development

The relationship between religion and family life education is especially strong in the area of ethics and values. Thornton (1989) observed that trends in family norms and trends in religious values and beliefs have followed similar paths, with both trends indicating an increasing emphasis on individual freedom rather than rigid conformity to established authority and behavioral standards. He suggested that "good theoretical reasons" lend support for the belief that "family and religious values are interrelated—with the causal influences being reciprocal" (p. 890).

Values are involved in family life education in at least three ways. The most obvious way is through the direct incorporation of values as a topic of study within the curricula of family life education programs. A second way is related to how values come into play as educators select and approach content. Third, the nature of the relationships in the educational setting may reflect certain values. (For further discussion regarding values in family life education, see Chapter 4.)

When family life education is presented in the context of a religious setting, religious values can be expressed freely. In other contexts, such as public schools, however, dealing with religion and values can be much more complex. Sometimes the links between religious values and family life education are explicit, as in the citation of a particular denominational stance in a discussion of a topic such as contraception, abortion, homosexuality, or divorce. Often, however, the links are subtle and may not be recognized by participants in the forum, as in discussions of family solidarity (emphasized in religious traditions ranging from Christianity to Confucianism) or family violence (denounced within the fundamental cultural assumptions of the combined Jewish and Christian perspective prominent in Western society).

Certain values are central to most, if not all, religions. Probably foremost on this list is love, although the emphasis placed on love for God, others, and self may vary. From one perspective, Browning and Browning (1991) suggested that the central ethic of Christian love should be equal regard, a concept that obviously has important implications in family life education, setting a standard that may be interpreted not only for relationships within the family but also for support of different life-style choices and family forms (Vos, 1991). Recognizing, however, the potential destructiveness of love in a family setting where a balanced perspective is not maintained, D. D. Williams (1978) observed that "unless tensions between self-protection and obligation to the community are acknowledged, family love can become a self-centered existence, protected from learning the larger demands of love by its internal satisfactions" (p. 239).

Values such as justice and mercy also are central to many belief systems. At the same time, such interpersonal strategies as self-affirmation, self-assertion, mutuality, and self-sacrifice are interpreted differently within different religious traditions.

The interpretation of various life experiences is dependent on personal values and the philosophical/theological framework within which the individual operates. For example, loneliness may be experienced either socially or existentially. The negative effects typically associated with loneliness, stemming from perceived social rejection by friends or family, is a different experience from existential loneliness, which may be viewed from a religious perspective as a part of the human condition and a significant part of the tradition of many religions (Collins, 1989).

Related to the study of values as a component of family life education has been the study of morality. Again, questions have been raised about the theoretical and/or pragmatic independence of that concept from the domain of religion. Dominating the study of moral development has been the empirical and theoretical work of Kohlberg (1981), who based his model on the cognitive-constructive developmental work of Piaget. Some aspects of Kohlberg's work have been called into question in recent years by Gilligan (1982) and her associates (Gilligan, Lyons, & Hanmer, 1990; Gilligan, Ward, & Taylor, 1988), who have asserted that Kohlberg's work was focused on the moral development of males (who tend to focus primarily on rights and fairness) and ignored the experience of females (who tend to focus primarily on responsibilities and caring). Although Kohlberg initially claimed that morality is independent from religion, Hanson (1991) has shown that the study of the development of moral reasoning cannot ignore significant, though perhaps complex and subtle, interrelationships with religion.

Faith Development

Just as the work on moral development has been dominated by Kohlberg, the study of faith development has been dominated by Fowler (1981, 1984). Beginning with the initial presentation of a model for faith development derived from a cognitive developmental/structuralist perspective (Fowler, 1981), this work has led to what is likely the most frequent explicit incorporation of a "religious" component into secular studies of human development and family relationships. At the same time, it has provided the basis for the use of an empirical/scientific model for examining various theological issues in general and religious education in particular. Even when other perspectives are put forward, they typically are presented as alternatives to Fowler (Dykstra & Parks, 1986).

Spirituality

The integration of theological and psychological perspectives also is evident in discussions about spirituality. Although the concept is age-old and fundamental to all religions (especially those with a mystic tradition), the term has come into popular usage in recent years through the "new age," self-help, and feminist movements. The essence of spirituality may be described as the way people experience themselves in relation to what they designate as the source of ultimate power and meaning in their lives and how they live out these relationships (Thayer, 1985) or, more simply, as their relationships with themselves, others, and the universe (Whitfield, 1984). It has been contrasted with religiosity "in that the spiritual dimension is more commonly associated with 'a state of being,' while religiosity is more commonly associated with a 'a state of doing,' or a specified unified system of practices associated with a particular religion or denomination" (Farran, Fitchett, Quiring-Emblen, & Burck, 1989, p. 187).

Attention to spirituality is seen both in contemporary writings and in classic works on the role of religion in the development of an individual's orientation to life. Berger (1967) laid a theoretical foundation for this relationship in his writing on the importance of family and religion in developing and sustaining a worldview. More recent empirical work has been focused on the relationship between specific life events and religious faith (Albrecht & Cornwall, 1989). The considerable attention being given today to the spiritual element in common human experiences may suggest that the universality of human experiences lies to a great degree in their spiritual aspects. Bregman (1989), for instance, has examined the moral and spiritual assumptions behind classic models of the human experience of dying.

Both Eastern and Western models of spirituality have been used for examining a variety of issues relevant to family life education. The relationship between self and others (and, or in the context of, a spiritual source) has been examined by Bolen (1979), who identified common elements from various religious traditions that have been presented under such labels as Tao, the kingdom of God, and karma. A similar integration, applied to a more specific issue, was proposed by Cox (1989), who suggested a framework for responding to family violence through the combined application of the Hindu concept of karma (for example, by recognizing that disruption of the family results from behavior of individual family members who are responsible for their deeds and must bear the consequences thereof) and the Christian idea of redemption (with its emphasis on the potential for perpetrators to change, to be treated effectively, to learn new behaviors, and to do penance for their behavior, thus producing positive results for themselves and perhaps for their victims as well as for future relationships or family situations in which they may be involved). In this way, both justice and forgiveness are reflected in a framework incorporating both reality and hope—a framework that has application as well to family issues other than violence.

Some writers have examined spirituality specifically within the context of family life. The potential significance of ordinary events that are part of living in families has been described by several writers (Boyer, 1984; Leckey, 1982; Wright, 1989). Integrating concepts from the study of spirituality and families, Boyer (1984) proposed that two ways of being in the world ("life on the edge" and "life at the center") may be complementary rather than mutually exclusive and that they have significant commonalities (such as attention to the love of God and neighbor as the ultimate spiritual lesson).

Although the primary emphasis in family life education is the prevention of dysfunctionality rather than its treatment, it is important for family life educators to be aware of the prominence given to spirituality in various programs dealing with dysfunctional families today, particularly in the recovery movement. The 12-step model often used in addiction treatment programs is premised on the idea that spiritual transformation is essential for recovery. This program involves several traditional spiritual disciplines, including confession, testimony, making amends, and prayer (Maudlin, 1991). Use of this model as a framework for spiritual healing has been discussed extensively by J. K. Miller (1991).

Religiosity

Religiosity (religious beliefs and/or practices) is a notable concept not only because of its theoretical and applied significance but also because of the attention devoted to it in the empirical literature. Among the variables that have been related to religiosity are health, sexuality, and social relationships.

A number of researchers have found religiosity to be predictive of marital satisfaction. This literature was reviewed by Dudley and Kosinski (1990) as a basis for their own research. They found that, in their sample of Seventh-Day Adventist couples, marital satisfaction was predicted best by family worship and congruence with the spouse on religiosity and church attendance. Also predictive of marital satisfaction were an intrinsic religious orientation, private and public ritualistic practices (such as prayer, Bible reading, family worship, church attendance, witnessing, and financially supporting the church), religious experience (sense of closeness to God), and salience of religious faith.

In their replication and extension of the classic "Middletown U.S.A." study of a midwestern city (Muncie, Indiana) decades after the original studies (Lynd & Lynd, 1929, 1937), Bahr and Chadwick (1985) found a strong link between religion and familism. They argued that "there is a relationship between family solidarity—family 'health' if you will—and church affiliation and activity," based on evidence "that the more religious residents of Middletown were more likely to be married, to remain married, to be highly satisfied with their marriages, and to have more children" (p. 413). They noted, however, that a causal relationship could not be inferred from their cross-sectional data: "It is not clear whether the direct relationship [between religiosity and familism] stems from the familistic being more apt to be religious or from those high in religiosity having stronger family bonds, or a combination of the two" (p. 407).

Religiosity also has been related to other family variables. For example, religiosity among Jewish married women in Israel was found to be related to pronatalistic tendencies, including number of children, expected family size, and age at marriage (Hartman, 1984). A strong relationship between religious involvement and fertility also has been found among Mormons (Heaton, 1988; Heaton & Goodman, 1985).

In his review of the relationship between religiosity and health, King (1990) concluded that religion generally has been associated with "health behaviors, health status [both physical and mental], and longevity" (p. 101). Among the areas often included in family life education programs that have been found to be associated with religiosity are developmental needs (Byrne & Price, 1979), stress (Brown, Ndubuisi, &

Gary, 1990; Pulisuk & Parks, 1983), mental health/distress (Crawford, Handal, & Wiener, 1989), sense of personal well-being (Hunsberger, 1985; Idler, 1987; Petersen & Roy, 1985), life-style (Phillips, Kuzma, Beeson, & Lotz, 1980), and drug use (Perkins, 1985). On the other hand, Bergen (1991) cited evidence that there is no relationship between religiosity and mental illness, suggesting that religiosity is multidimensional, reflecting both healthy and unhealthy ways of being religious.

An association between religiosity and social relationships also has been found by several researchers. For example, Johnson and Mullins (1989) found that "greater involvement in the social aspects of religion was significantly related to less loneliness" (p. 13) in their sample of elderly people who were living independently. The social dimension of religiosity "included membership and attendance at religious services as well as getting together socially with friends from one's religious group" (p. 13). In contrast, "the subjective dimension of religious commitment was not significantly related to loneliness" (p. 13).

Religion's Contributions to Families

Abbott et al. (1990) have referred to the numerous studies that have led family professionals to "note the correlation of religiosity with a variety of family phenomena (e.g., personal well-being, marital happiness, family affection and time spent together, noncoercive child discipline, family strengths, family identity, and commitment and the management of family stress and crisis)" (p. 443). At the same time, according to these authors, family professionals have tended not to give serious attention to how religious belief and practice may be beneficial for families and have suggested five ways that religion may promote family well-being: "(a) by enhancing the family's social support network, (b) by sponsoring family activities and recreation, (c) [by indoctrinating individuals] in supportive family teachings and values, (d) by providing family social and welfare services, and (e) by encouraging families to seek divine assistance with personal and family problems" (p. 443). Using a purposive sample of 200 married adults from 20 major U.S. religious denominations, Abbott et al. found that two of these were particularly important; level of social support and a sense of divine intervention in the respondents' lives were predictive of level of family satisfaction.

Various researchers have found that spirituality and/or religious faith have been related to effective coping with family stressors. For example, Ratcliff (1990) noted that personal faith helps families in coping with the stresses of having a mentally retarded child. The buffering role of religion in raising a retarded child was identified by Fewell (1986) as stemming not from church organizations but from three components: faith, belief in God, and prayer. Other researchers have shown *both* personal faith and association with a supportive religious community to be important coping resources for parents of disabled children (Abbott & Meredith, 1986; Crnic, Friedrich, & Greenburg, 1983; Weber & Parker, 1981).

Religion also has been identified as a predictor of effective functioning for families in general. A shared religious core was 1 of the 15 traits of healthy families identified by Curran (1983). Several other items also reflect the religious beliefs and practices of many families: family rituals and traditions, service to others, ethical teachings, respect for others, shared responsibility, sense of trust, and mutual support. Completing the set of traits are items with less explicit religious content but that are consistent with the teachings of many religious groups as well; these include communication and listening, mealtime interaction, a sense of play and humor, balanced interaction among members, shared leisure time, respect for each other's privacy, and willingness to face problems and seek help with them.

Taking an applied perspective directed specifically to Jewish families but pertinent for other families also, Bogot (1988) pointed out that "Jewish sources reveal at least eight value words/phrases that when mobilized can transform the home into a unique setting for religious living" (p. 511). The list contained (a) empathy, (b) helping others achieve their potential, (c) consistent caring, (d) mutualism versus rivalism, (e) decision making as tension between justice and mercy, (f) self-esteem, (g) etiquette, and (h) debate. Bogot suggested that the list can be used by families as a "checklist," serving as "a vehicle for quality control" (p. 511). The qualities in this list as well as those listed by Curran fit well with the general purpose of family life education as being "to strengthen and enrich individual and family well-being" (J. Thomas & Arcus, 1992, p. 7).

Religion-Related Problem Areas in Family Life Education

When family life education takes place in a religious setting, the presentation of values does not present a problem. In other contexts, such as public schools, the question of religion and values can be considerably more complex, and much controversy has swirled around the topic. According to Arcus (1986), the concerns of opponents of family life education are "(1) that family life education in the schools will violate family values; (2) that family life teachers cannot adequately handle the value differences that might exist in the classroom, and (3) that, in fact, it is not possible to teach values in the classroom" (p. 351).

Thornton (1989) has pointed out the "growing pluralism in religious beliefs and a reduction of shared morality" in the United States (p. 890). Thus objections to teaching sectarian values in public education are to be expected. But, on the other side, discussion of "secular values" raises many concerns from those who assume such values to be synonymous with "secularism" or "secular humanism" and therefore to be anti–theistic-religion (Van Dale, 1985). The feasibility of basing instruction on universal or nonsectarian moral or spiritual values has been questioned, although this is the solution advocated by some religious groups.

Maintaining separation of church and state does not mean exclusion of any references to religion that may be intrinsic to secular studies, but valuational topics such as family life education pose a particularly difficult case. Warshaw (1986) has suggested a general set of guidelines for teaching about religion in public schools that could be applicable to family life education programs. They include the teacher's careful prep-aration, efforts to present information empathically, maintaining ground rules such as permitting no ridicule either of other people's religious beliefs and practices or of pure secularism, being aware of community and school attitudes, and being aware of the assumptions of both teacher and students that are brought into the classroom.

Kenny and Orr (1984) have reported various polls indicating strong public support for family life education in the schools as well as a firm conviction that parents should have primary responsibility for the sex-uality education of their children. A parent and community partnership with the schools is crucial in successful implementation of such pro-grams. Steinhausen and Steinhausen (1983) have described ways that agencies concerned with family life issues, such as Planned Parenthood, sometimes have been able to work with religious groups, bringing sexuality education training directly to churches and synagogues.

Much opposition to family life education comes from the religious right, and the influence of this constituency has been strong in recent years. Scanzoni (1985) has pointed out that the reactionary religious mind-set characterizing persons of this persuasion demands that the world be viewed in a certain rigid and legalistic way. "When what is considered to be a settled arrangement ('God's order') is questioned in any way, the equilibrium is disturbed and one's secure world is thrown into disarray" (p. 5). Thus "the religious right attempts to preserve and protect its construction of reality primarily through three control mech-anisms: (1) the squelching of diversity, (2) the building of a separate subculture, and (3) efforts to force society to conform to its viewpoint"

(p. 5). Working with people of this persuasion is facilitated by understanding the intense fear that lies behind much of their opposition to family life education.

Lawrence (1989) has pointed out that fundamentalism not only is found among Christians but is characteristic of certain groups within the Muslim, Jewish, Buddhist, Sikh, Hindu, and Baha'i traditions as well. Fundamentalists of all faiths "are above all religiously motivated individuals, drawn together into ideologically structured groups, for the purpose of promoting a vision of divine restoration" (p. 1). Lawrence stated that fundamentalism "is expressed through the collective demand that specific creedal and ethical dictates derived from scripture be publicly recognized and legally enforced" (p. 27).

Some members of the religious right have tried to exert increasing influence over public schools in various parts of the United States, recognizing the schools' crucial role in children's socialization. Others remove their children from public schools and enroll them in religiously based schools. Still others have elected to school their children at home.

The home schooling movement of the New Christian Right has created a relatively recent controversy in the relationships among the educational, religious, family, and political institutions in the United States. Although not all families that support or practice home schooling are part of this movement, the largest segment, as well as the most visible and politically active, are. Among the primary reasons given by families participating in the home schooling movement is their belief in "family values" (Bates, 1991). Their rationale includes upholding the family as the major (and most exclusive) agent of children's socialization, the desire to integrate religious beliefs into the educational process, the desire to avoid negative peer influences, and the belief in specific values (including many typically falling within the domain of family life education) that are seen as inconsistent with those presented in public or even private schools with religious sponsorship or orientation.

Religious Teachings in Conflict With Family Life Education

Heise and Steitz (1991) have called upon counseling professionals "to be more aware of the manner in which some young children and adults are taught morality from a biblical perspective" (p. 17). They asserted that misinterpretation and misuse of the Bible at times may lie behind the poor self-concept, self-destructiveness, dysfunctional patterns in interpersonal relationships, addictions, and discontent found in certain clients. More positive religious images and interpretations might help such individuals. On a similar note, Heggen and Long (1991) observed a linkage between depression in many Christian women and the traditional gender role conditioning and negative view of anger emphasized in conservative Christian circles. Balswick and Balswick (1990) presented survey data showing some changes in traditional gender role attitudes among the largely evangelical readership of the periodical *Christianity Today* but stated that, in comparison with a Roper poll, the *Christianity Today* respondents were "more traditional than the national opinion poll respondents on every gender-role issue" (p. 18).

Indeed, family life education and religion are inextricably linked. As they intersect in many ways, they sometimes work together cooperatively and sometimes seem to be at cross-purposes. Any comprehensive approach to family life education, however, necessarily includes concepts and issues related to religion, regardless of the context in which it occurs.

FAMILY LIFE EDUCATION IN RELIGIOUS INSTITUTIONS

Religious institutions provide the basis for a large proportion of family life education. Increasingly, family life education topics are the basis for explicit and intentional programs. Perhaps even more socialization on these topics, however, comes in a variety of subtle and implicit ways through other programs of the church, such as liturgy and church doctrine.

Whether implicit or explicit, a theology for the family is the basis for family life education within religious institutions. Development of an intentional theology, however, can help facilitate the consistency, relevance, and effectiveness of these programs.

According to Anderson (1984), the inevitable diversity of family forms that evolve to meet new social circumstances means that "theologically normative statements about the family are most accurate when they are paradoxical" (p. 14). He suggested that such a theology is developed by identifying relevant themes from the religious tradition without absolutizing either the family or the theological tradition. Furthermore, a theology of family must recognize that human identity requires *both* autonomy and an experience of belonging:

> The systems perspective on family life enables us to acknowledge that growth toward autonomy is most likely to occur in families where the rules are flexible, the roles interchangeable, and the rituals dependable. It is the call to discipleship, however, that pushes us out of such nurturing communities into those ever-enlarging circles of interaction and concern in which God continues to make all things new. (pp. 122-123)

Life-Cycle Ceremonies

One way religious institutions affirm the importance of families is through life-cycle ceremonies. The role of churches in rituals associated with "hatching, matching, and dispatching" (i.e., baptisms or infant dedications, weddings, and funerals) is recognized widely and touches the lives even of individuals and families with relatively low levels of formal religious involvement. Friedman (1985) has noted that "modern society seems to be producing three other nodal points of consequence for the life cycle: divorce, retirement, and geographical uprooting" (p. 188). Although these events traditionally have provided fewer opportunities for ceremonial involvement, they are significant in their impact on families and need to be acknowledged in a comprehensive perspective of family process.

Anderson (1984) has pointed out that in each major period of the family life cycle, there are religious rituals corresponding to the family's main task. First, during the stage of *forming the family*, religious institutions assist not only by providing the setting for weddings but also by making available premarital counseling, called by Summers and Cunningham (1989) "a key link between church and family" (p. 327). In the next stage, *enlarging the family*, the religious institution again is involved through baptism, infant dedication, ritual circumcision, or baby naming and has the opportunity to focus on the family's adaptation to the child. In the stage of *expanding the family*, the opportunity exists to enhance the process of individuation through such religious rituals as first communion, confirmation, and bar and bat mitzvah. As the period of *extending the family* is reached, the religious organization is involved again through the marriage of children and can provide help and support for parents as they let go of the child who is leaving. When the stage of *reforming the family* is experienced, the religious organization is there to provide funeral and grief counseling upon the death of parents and has the opportunity to help couples achieve new intimacy in the marital dyad. Life-cycle ceremonies underscore Anderson's point about the importance of both being incorporated into a community and the fostering of individuation. (For further discussion of these forms of family life education, see the relevant chapters in Volume 2 of the *Handbook of Family Life Education*.)

These major stages in the individual and family life cycles that are marked with religious ceremonies may provide opportunities for specific programs in family life education as well, although attention to them is quite uneven. In most programs, for example, more attention tends to be given to birth than to death, a bias that appears to be even more pronounced in Jewish than Christian programs (perhaps reflecting theological differences between the two faiths). In religious schools, a life-cycle component often is included in the curriculum. In a Jewish school, topics typically include "*britmilah* (ritual circumcision), baby naming, *pidyon haben* (redemption of the first born), bar-bat mitzvah, marriage, and sometimes even divorce" (Schoenberg, 1983)—but not death. Gorr (1990), in discussing Reform Jewish education, noted that "in the study of the various stages of life, the same teachers who have so much to say about love and marriage, or concerning one's responsibilities to the community, never seem to have the time and wherewithal to address the issues surrounding death" (p. 548).

Formal Family Life Education Programs Within Religious Settings

Many programs offered through religious institutions are focused specifically on family life education topics, including both normative and nonnormative family situations. Sometimes such programs are based on standardized curricula and other materials available through religious publishing companies.

The marriage enrichment movement, which began in the early 1960s as a grass-roots movement, received early support from churches and has come to be associated primarily with religious sponsorship. Leaders and participants are married couples with a general goal of working "for better marriages, beginning with [their] own" (Mace & Mace, 1977, p. 159). Many of the programs from the movement's early years have been described by Otto (1976). Worldwide Marriage Encounter is predominately Catholic; National Marriage Encounter sponsors programs primarily for Protestant and Jewish couples. Both groups have "encouraged the development of local and regional groups [that], focused in the parish systems of the churches concerned, seek to support ongoing growth among the 'encountered' couples" (Mace & Mace, 1977, p. 160).

A frequent topic for specific family life education programs presented in religious settings is parenting education. Sometimes fairly standard parent education programs such as Systematic Training for Effective Parents (STEP) or Parent Effectiveness Training (PET) are used, and at other times there is a focus on scriptural teachings about parenting.

A foundation for parent education in the church was presented by Lee (1991). Focusing on the issue of behavioral discipline, he suggested that the goal should be "to help parents understand a broader biblical view of the parent-child relationship that transcends the immediate discipline situation" (p. 268). He proposed that parent education programs be based upon the idea of parenting as *discipleship*, a point also made by Eggebroten (1987). In such a context, discipline does not mean punishment but means providing children with wise parental guidance, teaching, and training in a nurturing environment.

Program materials on sexuality education within religious settings have been available for decades. Some are designed for children and youth of various ages, and others are designed for parents (Sex Information and Education Council of the U.S., 1985). All include emphasis on teaching about sexuality issues according to the basic theological guidelines of the sponsoring religious group.

Recently, many churches also have instituted divorce recovery programs for both children and adults. For example, Morgan (1985) has proposed ways churches can minister to divorcing couples (and those who care about them) through a Christian theology of divorce, rituals of separation and divorce, divorce support groups, and educational seminars for the congregation to aid in understanding and supporting persons who experience divorce.

Programs for individuals experiencing various traumatic family situations such as sexual and domestic violence also are being given increasing attention in religious settings. Alsdurf and Alsdurf (1989) have exposed the seriousness of wife battering in religious circles and have shown how certain religious teachings have been used to foster rather than deter violence. Similarly, Feldmeth and Finley (1990) have confirmed that religious homes are not immune to the tragedy of childhood sexual abuse and have offered counsel for adult survivors who are tortured by memories of such abuse. Fortune (1983) has provided an ethical and pastoral perspective on rape and child sexual abuse. She also has written a booklet addressed specifically to the abused Christian woman who is likely to find that "her experience of violence in her family will not only be a physical and emotional crisis but also a spiritual crisis" (Fortune, 1987, p. 2). Also writing from a Christian faith perspective, Wright (1989) included the topic of domestic violence in her discussion of spirituality within the context of family life, highlighting concerns such as confronting those who perpetrate violence within the family, holding offenders accountable, and considering the spiritual relevance of forgiveness in such circumstances. A different way of relating spirituality to healing from incest, rape, and battering has been presented by Jacobs (1989), who studied "women-centered rituals" in a women's spirituality group that learned "images of female strength from ancient symbols of the goddess" (p. 265).

Religious Education Programs

In addition to religious sponsorship of programs focused specifically on family life education, there are often judgments and assumptions about families that are conveyed through other education efforts that are part of the standard calendar of religious institutions. Such programs include Sunday school, vacation Bible school, confirmation classes, and youth groups as well as the informational component of regular worship services.

One of the persistent controversies in Christian education is the extent to which programs should be based on or incorporate contemporary psychological understandings of human beings versus scriptural content and theological explanations. The work of Fowler (1981) on stages of faith development, for example, has become the basis of a number of Christian education programs. More recently, this work has been expanded with the development of a model integrating family systems theory and faith development theory (Fowler, 1987).

Coming from a religious education perspective, Westerhoff (1976) also has contributed substantially to the literature on faith development. He has focused specifically on the role of adults in children's faith, summarizing his position with the idea that "our children will have faith if we have faith and are faithful" (p. 126). If parents are not believers, the church serves as the major socializing agency aiding children in faith development. Loder (1981), however, has challenged the assumption that a positive environment and adequate adult models for faith will ensure faith in children.

What children and adults learn in Sunday school and other classes sponsored by their religious institutions is determined to a large extent by the curricular resources published by their particular groups. In summarizing the variation in denominational influence of Christian education programs, Bowman (1991) has shown that some denominations exercise tight control over what is taught and how it is taught, whereas others allow much more freedom.

Doctrinal Statements

Religious doctrine, "law," or "discipline" often contains components dealing directly or indirectly with family-related matters. Such principles often are among the most controversial within religious groups and also in relation to the larger society. Official pronouncements by religious bodies on such topics as contraception, abortion, masturbation, homosexuality, divorce, remarriage after divorce, nonmarital sexuality, the role of women, and the marital status of clergy all have been debated over the years and continue to receive much attention in both the religious and the popular media. Scripture, religious traditions, human experience (including insights from the social and behavioral sciences), and political considerations all figure into the formation of such statements, and religious teachings and policies on such topics often undergo many changes over time. Kennedy (1970), for example, has shown how Protestant churches gradually moved to an acceptance of contraception after denouncing family use of birth control earlier. Similarly, Morgan (1985) has described the revisions made over time by both Protestants and Roman Catholics in their official statements on divorce.

Sacred Writings

The theological bases of religions typically are found in their scriptures. Both positive and negative images of family relationships are portrayed in the Bible. Indeed, Mann (1991) has suggested that this concern with families establishes the theological unity of Genesis, a central element of which is that "family systems are the basic matrix within which people become alienated, and the primary locus of therapeutic transformation" (p. 341). From a different perspective, Anderson (1984) has pointed out that in the New Testament the sanctity of the family was limited, for although "Jesus accepted and even guarded the family, he refused to absolutize it" (p. 13). A similar point has been made by Ruether (1983a).

Scriptures have an indirect influence on family life education programs through their permeation of the culture (e.g., "Spare the rod and spoil the child"). Scriptural teachings also often are used as direct references in family life education programs, bringing with them the usual difficulties of interpreting material from other cultures and historical periods for relevance to modern-day families. For example, it is doubtful that many people in today's society would advocate following the levirate requirement that a surviving brother father children for his brother's widow to ensure that she not suffer the shame of childlessness and that the brother's lineage be maintained—or the teaching that a rebellious child should be stoned to death—or the requirement that a rapist pay a bride price to the father of the woman he violated and then marry the woman. There is considerable controversy, however, about maintaining other conventions in which scriptural injunctions are even less clear or specific, such as those regarding divorce, abortion and contraception, or sexual orientation.

One of the greatest difficulties encountered with the use of certain scriptural references occurs in situations where the contemporary reader has a history of negative or dysfunctional family experiences. Emphasizing that religious educators need to be sensitive about children's family situations and take care about how they represent God to them, Vogel (1990) has avowed, "I would never tell a child who had been deserted or abused by her father that God is like a father. That child's experiences of 'father' do not reflect the qualities of the God of Abraham and Sarah, Mary and Joseph" (p. 11).

Survivors of childhood physical, psychological, and sexual abuse typically find the commandment to "honor your father and your mother" especially troubling. Obedience to parents may have been held up as a rule never to be questioned—no matter what a parent demanded of them or did to them. Many mental health professionals and others concerned with family life have written about the destructive influence of religion when biblical and theological factors are used to justify abuse in families (Leehan, 1989; A. Miller, 1983, 1990; Scanzoni, 1983, 1988).

Also troubling to many adult children of dysfunctional families, rape survivors, and women who have been battered by boyfriends or husbands are scriptural injunctions to "turn the other cheek" or to identify with a savior who is portrayed as accepting suffering as divine will and a redemptive experience. Typically, when such injunctions are cited, there is no differentiation between voluntary and involuntary suffering (a clear distinction between the suffering of Christ on the cross, as interpreted in Christian theology, and the suffering of a child abused emotionally by alcoholic parents or sexually by an older sibling or other relative). Nor is it typically emphasized that not all suffering is redemptive (Price, 1991).

Scott (1988) has noted the relative silence of the scriptures on the subject of abuse, other than the injunction of the Torah against incest, and has pointed out that there are even stories that appear to accept or even commend violence. In *Texts of Terror*, Trible (1984) has presented a number of scriptural stories in which such family violence is portrayed. Clergy, counselors, and other educators often are faced with the challenge of presenting alternative interpretations and providing other scriptural images. Scott (1988) has identified various illustrations of God as a good parent, both "as a loving Father, who feels for his children . . . (Psalm 103:13) . . . [and] as a loving, supporting mother [Isaiah 49:15]" (p. 144). He also has identified scriptural references to appropriate parenting by human parents.

In dealing with scripture passages that raise questions that can be unsettling to faith, religious educators emphasize hermeneutics, the science of interpretation. Swartley (1983) presented a detailed study of four topics about which the Bible can be said to give "mixed signals" and about which Christians have disagreed in their understandings of biblical teachings: slavery, the Sabbath, war, and women. Interpretations of scriptural teachings on the role of women are particularly pertinent today because of the controversy around gender role issues. According to Swartley (1983), interpreters of scripture tend to take one of two opposing positions: "Hierarchical" interpreters believe men should be dominant and women subordinate, and "liberationist" interpreters believe the Bible liberates from hierarchical gender patterns. These sides understand various scriptural texts differently, and the differences affect the way various religious groups teach about gender-related (and thus family-related) issues.

A similar distinction may be found in Muslim interpretations of the Koran. Hassan (1987), a direct descendant of Muhammad, has shown from examining the Koran that woman and men originally were intended to be equal before Allah. She has argued that misinterpretations of various texts, disseminated through commentaries influenced by other traditional writings, have given force to laws and customs that have oppressed women under Islam. Hassan has prepared a detailed study of Koran texts dealing with women to show that the intention of such texts has been greatly misunderstood on such topics as attitudes toward female children, male-female relationships (especially in marriage), polygamy, family planning, and purdah (keeping women secluded from the eyes of men).

Trible (1984), speaking of Jewish and Christian scriptures, has suggested a feminist hermeneutic that uses scripture to interpret scripture, providing a critique of patriarchy and a challenge to sexism. Also, Vogel (1990) urged religious educators to use curriculum materials that highlight the women in scripture as well as the men so familiar in Bible stories. She also showed ways gender equality can be modeled in Sunday school classes (such as through assigned tasks and decision making and the avoidance of lesson materials that enforce gender stereotypes). Similar suggestions have been made by Larkin (1983).

Ritual and Liturgy

The growing ferment in religious institutions as they deal with gender issues has affected not only formal religious education programs but also the rituals, liturgies, and symbols that form important parts of worship. These elements of worship essentially compose a "hidden curriculum" that also transmits educational messages indirectly, including particular viewpoints on family life. For example, Cunningham, McClurg, Robinson, and Summers (1989) have shown how a content analysis of hymns yields numerous examples of family concepts, many of which portray traditional gender roles.

Rituals

Religious rituals convey a variety of meanings, both sacred and secular (Manuel, 1991). Some rituals are performed in the corporate worship of a religious group (e.g., baptism), others are carried out privately by individuals (e.g., prayer), and others typically are carried out within a family setting (e.g., reciting a blessing at mealtimes). Instruction regarding rituals may be done in a formal educational setting (e.g., confirmation classes), on an individual basis (e.g., pastoral counseling), or through example (e.g., in religious services). Such instruction typically conveys messages of both an explicit and an implicit nature, many of which are related to family life education issues. Della Fave (1991) has reiterated the ways that ritual powerfully reinforces beliefs and norms through repetition and participation in a group that shares closeness in a collective experience and is aroused emotionally by symbols.

Symbols

"Every sentiment, every ideal, every institution associated with the phenomenon of religion, be it noble or ignoble, subsists in an atmosphere of symbols" (Heisig, 1988, p. 198). As Tillich (1960) noted, the innate power of a symbol is its most important characteristic. Closely related are the various connotations, and it is these connotations in religious symbols that often carry powerful messages about important topics in family life education. The Christian doctrine of the Trinity, for example, traditionally has represented masculinist imagery of God in the role of father and Jesus Christ as son.

Another symbolic representation of a family role is Mary, mother of Jesus. Coll (1985) has traced historical changes in the symbolic portrayal of Mary. Discussing the negative effects of earlier interpretations of Mary as a virgin, Coll speculated that this image was a religious expression of treatment of all "women as objects, to be restricted, guarded so that they may serve for the edification of men" (p. 381). By contrast, contemporary women are reclaiming ancient interpretations of the symbol of Mary as virgin—a person complete in herself, whose identity is derived from personal integrity and wholeness rather than belonging to a man. Weaver (1985) has emphasized the humanness of Mary, that "she is one of us," stating that "her predicament as an unwed mother has been used by missionaries trying to appeal to poor women and prostitutes in

Mexican slums" (p. 206). Ruether (1977) has spoken of reconceptualizing the symbol of Mary so that she is viewed as a symbol of empowerment and liberated humanity and *not* as a symbol of passivity, docile submission, and suppressed personhood.

Liturgy

One aspect of liturgy is its presentation of theological perspectives and principles. For example, recitation of the Lord's prayer conveys a model of a father who is holy, powerful, forgiving, and provident. Other elements of worship (e.g., confession, absolution, and blessing) also convey subtle but powerful messages about significant relationships, particularly in religious traditions with explicit use of family "titles" for individuals in the religious community (e.g., father, mother, brother, sister).

Some liturgical traditions have arisen not so much from sacred as from secular traditions. These include celebration of family-focused holidays (e.g., Mother's Day, Father's Day), designation of services or occasions for specific groups (e.g., Women's Day, Youth Day), and incorporation into worship of elements designated for certain groups (e.g., children's sermon).

At times, elements of the liturgy may reinforce or run counter to information from other sources about family-related issues. For example, Mitchell (1988) editorialized on the role of secrets in both religion and families. Noting the family systems perspective on the potential destructiveness of keeping family secrets, he then described a litany from the *Worshipbook* of the Presbyterian churches in which worshippers give thanks for the keeping of secrets. On the other hand, he also noted the secrecy reflected and celebrated in the mystery that is a part of much theological understanding and experience.

Language

One of the most controversial issues in the realm of liturgy concerns inclusive language. The debate centers on traditional language (use of the generic masculine to refer to the people of God as well as use of masculine pronouns to refer to God) versus language that is not gender specific and that makes the inclusion of both sexes clear and precise (Daly, 1973; Ruether, 1983b; Watkins, 1981).

The influence of feminist theology on ritual and liturgy is seen not only in the Christian churches, both Roman Catholic and Protestant, but it is also found within Judaism. Jewish women have held all-women

Passover seders, in which the questions of God's deliverance are asked by daughters rather than sons and in which a place is set for the prophet Miriam instead of for the prophet Elijah (Pogrebin, 1991). There has been a rediscovery of mystic Judaism with its emphasis on Shekhinah, the female aspect of God, with emphasis on God's indwelling presence (Litwoman, 1990). Rosh Hodesh women's groups have sprung up to revive an ancient tradition of celebrating a special holiday for women on the first of each month according to the Hebrew calendar (the time of the new moon). Some groups are applying these celebrations to life-cycle events. As Angelou and Bandes (1989) have written, "Women wanted a Jewish way to mark important events in their lives and began creating rituals for pregnancy, miscarriage and birth; the onset and cessation of menstruation; and the deaths of loved ones. In addition, they started celebrating personal milestones" (p. 8). Various Jewish educators have begun taking a new look at women's place in Judaism (Plaskow, 1989) and are composing new blessings in Hebrew and English as means toward new theological images (Falk, 1989).

"Extracurricular" Religious Education Endeavors

In addition to the religious education endeavors inside religious institutions, there are "extracurricular" religious education experiences as well. These may come from religious radio and television programming and from the spate of religious books and magazines, both denominational and nondenominational, many of which are designed to provide advice on marriage, parenting, and other family life topics.

Norrell and Langford (1987) monitored broadcasts of several syndicated religious television programs (two of which were touched later by sex and money scandals) and found that family issues often were discussed. Family love, commitment, and marital permanence were emphasized by all the speakers. Programs dealing with marital roles, however, emphasized hierarchy, with wives submitting willingly to husbands and with a mother's authority over her children being derived from her husband, the head of the family. Some speakers emphasized the innate sinfulness of children and their need for loving discipline (including spanking); at the same time, some stressed love for children and building their self-esteem and sense of belonging. In discussion of other family-related issues (e.g., divorce, abortion, and homosexuality), the stance taken was conservative, often strongly condemning.

Sorenson and Sorenson (1985) found in their study of 37 "Christian" books on marriage that three fourths emphasized traditional gender roles and a hierarchical structure for marriage and claimed to have derived their views from the Bible. The majority (over two thirds) included sexist language and sexist examples. Most authors viewed the state of marriage in contemporary American society as a cause for alarm and tended to blame this disturbing state on husbands' failure to exercise leadership in the home. Sorenson and Sorenson pointed out the dangers of wife victimization under the model advocated.

In their content analysis of evangelical child-rearing books, however, Sorenson and Sorenson (1986) found evidence of movement away from earlier more rigid emphases in such books for Christian parents. Authoritarianism was stressed less than was once the case, with more authors emphasizing democratic or authoritative child-rearing patterns. The needs of children for affection, warmth, and encouragement were emphasized, even when advice given might have seemed authoritarian. Most of the books were written after 1979 and reflected the cultural emphasis on less stereotypical roles for women. Further, although the majority of the authors claimed to have gleaned their insights from scripture, some also acknowledged having used material from child development literature and social science research.

Religious Groups as Communities of Care

The interrelatedness of humans to each other, a fundamental principle of most religions, is illustrated by and often has been described in relation to the concept of family. References to the "church family" (or sometimes "faith family") or the church as a "family of families" (Bender, 1982) are common, applied variously at the level of a particular congregation, a denomination, or an entire religion. The family analogy is used in many ways, such as the description by Stewart (cited in Frame, 1991) of the 1991 Presbyterian controversy over the proposed report on sexuality that the central issue was whether the diverse segments of the denomination wanted "to continue to be family to each other" (p. 37). Perhaps the most extensive analysis of this model is reflected in the work of Friedman (1985), who used family systems theory to analyze the processes of congregational dynamics. Looking at the families within the congregation, the congregation as a family system, and the personal families of the clergy, he concluded that clergy often can do more to help families by the way they lead their congregations than they can through formal sessions with families.

In their classic sociological study of churches, Glock, Ringer, and Babbie (1967) conceptualized the church as a "family surrogate" for single people and childless married couples, arguing that the church serves the role of the family in meeting various social and emotional needs for these groups. This "family surrogate" model has been tested empirically (Christiano, 1986; Roof & Hoge, 1980). Even though demographic analyses of church participation have not supported this specific conceptualization (Roof & Hoge, 1980), the church continues to serve as an important component of a social support system for many individuals. Although the family metaphor is evident, it is not clear to what extent the church is teaching about a nurturing approach to family development and interaction through this model and the extent to which the family model is being adopted by the church as a means of meeting its members' needs. In either case, members are receiving reinforcement—and in many cases direct instruction—in relationship development and maintenance.

Pastoral care in general and pastoral counseling in particular provide many family life education opportunities. Despite the professionalization of mental health care, clergy continue to be identified as the most popular source of help for personal problems, many of which are family related (Chalfant et al., 1990; Gurin, Veroff, & Feld, 1960; Lowe, 1986; Quackenbos, Privette, & Klentz, 1985; Ruppert & Rogers, 1985; Veroff, Kulka, & Douvan, 1981; Virkler, 1979). As Wynn (1987) noted, "Clergy have no choice about performing family counseling in [their] ministry; [the] only choice is whether [to] do so intelligently or carelessly" (p. 15). Most clergy, however, have very limited training in psychotherapy (Linebaugh & DiVivo, 1981; Orthner & Morley, 1986), knowledge of psychopathology (Domino, 1990), or knowledge of family science (Cunningham & Weddle, 1987).

Models of pastoral care typically emphasize the importance of the relational model (Avery, 1986), an orientation to ministry that has been associated particularly with female clergy (Stevens, 1989). Descriptions of congregational care by laity as well as clergy typically follow this model (Sunderland, 1988). Often such programs are specifically family focused, either in their description using family as metaphor and/or in centering their organization around family-type units or "clusters" (Sawin, 1979, 1982).

The clergy family is another potential source of family life education for families in religious congregations. In view of their potential impact as role models, there often exists an explicit expectation that religious leaders and their families will set a good example in various areas of their lives. Norell (1989, 1991) has pointed out many of the stresses and strains experienced by clergy families because of work and family conflicts and has found higher family life satisfaction among clergy families that established firm boundaries between the demands of their churches and their own family lives. In wisely balancing work and family time and energy distribution, clergy families have another opportunity for positive role modeling. Friedman (1985) emphasized that the potential effect on members of the congregational community is enhanced because it occurs through a natural process derived from the nature of the clergy's connectedness rather than a conscious modeling of a role.

One aspect of congregational care often emphasized is responding to the needs of families in crisis. Such intervention typically includes counseling, often implicitly drawing on family stress theory (Mullen & Hill, 1990). Crises often present the opportunity for providing informational as well as emotional support to the families involved. Information may be in the domain of faith and theological perspectives but also may include assistance with areas such as communication, family resource management, and other aspects of family functioning designed not only to assist the family in coping with their immediate situation but also providing the possibility of generalization to later adjustment and/or coping with future crises.

In education, the "teachable moment" often occurs at a point of crisis, and this general principle is as true in family life education as in other areas. In fact, religious institutions are in a particularly opportune position to assist families in this way, because even families with relatively limited formal religious involvement may come into contact with a religious representative (e.g., hospital chaplain, parish priest, layperson involved in prison ministry) during a time of crisis. Crises experienced by families within a faith community also provide an educational opportunity for other members of that community. Some of this education may be relatively content oriented. For example, the experience of a family struggling with discovering the substance abuse of one of its members may provide the catalyst for an entire congregation to learn more about chemical addictions. Or learning about a family member testing positive for HIV may provide an opportunity for church groups to become better educated about AIDS and its transmission and perhaps develop an outreach ministry for people suffering from AIDS. Or the arrest of a member of a congregation may provide the opportunity not only for discussions of grace and forgiveness but also for discussions of family stress and family communication.

One of the challenges facing all educators today is that of dealing with diverse audiences. This challenge may be particularly difficult when combined with a religious tradition that often has idealized a particular family form—the two-parent family (one adult male and one adult female) with their biological children that has continuing contact with an extended family (based on biological relationships). More adults now, however, are remaining single longer or becoming single again after marriage, and 1 in 4 children under age 18 are being raised in a single-parent home. The figures are even more pronounced for minority families. And more than a million babies each year are born to unmarried women.

The black church has a tradition of involvement in the social development of minorities (Curry, 1991). This role is receiving new emphasis both within the black community and also from government. Speaking at the Chicago '91: National Conference on the Family, Secretary of Health and Human Services Louis Sullivan encouraged the formation of a coalition among the black church, government, and other community groups to "strengthen our families and those institutions and community organizations—like our schools and our churches—which help to instill and reinforce values" (cited in Lawton, 1991, p. 39). At the same time, a policy-oriented briefing on the "restoration of the black family" emphasized political involvement of black churches, especially on "traditional values" and profamily issues (Lawton, 1991, p. 39). Evident in both cases is the incorporation of family life education within the church and also the church's involvement in a social education process at the community and national levels.

The institutional church appears to have been more successful in responding to the needs of some demographic groups than others. Religious institutions, which have been praised for their role as a stabilizing force and carrier of tradition within society and also criticized for their resistance to change, have been slow to revamp programs to address the demographic diversity of society. Traditionally, most church programs have been focused on the traditional nuclear family. Recently, the realities of demographic changes have led some churches to develop programs targeted specifically to other family configurations (e.g., divorced individuals, single parents, gay and lesbian individuals and couples). Such developments not only have brought changes in the emphases of family life education programs that include these groups but also have brought educational opportunities for other members of the congregations to learn about the special concerns of these family situations in a way that has a special impact because of the interactional nature and shared group membership in a community of faith.

Social Action and Social Justice Programs

One area of ministry undertaken by many contemporary religious groups is that of social action/social justice programs. Such programs provide opportunities for family life education to population groups not typically represented in the congregations and also for educating members of the sponsoring congregations about issues in family life education to which they might not be exposed otherwise. Examples of such programs are prison ministries and community-based aftercare (e.g., half-way houses). Also, churches and synagogues can work with community service agencies in the meeting needs of populations such as the elderly (Tobin, Ellor, & Anderson-Ray, 1986), the homeless, and the mentally ill.

In addition to direct programs for different populations, religious groups may engage in political action on behalf of families. For example, a congregation sensitized to the needs of divorced families might advocate "for day care, for tax credits to allow a parent to stay home with young children, and for natural fathers to be named and held financially responsible for their offspring . . . [as well as] legislation supporting joint custody, divorce mediation, adequate levels of child support and equal wages for equal work" (Vos, 1991, p. 1062).

IMPLICATIONS AND RECOMMENDATIONS

Much additional research is needed on the intersection of religion and family life education. A number of implications for family life education can be identified, however.

In religious settings, for example, it is important to recognize the many subtle ways in which family life education occurs and to evaluate whether the messages conveyed are those that are desired. There also are many opportunities for direct education of and about families. Among them are the following:

1. In pastoral care, families can be empowered to function more effectively in everyday life as well as in crisis situations by combining emotional and spiritual support with direct and indirect instruction.

2. Congregational care can be structured in a way that includes the diversity of family forms represented in contemporary society, thereby providing instruction in accepting and respecting differences and demonstrating love toward all persons and family groups.

3. Religious education programs can be enhanced by ensuring that educators are sensitive to the special circumstances and needs of both children and adults from diverse family forms.

4. Social and political action activities can be undertaken to advocate for family needs. Congregations can be educated to become more aware of possibilities for such service.

5. Recovery and support groups with a spiritual model can provide information and guidance to empower families faced with family violence, substance abuse, or whatever other problems members of the congregation and larger community may be experiencing.

In settings outside religious institutions, it is important to recognize the many subtle ways in which religious/spiritual/theological concepts are involved, again evaluating such programs to ensure consistency of these messages with program goals. Opportunities for more direct incorporation of such concepts into family life education include the following:

1. It is important for educators to seek out resource persons from various religious traditions who are committed to the goals of family life education and who understand how any perceived gap between those religious traditions and family life education can be bridged.

2. Awareness of religious concerns and efforts to recruit religious leaders in family life education efforts can help gain necessary community support for family life education programs.

3. Awareness of religious beliefs and practices and of stage in faith and spirituality development of family life education program participants can aid in designing curricula and programs relevant to the precise questions and concerns of those whom educators wish to reach.

4. By attempting to understand the religious sensitivities and fears of persons who worry about compromising their religiously based personal value systems through participation in family life education programs, educators can show respect, provide reassurance, and point out areas of common concern. An adversarial stance is counterproductive in facing areas of disagreement.

5. Educators need to plan carefully how to incorporate relevant religious dimensions into family life education curricula. Examples include how religious values relate to decision making, relationship concerns, conflict resolution, sexuality, marriage, and parenting.

Clearly, there is a need to design family life education programs with an understanding of the religious concerns of participants, just as there is a need to consider insights from family studies research in designing religious education programs. It works both ways. Religion has something to say to family life education, and family life education has something to contribute to religion. The needs of individuals and families will be served most effectively if attention is given to the importance of an integrative and collaborative approach, recognizing that ultimately the goals of religion and family life education are complementary rather than contradictory.

REFERENCES

Abbott, D. A., Berry, M., & Meredith, W. H. (1990). Religious belief and practice: A potential asset in helping families. *Family Relations, 39,* 443-448.

Abbott, D. A., & Meredith, W. H. (1986). Strengths of parents with retarded children. *Family Relations, 35,* 371-375.

Albrecht, S. L., & Cornwall, M. (1989). Life events and religious change. *Review of Religious Research, 31,* 23-38.

Alsdurf, J., & Alsdurf, P. (1989). *Battered into submission: The tragedy of wife abuse in the Christian home.* Downers Grove, IL: InterVarsity.

Anderson, H. (1984). *The family and pastoral care.* Philadelphia: Fortress.

Angelou, M., & Bandes, H. (1989, July/August). Jewish women reclaim rituals. *New Directions for Women,* p. 8.

Arcus, M. (1986). Should family life education be required for high school students? An examination of the issues. *Family Relations, 35,* 347-356.

Avery, W. O. (1986). Toward an understanding of the ministry of presence. *The Journal of Pastoral Care, 40,* 342-353.

Bahr, H. M., & Chadwick, B. A. (1985). Religion and family in Middletown, U.S.A. *Journal of Marriage and the Family, 47,* 407-414.

Balk, D. E. (1991). Death and adolescent bereavement: Current research and future directions. *Journal of Adolescent Research, 6,* 7-27.

Balswick, J., & Balswick, J. (1990, July 16). Adam and Eve in America. *Christianity Today,* pp. 15-18.

Bates, V. L. (1991). Lobbying for the Lord: The New Christian Right home-schooling movement and grassroots lobbying. *Review of Religious Research, 33,* 3-17.

Bender, R. T. (1982). *Christians in families.* Scottdale, PA: Herald.

Bergen, A. E. (1991). Values and religious issues in psychotherapy and mental health. *American Psychologist, 46,* 394-403.

Berger, P. (1967). *The sacred canopy: Elements of a sociological theory of religion.* Garden City, NY: Doubleday.

Bogot, H. I. (1988). Making God accessible: A parenting program. *Religious Education, 83,* 510-517.

Bolen, J. S. (1979). *The tao of psychology: Synchronicity and the self.* San Francisco: Harper & Row.

Bowman, L. E., Jr. (1991). Call for a serious Christian education summit meeting. *Anglican Theological Review, 73,* 106-112.

Boyer, E., Jr. (1984). *A way in the world: Family life as spiritual discipline.* San Francisco: Harper & Row.

Bregman, L. (1989). Dying: A universal human experience? *Journal of Religion and Health, 28,* 58-69.

Brown, D. R., Ndubuisi, S. C., & Gary, L. E. (1990). Religiosity and psychological distress among blacks. *Journal of Religion and Health, 29,* 55-68.

Browning, D., & Browning, C. (1991, August 7-14). The church and family crisis: A new love ethic. *The Christian Century*, pp. 746-749.

Byrne, J. F., & Price, J. H. (1979). In sickness and in health: The effects of religion. *Health Education, 13*, 25-27.

Chalfant, H. P., Heller, P. L., Roberts, A., Briones, D., Aguirre-Hochbaum, S., & Farr, W. (1990). The clergy as a resource for those encountering psychological distress. *Review of Religious Research, 31*, 305-313.

Christiano, K. J. (1986). Church as a family surrogate: Another look at family ties, anomie and church involvement. *Journal for the Scientific Study of Religion, 25*, 339-354.

Coles, R. (1990). *The spiritual life of children.* Boston: Houghton Mifflin.

Coll, R. (1985). Challenging and reclaiming symbols. *Religious Education, 80*, 373-382.

Collins, W. E. (1989). A sermon from hell: Toward a theology of loneliness. *Journal of Religion and Health, 28*, 70-79.

Cornwall, M. (1988). The influence of three agents of religious socialization: Family, church, and peers. In D. L. Thomas (Ed.), *The religion and family connection: Social science perspectives* (pp. 207-231). Provo, UT: Brigham Young University, Religious Studies Center.

Cox, J. L. (1989). Karma and redemption: A religious approach to family violence. *Journal of Religion and Health, 28*, 16-25.

Crawford, M. E., Handal, P. J., & Wiener, R. L. (1989). The relationship between religion and mental health/distress. *Review of Religious Research, 31*, 16-22.

Crnic, K. A., Friedrich, W. N., & Greenburg, M. T. (1983). Adaptation of families with mentally retarded children: A model of stress, coping, and family ecology. *American Journal of Mental Deficiency, 88*, 125-138.

Cunningham, J. L., McClurg, T., Robinson, L., & Summers, R. (1989, November). *The hidden curriculum of the church: Family concepts in hymns.* Paper presented at the meeting of the National Council on Family Relations, New Orleans.

Cunningham, J. L., & Weddle, K. G. (1987, April). *Clergy as premarital counselors: Their knowledge and focus.* Paper presented at the meeting of the Texas Council on Family Relations, San Antonio.

Curran, D. (1983). *Traits of a healthy family.* New York: Ballantine.

Curry, B. P. (1991). The role of the church in the educational development of black children. In M. Parker & L. N. June (Eds.), *The black family: Past, present, and future* (pp. 115-124). Grand Rapids, MI: Zondervan.

Daly, M. (1973). *Beyond God the father.* Boston: Beacon.

D'Antonio, W. V. (1985). The American Catholic family: Signs of cohesion and polarization. *Journal of Marriage and the Family, 47*, 395-405.

Della Fave, L. R. (1991). Ritual and the legitimation of inequality. *Sociological Perspectives, 34*, 21-38.

Domino, G. (1990). Clergy's knowledge of psychopathology. *Journal of Psychology and Theology, 18*, 32-39.

Dudley, M. G., & Kosinski, F. A., Jr. (1990). Religiosity and marital satisfaction: A research note. *Review of Religious Research, 32*, 78-86.

Dykstra, C., & Parks, S. (Eds.). (1986). *Faith development and Fowler.* Birmingham: Religious Education Press.

Eggebroten, A. (1987, April). Sparing the rod: Biblical discipline and parental discipleship. *The Other Side*, pp. 26-33, 42.

Everett, W. J., & Everett, S. J. (1985, November). *The oikos project on work, family, and faith.* Paper presented at the meeting of the National Council on Family Relations, Dallas.

Falk, M. (1989). Notes on composing new blessings: Toward a feminist-Jewish reconstruction of prayer. In J. Plaskow & C. Christ (Eds.), *Weaving the visions* (pp. 128-138). San Francisco: Harper & Row.

Farran, C. J., Fitchett, G., Quiring-Emblen, J. D., & Burck, J. R. (1989). Development of a model for spiritual assessment and intervention. *Journal of Religion and Health, 28,* 185-194.

Feldmeth, J. R., & Finley, M. W. (1990). *We weep for ourselves and our children: A Christian guide for survivors of childhood sexual abuse.* San Francisco: Harper.

Fewell, R. (1986). Supports from religious organizations and personal beliefs. In R. Fewell & P. Vadasy (Eds.), *Families of handicapped children* (pp. 3-34). Austin: Pro-ed.

Fortune, M. M. (1983). *Sexual violence: The unmentionable sin.* New York: Pilgrim.

Fortune, M. M. (1987). *Keeping the faith: Questions and answers for the abused woman.* San Francisco: Harper & Row.

Fowler, J. W. (1981). *Stages of faith.* New York: Harper & Row.

Fowler, J. W. (1984). *Becoming adult, becoming Christian.* San Francisco: Harper & Row.

Fowler, J. W. (1987, November). *The family as ecology of selfhood and faith.* Paper presented at the meeting of the National Council on Family Relations, Atlanta.

Frame, D. (1991, July 22). Presbyterian assembly rejects sexuality report. *Christianity Today,* pp. 37-38.

Friedman, E. H. (1985). *Generation to generation: Family process in church and synagogue.* New York: Guilford.

Garrett, W. R. (1989). [Review of *The religion and family connection: Social sciences perspectives*]. *Review of Religious Research, 31,* 106-107.

Gilligan, C. (1982). *In a different voice: Psychological theory and women's development.* Cambridge, MA: Harvard University Press.

Gilligan, C., Lyons, N. P., & Hanmer, T. J. (1990). *Making connections.* Cambridge, MA: Harvard University Press.

Gilligan, C., Ward, J. V., & Taylor, J. M. (Eds.). (1988). *Mapping the moral domain.* Cambridge, MA: Harvard University, Graduate School of Education.

Glock, C. Y., Ringer, B. B., & Babbie, E. R. (1967). *To comfort and to challenge: A dilemma of the contemporary church.* Berkeley: University of California Press.

Gorr, A. (1990). What to do with death: The end of life in reform Jewish education. *Religious Education, 85,* 548-556.

Gurin, G., Veroff, J., & Feld, S. (1960). *Americans view their mental health.* New York: Basic Books.

Hanson, R. A. (1991). The development of moral reasoning: Some observations about Christian fundamentalism. *Journal of Psychology and Theology, 19,* 249-256.

Hartman, M. (1984). Pronatalistic tendencies and religiosity in Israel. *Sociology and Social Research, 68,* 247-258.

Hassan, R. (1987). Women in the context of change and confrontation within Muslim communities. In V. R. Mollenkott (Ed.), *Women of faith in dialogue* (pp. 96-109). New York: Crossroad.

Hauerwas, S. (1985). The family as a school for character. *Religious Education, 80,* 272-285.

Heaton, T. B. (1988). Four C's of the Mormon family. In D. L. Thomas (Ed.), *The religion and family connection: Social science perspectives* (pp. 107-124). Provo, UT: Brigham Young University, Religious Studies Center.

Heaton, T. B., & Goodman, K. L. (1985). Religions and family formation. *Review of Religious Research, 25,* 103-114.

Heggen, C. H., & Long, V. O. (1991). Counseling the depressed Christian female client. *Counseling and Values, 35,* 128-135.

Heise, R. G., & Steitz, J. A. (1991). Religious perfectionism versus spiritual growth. *Counseling and Values, 36*, 11-18.

Heisig, J. W. (1988). Symbolism. In M. Eliade (Ed.), *The encyclopedia of religion* (Vol. 14, pp. 198-207). New York: Macmillan.

Hoge, D. R., Petrillo, G. H., & Smith, E. I. (1982). Transmission of religious and social values from parents to teenage children. *Journal of Marriage and the Family, 44*, 569-580.

Hunsberger, B. (1985). Religion, age, life satisfaction, and perceived sources of religiousness: A study of older persons. *Journal of Gerontology, 40*, 615-620.

Idler, E. L. (1987). Religious involvement and the health of the elderly: Some hypotheses and an initial test. *Social Forces, 66*, 226-238.

Jacobs, J. L. (1989). The effects of ritual healing on female victims of abuse: A study of empowerment and transformation. *Sociological Analysis, 50*, 265-279.

Johnson, D. P., & Mullins, L. C. (1989). Subjective and social dimensions of religiosity and loneliness among the well elderly. *Review of Religious Research, 31*, 3-15.

Kennedy, D. M. (1970). *Birth control in America: The career of Margaret Sanger.* New Haven, CT: Yale University Press.

Kenny, A. M., & Orr, M. T. (1984, March). Sex education: An overview of current programs, policies, and research. *Phi Delta Kappan*, pp. 491-496.

King, D. G. (1990). Religion and health relationships: A review. *Journal of Religion and Health, 29*, 101-112.

Kohlberg, L. (1981). *The philosophy of moral development* (Vol. 1). New York: Harper & Row.

Kollar, N. (1986). Personality theories, religious education and older adults. *Religious Education, 81*, 609-624.

Koteskey, R. L., Walker, J. S., & Johnson, A. W. (1990). Measurement of identity from adolescence to adulthood: Cultural, community, religious, and family factors. *Journal of Psychology and Theology, 18*, 54-65.

Kubler-Ross, E. (1969). *On death and dying.* New York: Macmillan.

Lamm, M. (1980). *The Jewish way in love and marriage.* San Francisco: Harper & Row.

Larkin, G. (1983). Influence by example. *Religious Education, 78*, 275-278.

Lawrence, B. B. (1989). *Defenders of God.* San Francisco: Harper & Row.

Lawton, K. A. (1991, August 19). Giving black families a boost. *Christianity Today*, pp. 38-39.

Leckey, D. R. (1982). *The ordinary way: A family spirituality.* New York: Crossroad.

Lee, C. (1991). Parenting as discipleship: A contextual motif for Christian parent education. *Journal of Psychology and Theology, 19*, 268-277.

Leehan, J. (1989). *Pastoral care for survivors of family abuse.* Louisville, KY: Westminster/John Knox.

Linebaugh, D. E., & DiVivo, P. (1981). The growing emphasis on training pastor-counselors in Protestant seminaries. *Journal of Psychology and Theology, 9*, 266-268.

Litwoman, J. (1990, July/August). Reclaiming the Shekhinah. *New Directions for Women*, pp. 1, 21.

Loder, J. E. (1981). *The transforming moment.* San Francisco: Harper & Row.

Lowe, D. W. (1986). Counseling activities and referral practices of ministers. *Journal of Psychology and Christianity, 5*(1), 22-29.

Lynd, R. S., & Lynd, H. M. (1929). *Middletown.* New York: Harcourt, Brace.

Lynd, R. S., & Lynd, H. M. (1937). *Middletown in transition.* New York: Harcourt, Brace.

Mace, D., & Mace, V. (1977). *How to have a happy marriage.* Nashville: Abingdon.

Majka, F. (1986). Educating for cult (and Christian) awareness. *Religious Education, 81*, 280-287.

Mann, T. (1991). "All the families of the earth": The theological unity of Genesis. *Interpretation, 45*, 341-353.

Manuel, G. M. (1991). Group process and the Catholic rites of reconciliation. *Journal of Religion and Health, 30,* 119-129.

Maudlin, M. G. (1991, July 22). Addicts in the pew. *Christianity Today,* pp. 19-21.

Miller, A. (1983). *For your own good.* New York: Farrar, Straus & Giroux.

Miller, A. (1990). *Banished knowledge.* New York: Doubleday.

Miller, J. K. (1991). *Hunger for healing: The twelve steps as a classic model for Christian spiritual growth.* San Francisco: Harper.

Mitchell, K. R. (1988). Shadows and secrets. *The Journal of Pastoral Care, 42,* 1-2.

Morgan, R. L. (1985). *Is there life after divorce in the church?* Atlanta: John Knox.

Mullen, P. M., & Hill, E. W. (1990). Family stress theory: A perspective on pastoral care. *Journal of Religion and Health, 29,* 29-39.

Norrell, J. E. (1989). Clergy family satisfaction. *Family Science Review, 2,* 337-346.

Norrell, J. E. (1991). *Clergy families, family life satisfaction, religious orthodoxy, and boundary maintenance.* Unpublished manuscript, Erskine College, Due West, SC.

Norrell, J. E., & Langford, M. (1987, November). *Televised religion and the family.* Paper presented at the meeting of the National Council on Family Relations, Atlanta.

O'Brien, J. M., Goodenow, C., & Espin, O. (1991). Adolescents' reactions to the death of a peer. *Adolescence, 26,* 431-440.

Orthner, D., & Morley, R. (1986, November). *Attitudes toward personal and family counseling among clergy.* Paper presented at the meeting of the National Council on Family Relations, Dearborn, MI.

Otto, H. (1976). *Marriage and family enrichment: New perspectives and programs.* Nashville: Abingdon.

Parks, S. (1986). *The critical years: The young adult search for a faith to live by.* San Francisco: Harper & Row.

Perkins, H. W. (1985). Religious traditions, parents, and peers as determinants of alcohol and drug use among college students. *Review of Religious Research, 27,* 15-31.

Petersen, L. R., & Roy, A. (1985). Religiosity, anxiety, and meaning and purpose: Religion's consequences for psychological well-being. *Review of Religious Research, 27,* 49-62.

Phillips, R. L., Kuzma, J. W., Beeson, W. L., & Lotz, T. (1980). Influence of selection versus lifestyle on risk of fatal cancer and cardiovascular disease among Seventh-Day Adventists. *American Journal of Epidemiology, 112,* 296-314.

Plaskow, J. (1989). Jewish memory from a feminist perspective. In J. Plaskow & C. Christ (Eds.), *Weaving the visions* (pp. 39-50). San Francisco: Harper & Row.

Pogrebin, L. C. (1991). *Debra, Golda, and me: Being female and Jewish in America.* New York: Crown.

Price, T. (1991, November 13). Peace churches and violence against women. *The Christian Century,* pp. 1052-1053.

Pulisuk, M., & Parks, S. H. (1983). Social support and family stress. *Marriage and Family Review, 6,* 137-156.

Quackenbos, S., Privette, G., & Klentz, B. (1985). Psychotherapy: Sacred or secular? *Journal of Counseling and Development, 63,* 290-293.

Ratcliff, D. E. (1990). Counseling parents of the mentally retarded: A Christian perspective. *Journal of Psychology and Theology, 18,* 318-325.

Roof, W. C., & Hoge, D. (1980). Church involvement in America: Social factors affecting membership and participation. *Review of Religious Research, 21,* 405-426.

Roozen, D. A., McKinney, W., & Thompson, W. (1990). The "big chill" generation warms to worship: A research note. *Review of Religious Research, 31,* 314-322.

Ruether, R. (1977). *Mary: The feminine face of the church.* Philadelphia: Westminster.

Ruether, R. (1983a). An unrealized revolution: Searching the scripture for a model of the family. *Christianity and Crisis, 43,* 399-404.

Ruether, R. (1983b). *Sexism and God-talk: Toward a feminist theology.* Boston: Beacon.

Ruppert, P. P., & Rogers, M. L. (1985). Needs assessment in the development of a clergy consultation service: A key informant approach. *Journal of Psychology and Theology, 13,* 50-60.

Sawin, M. M. (1979). *Family enrichment through family clusters.* Valley Forge, PA: Judson.

Sawin, M. M. (Ed.). (1982). *Hope for families.* New York: Sadlier.

Scanzoni, L. D. (1983, November/December). Beware: Patriarchy is hazardous to children. *Daughters of Sarah,* pp. 4-8.

Scanzoni, L. D. (1985, March). Understanding the reactionary religious mind. *SIECUS Report,* pp. 5-6.

Scanzoni, L. D. (1988). Contemporary challenges for religion and the family from a Protestant woman's point of view. In D. L. Thomas (Ed.), *The religion and family connection: Social science perspectives* (pp. 125-142). Provo, UT: Brigham Young University, Religious Studies Center.

Schoenberg, E. S. (1983). Jewish education and dying. *Religious Education, 78,* 210-216.

Scott, M. S. (1988). Honor thy father and mother: Scriptural resources for victims of incest and parental abuse. *The Journal of Pastoral Care, 42,* 139-148.

Sex Information and Education Council of the U.S. (1985, March). Bibliography of religious publications on sexuality and sex education. *SIECUS Report,* pp. 7-10.

Sirkin, M. I. (1990). Cult involvement: A systems approach to assessment and treatment. *Psychotherapy, 27,* 116-123.

Sorenson, J. D., & Sorenson, R. S. (1985, November). *Images of marriage in religious literature.* Paper presented at the meeting of the National Council on Family Relations, Dallas.

Sorenson, J. D., & Sorenson, R. S. (1986, November). *A content analysis of Christian childrearing books.* Paper presented at the meeting of the National Council on Family Relations, Detroit.

Steinhausen, M. S., & Steinhausen, G. W. (1983, Winter). The church/synagogue as a setting for sexuality education. *Family Life Educator,* pp. 21-22.

Stevens, L. (1989). Different voice/different voices: Anglican women in ministry. *Review of Religious Research, 30,* 262-275.

Stott, G. N. (1988). Familial influence on religious involvement. In D. L. Thomas (Ed.), *The religion and family connection: Social science perspectives* (pp. 258-271). Provo, UT: Brigham Young University, Religious Studies Center.

Summers, J. R., & Cunningham, J. L. (1989). Premarital counseling by clergy: A key link between church and family. *Family Studies Review, 2,* 327-336.

Sunderland, R. D. (1988). Lay pastoral care. *The Journal of Pastoral Care, 42,* 159-171.

Swartley, W. M. (1983). *Slavery, sabbath, war, and women.* Scottdale, PA: Herald.

Thayer, N. S. T. (1985). *Spirituality and pastoral care.* Philadelphia: Fortress.

Thomas, D., & Cornwall, M. (1990). Religion and family in the 1980s: Discovery and development. *Journal of Marriage and the Family, 52,* 983-992.

Thomas, J., & Arcus, M. (1992). Family life education: An analysis of the concept. *Family Relations, 41,* 3-8.

Thompson, M. J. (1989). *Family: The forming center.* Nashville: Upper Room Books.

Thornton, A. (1985). Reciprocal influences of family and religion in a changing world. *Journal of Marriage and the Family, 47,* 381-394.

Thornton, A. (1989). Changing attitudes toward family issues in the United States. *Journal of Marriage and the Family, 51,* 873-893.

Thornton, A., & Camburn, D. (1989). Religious participation and adolescent sexual behavior and attitudes. *Journal of Marriage and the Family, 51,* 641-653.

Tillich, P. (1960). The religious symbol. In R. May (Ed.), *Symbolism in religion and literature* (pp. 75-98). New York: George Braziller.

Tobin, S. S., Ellor, J. W., & Anderson-Ray, S. M. (1986). *Enabling the elderly: Religious institutions within the community service system.* Albany: State University of New York Press.

Trible, P. (1984). *Texts of terror.* Philadelphia: Fortress.

Udry, J. R. (1988). Biological predispositions and social control in adolescent sexual behavior. *American Sociological Review, 53,* 709-722.

Van Dale, R. L. (1985). Religious values and secular humanism in the schools. *Religious Education, 80,* 12-28.

Veroff, J., Kulka, R. A., & Douvan, E. (1981). *Mental health in America: Patterns of help-seeking from 1957-1976.* New York: Basic Books.

Virkler, H. A. (1979). Counseling demands, procedures, and preparation of parish ministers: A descriptive study. *Journal of Psychology and Theology, 7,* 271-280.

Vogel, L. J. (1990, September/October). "Teach these words to your children": Inclusivity in Christian education. *Daughters of Sarah,* pp. 10-11.

Vos, B. (1991, November 13). Practicing a love ethic for all families. *The Christian Century,* pp. 1060-1062.

Warshaw, T. (1986). Preparation for teaching about religions in public schools. *Religious Education, 81,* 79-92.

Watkins, K. (1981). *Faithful and fair: Transcending sexist language in worship.* Nashville: Abingdon.

Weaver, M. J. (1985). *New Catholic women.* San Francisco: Harper & Row.

Weber, G., & Parker, C. (1981). A study of family and professional views of the factors affecting family adaptation to a disabled child. In N. Stinnett, J. Defrain, K. King, P. Knaub, & G. Rowe (Eds.), *Family strengths 3: Roots of well-being* (pp. 379-395). Lincoln: University of Nebraska Press.

Westerhoff, J. (1976). *Will our children have faith?* New York: Seabury.

Whitfield, C. L. (1984). *Alcoholism and spirituality.* Baltimore: Resource Group.

Williams, D. D. (1978). *The spirit and the forms of love.* New York: Harper & Row.

Williams, R. B. (1987, March 11). Hinduism in America. *The Christian Century,* pp. 247-249.

Wright, W. M. (1989). *A spirituality of family life.* New York: Crossroad.

Wynn, J. C. (1987). *The family therapist: What pastors and counselors are learning from family therapists.* Old Tappan, NJ: Fleming H. Revell.

9

Looking Ahead in Family Life Education

Margaret E. Arcus

WHAT LIES AHEAD for family life education? What issues and problems need to be addressed and what critical challenges must be surmounted if the movement is to continue to serve families well? In this volume of the *Handbook of Family Life Education,* some of the key foundational areas of family life education have been examined. Attention has been directed to the nature of family life education, its evolution, and its progress toward professionalization. The central theme of values and the central tasks of planning, implementing, and evaluating programs have also been addressed. As well, the key variables of gender, ethnicity, and religion have been examined.

In chapters dealing with each of these topics, authors have reviewed, discussed, and challenged key literature to better inform those involved in family life education scholarship and practice. Because the major purpose of this handbook is to indicate the evolution and current status or "state of the art" of these various dimensions of family life education, it is useful in this final chapter to summarize, discuss, and integrate the key ideas and challenges presented in each of the preceding chapters.

THE NATURE OF FAMILY LIFE EDUCATION

As noted in Chapter 1, the issue of definition and clarification of the concept of family life education has been problematic since the inception of the field. In spite of early attempts to gain some consensus, family life educators have continued to struggle with the meaning of the term, and many different definitions have been proposed by individual family life educators. Recent attempts to overcome the limitations of definitions have focused on the use of methods of analytical inquiry and have resulted in the clarification of at least some of the "features" of family life education. In Chapter 1, Arcus, Schvaneveldt, and Moss focus attention on four of these features: rationale, purpose, content, and what the authors term *operational principles*. To summarize these features briefly, they report that three different but related rationales (dealing with problems, preventing problems, developing potentials) have been influential in the development of family life education, that the general purpose of the field is to strengthen and enrich individual and family well-being, and that the Framework for Life-Span Family Life Education (see the Appendix) is a defensible conception of the content of family life education. They further identify seven "operational principles" relevant to family life education practice. Of the four features examined, the purpose and the content of family life education appear to have the most well-established scholarly basis, while the rationale and operational principles are primarily descriptive of the literature and thus somewhat speculative.

One of the points that stands out in Chapter 1 is that many of the questions and issues of family life education have been persistent ones over time. Should family life education focus on the individual or on the family unit? Should programs be functional or academic ones? How is education distinct from instruction or from therapy? Are the goals and objectives of family life education too broad, diluting the energies of family life educators and thus the potential impact of these programs? Does the breadth of family life education make the preparation of educators problematic? Although these questions have been persistent ones, family life educators have apparently given few of them any serious scholarly scrutiny. Thus it is not clear whether the persistence of the questions reflects the lack of scholarly attention or whether, in fact, such issues are simply enduring ones, embedded in the nature of family life education.

Other questions and issues arising from the discussion in Chapter 1 also should be addressed. There is a need to give serious and critical attention to the diversity of goals in family life education and to establishing some priorities among them. This not only would help to clarify the nature of family life education but also would provide some guidance to family life educators (particularly in times of scarce resources and competing needs) to ensure that the most important goals are being addressed.

To what extent are the operational principles identified in Chapter 1 actually reflected in family life education practice, and what are the implications of using or endorsing these various principles? What if, for example, respecting individual and family values results in endorsing dominance over and violence against women and children? What does it mean to be educational rather than therapeutic? Would the examination of any legitimate *conceptual* distinctions between education and therapy help to resolve the tensions that currently exist between these two approaches, and would it then make any difference to the practice of family life education? What assumptions and normative beliefs underlie family life education, and to what extent are these justified, either empirically or analytically? Does family life education in fact *prevent* problems? What conditions make "problem prevention" likely or unlikely?

THE EVOLUTION OF FAMILY LIFE EDUCATION

Lewis-Rowley, Brasher, Moss, Duncan, and Stiles, in Chapter 2, present a historical account of the unfolding of efforts to educate for family life. The influence of major social and cultural developments and the contributions of major academic foundational areas were addressed for each of several sequential time periods or eras. Thus the focus in this chapter coincides with what Thomas, Schvaneveldt, and Young call "program development" in Chapter 5—a discussion of the forces that contributed to the origin and evolution of education for family life over time.

The basic premise in Chapter 2 is that patterns of family life are embedded in ongoing social changes that become central in the development of education for family life. Among those social changes or forces that have been central to the evolution of family life education over the past 200 years are a growing concern for education, first for the elite and then for the masses; the early identification of the home as the central paradigm for family education, thus directing attention primarily to the education of women for their traditional roles and tasks; a belief that the problems of family life and those of society are connected; the influence of different disciplines (home economics, sociology, social work, social psychology) and of empirical and analytical research on the development and perspectives of family life education; and the impact of economic forces (the depressions of 1873 and of the 1930s and the recession of the 1970s), of political events (e.g., the Civil War, World Wars

I and II, the Korean and Vietnam wars), and of government policies (e.g., the Morrill Land Grant Act of 1862, the Smith-Lever Act of 1914, the National Mental Health Act of 1946).

Documenting these developments over such an extended period of time is a monumental task, and Chapter 2 provides a rich source of information regarding the evolution of education for family life. As such, this chronology not only illuminates the past but may also provide insights into the present, that is, why family life education is where it is at the current time. It is also possible that this historical accounting may be of value in helping family life educators to better shape the direction of family life education. What are the contemporary forces influencing family life education, and can (or how can) the lessons of the past assist family life educators in dealing with these forces?

Because the authors of Chapter 2 have chosen to focus on forces influencing family life education, they have not provided an account of the history of the family life education movement itself. (Given the limitations of a single chapter, it was not possible for them to do both.) Thus the task of examining the history of the family life education movement remains to be done. For example, what were the beliefs, the values, the motivations, the experiences of the early leaders of family life education? Was there conflict, and, if so, how was this handled? How did these leaders respond to or attempt to shape the various external influences? Writing such a history of the family life education movement will necessarily require access to early documents, many of which may no longer exist or may be difficult to find.

A historical perspective on family life education is not just its chronology, however. Neither should such a history be an end in itself. Rather, it should be a means of understanding the phenomenon of change as this occurs in family life education over time. In any future historical investigations, it will be important to examine not only what happened but also how and why it happened. Thus any historical research in family life education will need to be embedded in some kind of theory or framework. Thomas (1986), for example, used Cuban's theory of curricular determinants (Cuban, 1979) to examine both the process by which home economics curriculum had changed over time and the role played by professionals in this process. In her study, Thomas not only identified the forces that had influenced curriculum change but also determined that this process of change occurred in three "stages," beginning with broad social movements, which then led to political-legal decisions to influence the direction of education, which were then followed by the actions of interested groups and individuals who attempted both to influence and to implement the changes. It would be interesting to know whether changes in family life education followed a similar "three-stage" process. In another example, Daly (1973) studied the promotion of family life and sex education in Canada using Smelser's theory of collective behavior (Smelser, 1962). In this study, Daly not only identified family life and sex education as a particular kind of collective behavior (a norm-oriented movement) but was also able to "test" Smelser's theory using family life and sex education as a particular example. The information provided in Chapter 2 would appear to lay important groundwork for other theory-based historical studies in family life education.

In their conclusion to Chapter 2, Lewis-Rowley et al. indicate that the immediate decades will "probably" give attention to (a) teams of specialists and/or generalists, (b) refined theory and research, (c) intervention in private and/or public spheres, and (d) global in addition to national family policies. In the absence of supporting data, these claims must be taken as speculations about potential future forces in family life education. Some of these speculations make sense in light of historical trends in family life education (e.g., the development and use of refined theory and research). Other speculations, however, might be questioned. Although the authors of Chapter 2 clearly value coalitions and although this valued position can easily be understood, it does seem to be at odds with the competition among disciplines and perspectives that appears to be characteristic of contemporary family life education and that is discussed at least briefly in Chapter 2 and elsewhere (e.g., Chapters 1 and 3). How to move family life education from competition to the teamwork suggested in Chapter 2 during the next few decades will be a major challenge for the field.

PROFESSIONALIZATION

In Chapter 3, Czaplewski and Jorgensen note that a key component of any profession is the preparation of its practitioners. Although family life education meets some but not all of the criteria for classification as a profession, the preparation of its educators has been of major concern in family life education over time (a concern reported in nearly every chapter in this handbook), and educator preparation is the major focus of this chapter.

According to the authors, family life education can be characterized at the current time as having many beliefs and preferences but no commonly accepted model of educator preparation. They focus their attention on two aspects of preparation: the differing paradigms that underlie educator preparation (behavioristic, personalistic, inquiry oriented) and the subject matter considered to be essential for family life educators. In their view, both of these aspects are in need of serious scholarly attention.

In their introduction, Czaplewski and Jorgensen identify three issues and concerns of the mid-1960s regarding the family life educator: problems with recruitment and retention, the lack of formal training, and the diverse backgrounds of family life educators. Although they do not return directly to these themes in their conclusion, progress on these issues can be inferred from their chapter. These three issues will be used here as a "framework" around which to discuss additional challenges that require attention.

Because little attention in Chapter 3 was directed to questions of recruitment and retention, one might infer that this is an issue that has been "resolved" (or at least is no longer seen as a problem). Indeed, the authors suggest that there are currently "thousands" of family life educators. The question might be raised, however, whether these thousands are in fact family life educators who are trained in, conversant with, and committed to the philosophy and principles of family life education or whether they might more appropriately be described as individuals carrying out activities in the name of family life education but working primarily from a personally derived (rather than field-based) commitment and philosophy. Given the importance of the educator in the practice of family life education, amazingly little is known about these educators—who they are, how they came to be family life educators, the nature of their preparation and how this preparation has influenced their practice, to what extent these educators subscribe to the overall views of the field, and so on.

Czaplewski and Jorgensen indicate that there is no longer a lack of formal preparation for family life education and point to the number of undergraduate and graduate preparation programs that currently exist. They report, however, that little is known about the scholarly underpinnings of these programs and that few of them have been subjected to any scholarly examination. For example, to what extent are the various paradigms of preparation actually found in family life education practice (as opposed to its literature), either implicitly or explicitly? Can the paradigms appropriately be combined into some eclectic model, or are there contradictory assumptions underlying the paradigms that make such combination problematic? Are the elements currently included in preparation programs indeed essential in family life education, and to what extent can they actually be attained in preparation programs? Should family life educators be prepared as generalists or as specialists?

(And, given the integrated nature of the content of family life education discussed in Chapter 1, does it make sense to even ask this question any more?) The discussion in Chapter 3 makes it clear that one of the challenges facing family life education is the need for more critically designed and more carefully articulated preparation programs in higher education.

The third issue—the diverse backgrounds of family life educators—still appears to be problematic, reflected in questions concerning competing interests, differing perspectives, and issues of territoriality. Based on current evidence, it is unclear whether family life educators are unwilling or unable to overcome these issues. In light of this continuing difficulty, however, a major question must be addressed by family life educators: What does it take to make diversity a strength rather than an issue or a problem?

The authors of Chapter 3 also raise some important questions regarding ethical issues engendered by the process of professionalization in family life education. Because the certification of family life educators is relatively new, the comments of the authors are necessarily introductory, and many questions need to be pursued. What ethical values are central to family life education, and how can these be justified? What are the major ethical issues and problems in family life education practice that must be addressed in any code of ethics? When ethical values and principles come into conflict during practice (see Reamer, 1982, for some examples), does it make any difference how a practitioner resolves the conflict?

Czaplewski and Jorgensen report that certification programs benefit individuals through higher self-esteem, increased respect, greater remuneration, and other benefits. Given the newness of the certification program in family life education, this would appear to be an important time to begin to investigate such claims. How has the certification program benefited certified family life educators? What influence has it had (or not had) on academic preparation programs or on planned efforts for in-service education?

VALUES AND VALUES EDUCATION

The theme of values in family life education is addressed in Chapter 4. In this chapter, Arcus and Daniels discuss the importance of values within family life education (e.g., values development as a part of the role of the family life educator and the inclusion of specific values goals and experiences in family life programs) and note the problems that arise from confusion regarding this concept. In an attempt to reduce this confusion, the authors discuss several features of the concept of values: (a) They distinguish between values and related concepts such as attitudes, opinions, and preferences; (b) they explain the different kinds of values central to family life education (moral/ethical, cultural, religious, personal) and explore the relationships among them; (c) they examine the nature of value judgments; and (d) they describe the different levels of values and their relevance for family life education.

Arcus and Daniels discuss and critique several major approaches to values education: ignoring values (the "hidden curriculum"), indoctrination, values clarification, Kohlberg's moral development, and value reasoning. They express some concern that the major values education approach found in family life education (the Values Clarification approach) is both theoretically and methodologically flawed. Arcus and Daniels also discuss several values and values education issues: the schools as settings for values education, teacher preparation for values education, and the presumed parental prerogative for values education.

Chapter 4 begins with several central questions regarding values and family life education. What values should (or should not) be included in family life education programs? Should educators share their personal values with participants? What is the best way to handle controversial values questions? How should family life educators deal with potential differing values among the various family life education stakeholders—parents, children, the community, the state, the family life educator, and the field itself?

Many of these important questions remain to be answered. There is a major need in family life education to specify the normative beliefs or values of the field. This not only would help to clarify the concept of family life education (see Chapter 1) but would also be an important step in the development of a code of ethics (see Chapter 3). Recognizing the distinctions between personal and social values and the different levels of values would appear to be important in identifying and justifying these normative beliefs. Clarifying the normative beliefs of family life education would also be of value to family life educators in helping them to determine what values to teach or promote in their programs.

Important questions also remain about values education. Do family life educators promote particular values, and, if so, which ones? To what extent are these values promoted consciously? How do family life educators deal with controversial issues that arise within the educational setting? How do respondents experience the values content of family life education? It should be of major concern to family life education that many educators continue to use an educational approach that has been found to have both conceptual and empirical limitations. Thus improving the preparation of family life educators to deal with values is an essential task facing the field.

Several conceptual and empirical questions require attention. Given the diversity of family values in any community, what does it mean to "violate" family values (or indeed to respect them)? Must all values be respected equally? How does one deal with legitimate conflicts among values? Do values activities and experiences used in family life education make any difference in the lives of participants? What values are held by family life educators themselves, and how do these values influence programs? Should family life education (e.g., school-based programs, marriage preparation, parent education) be required, and, if so, how is this form of paternalism to be justified?

PROGRAMS IN FAMILY LIFE EDUCATION

In Chapter 5, Thomas, Schvaneveldt, and Young review the assumptions and practices associated with the major activities of program planning, implementation, and evaluation as these are reflected in the family life education literature. They also critique these assumptions and practices using relevant findings from contemporary educational theory and research. In general, Thomas et al. conclude that considerable family life education practice is based on outdated and unquestioned educational perspectives and practices and on a limited understanding of what is involved in the design, implementation, and evaluation of educational programs.

For example, program design in family life education appears to be based on a view of "curriculum as plan," with family life educators subscribing to a traditional view dominated by the Tyler model. This model, however, has been subjected to considerable criticism in the educational literature, and critics have argued in particular that behavior and behavior change (themes that appear often in family life education literature) may be deceptive as a criterion of learning. As well, the Tyler model has been criticized for perpetuating the mistaken notion that cognitive and affective learning occur separately and that their behavioral indicators will be different and will be easy to measure.

Family life educators also appear to have a narrow view of program implementation, with paramount concern for the introduction and adoption of programs ("program fidelity") and little attention to the actual use and interpretation of a program in practice ("program adaptation"). Many family life education programs appear to be based on the assumption that programs will be implemented and used faithfully by family life educators as intended by the developers. But recent educational research challenges this assumption, indicating that the interpretation of programs in practice may differ substantially from what was intended by the developers of the program document.

Although considerable concern in family life education is directed toward the evaluation of programs, Thomas et al. note that efforts to evaluate family life education programs are generally "one-sided"; that is, they are primarily concerned with measuring program outcomes in relation to prespecified program objectives (summative evaluation). For the most part, evaluation methods in family life education tend to be limited to surveys and experiments, with little use of qualitative methods. Given that educators may adapt rather than adopt programs, the authors suggest that the emphasis in family life education on measuring progress toward prespecified objectives may simply provide information about how well the objectives were implemented rather than providing evidence concerning what happened as a result of the program.

Many important questions are raised in Chapter 5. Are program goals in family life education both worthwhile (educationally justifiable) and realistic (attainable within the particular educational program)? Can the Framework for Life-Span Family Life Education (National Council on Family Relations, 1984) be justified on the basis of learning theories as well as on developmental theories? How do cognition and affect interact to influence behavior? How do learners actually experience programs, and how do they actively construct meaning in light of their past experiences? How do these personally constructed meanings influence program design, implementation, and evaluation?

Further, how do family life educators actually use or interpret programs, and does this change over time? What perceptions do participants have of the program, and how do these perceptions influence program outcomes? What situational and educator variables influence the use of a program in practice? What have participants learned as a result of the family life education program, and how does this differ (if it does) from what it was intended that they learn? What is the nature of the "hidden curriculum" in family life education?

The issues and challenges raised in Chapter 5 obviously have important implications for the preparation of family life educators. In particular, the chapter indicates the need for more comprehensive and more current instruction in the issues and perspectives of program development, implementation, and evaluation, with particular attention to the development of multiple perspectives and multiple strategies. Thus Chapter 5 extends the discussion of the preparation of professionals begun in Chapter 3. Thomas et al. also raise important issues regarding the politics of family life education, making particular reference to "whose interests are being served by evaluation studies." Although they do not expand on this issue, it does suggest that greater attention needs to be given in family life education to political forces and issues that affect family life education programs.

GENDER ISSUES

Bubolz and McKenry begin Chapter 6 by noting that gender issues have emerged as critical in family life education during the past decade. Although family life education developed originally as education by women for women to help them carry out their traditional roles, fundamental changes in the roles of both men and women during the past century have important implications for family life education. The major purpose in Chapter 6 is to discuss the gendered meanings of the behaviors and roles of males and females in relation to the content, goals, and delivery of family life education programs.

Bubolz and McKenry declare at the outset their commitment to the values and goals of egalitarianism, justice, self-determination, and responsibility. They indicate not only that these values should be taught directly in family life education but also that these values and goals should influence decisions about how, by whom, and for whom family life education is to be conducted. These authors see their views as consistent with contemporary feminism, in particular with the emphasis on the new scholarship of feminism (rather than with its force as a political movement).

Although Bubolz and McKenry justify the above values and goals on the basis of their perceived importance to family life education and the realities of contemporary family living, they acknowledge that not all professionals may be able to embrace all of the implications of the new scholarship that they present and on which they base their discussion. This potential difference of perspectives presents a major challenge for family life education. To what extent should the tenets of the new feminist scholarship (e.g., egalitarianism) be incorporated into family life education and be accepted as the perspective of the field? If family life educators disagree on such central values and goals, what holds family life education together as a movement or takes it beyond the personal beliefs of individual family life educators? Given the need in family life education to identify its normative beliefs (see Chapter 4), the explicit statement of Bubolz and McKenry provides an important step in this direction. Ideally, it will serve as the basis for important debate and discussion in family life education regarding this particular issue.

In their chapter, Bubolz and McKenry review the new scholarship of both the women's and the men's movements and summarize key issues arising from this scholarship (e.g., potential differences between the genders, the genesis of such differences, the possibilities for equality, and so on). They then discuss the implications of the new scholarship in relation to broad family life education content areas. For example, in education regarding sexuality, they highlight the importance of including social and historical influences on sexuality as well as biological ones. They indicate that education concerning relationship development not only needs to take into account changing gender roles and the changing status of women but also alternative ways of meeting intimacy needs and the dissociation between marriage and parenthood. They see issues of paid and unpaid work and the related matters of power, inequity, and caring as central gender issues in family life and thus central issues in family life education. They also discuss gender issues related to such topics as parenthood and child rearing, family transitions, and family crises and violence.

As Bubolz and McKenry note, one of the problems facing family life education is that much of the family science literature on which programs are based is incomplete and biased and thus is seriously flawed. How are educators to provide sound family life programs under such circumstances? Two major challenges emerge from this situation: (a) the need for educators to be aware of the limitations of the available literature and to monitor their practice accordingly and (b) the need for scholars to fill in the gaps and to overcome the biases in the literature on families.

Because this chapter was primarily concerned with the theoretical underpinnings of gender and the implications for family life education content, it has not focused in great depth on questions of practice such as pedagogy, curriculum and materials, and so on. That work remains to be done, and it presents a major challenge for contemporary family life education. Several important questions need to be examined. Are family life education programs perceived differently by males and by females? Do programs differ, depending upon the auspices under which they are offered? Should family life education be required for both males and females, and should such education be coeducational? Does the discourse of family life education inappropriately reflect either male or female experiences and patterns of speech? Does it matter if the family life educator is male or female? Are there feminist and nonfeminist or masculine pedagogies? If so, what are the implications of these for family life education?

Bubolz and McKenry move beyond a focus on traditional family life education content or boundaries when they indicate the importance of educating women for economic independence and thus empowerment. As they state in their conclusion, they endorse a paradigm for change in those social structures, norms, and beliefs that deny full equality and participation for the sexes, and they claim that family life education can contribute to this change and thus to a higher quality of family life and increased individual and societal well-being. Important questions will need to be addressed concerning the significance of extending family life education boundaries in new directions such as this. Consideration must also be given to the implications of not responding to such contemporary concerns.

ETHNICITY AND CULTURAL DIVERSITY

In Chapter 7, Hildreth and Sugawara address some of the critical challenges facing family life educators as they design and deliver family life education programs in culturally diverse societies. They identify and discuss several issues that have major implications for family life education: (a) the diversity of migrant experiences and expectations; (b) the conflicts and transitions attendant upon entering into a new cultural environment (e.g., reestablishing one's identity, reexamining values, forging new relationships); (c) the dual cultural dilemmas faced by families as they deal with the contrasting features of their traditional culture and that of the new environment; and (d) the emergence of bicultural (intergenerational) conflicts (those that arise between parents and children regarding family relationships, the socialization of children, and expectations and experiences related to education and employment). Numerous examples are provided that illustrate the centrality of these issues to the purposes and the content of family life education.

Hildreth and Sugawara challenge family life education to move away from what they see as its traditional practice of emphasizing uniformity rather than diversity, that is, emphasizing the norms and practices of the dominant culture. They discuss and critique several models of intergroup relationships (assimilation, amalgamation, cultural pluralism, ethnogenesis) that have been used to help individuals and families deal with cultural diversity. In their view, ethnogenesis, because of its emphasis on common cultural characteristics, unique cultural pasts, and emergent cultural characteristics, provides the best theoretical framework from which family life education programs should be developed. Although they make this case, how to put such a framework into practice is not discussed and thus remains a major challenge for contemporary family life educators.

The authors also address several aspects of designing and delivering programs for multicultural groups: understanding the needs, expectations, and strengths of diverse families; matching goals and objectives to these needs; designing and implementing appropriate programs; and evaluating the programs. Although these aspects are common to the development of all family life education programs, Hildreth and Sugawara draw attention to the special considerations to be taken into account regarding multicultural groups. Their use of specific examples from different ethnic groups is not exhaustive (nor was it intended to be), but it does provide a basis from which family life educators might begin to challenge their own awareness and sensitivity to issues of cultural diversity.

Some of the issues raised in Chapter 5 regarding programs would appear to be particularly relevant here. To what extent are family life education program documents sensitive to and reflective of issues of ethnicity and cultural diversity? Given the diversity that is likely to be present in any family life education group, how feasible is it to match goals to the needs of *all* in a particular family life program? How are these programs actually used in practice? How do participants from different ethnic backgrounds experience and respond to a particular program? The use of formative evaluation studies would appear to be particularly valuable in providing evidence of the extent to which family life education programs are actually meaningful to culturally diverse families.

Ethnicity and cultural diversity present important dilemmas for family life educators. How should family life educators respond in situations of intergenerational conflict (e.g., the high school girl who wants to date like others in her class but whose parents and culture discourage or do not allow that)? Is it the educators' responsibility to respond to the needs of the adolescent (thus meeting the needs of the participant), or should the educator respond to the values of the parents (thus respecting cultural values)? This is a clear example of the kind of values question raised in Chapter 4: How should family life educators deal with the differing values among the various family life education stakeholders?

What if participants do not agree with the dominant values of family life education? Most marriage preparation and marriage enrichment programs, for example, are based on a belief in companionate marriages. How should educators deal with program participants who come from cultural groups that have more traditional views regarding marriage roles and relationships? Such questions will become increasingly important in family life education as efforts are made in some settings to require participation in marriage preparation (or other) programs.

Another important challenge for family life educators is related to the fact that cultures are not static but are in a constant state of change. Thus it will not be sufficient simply to become more aware or to gain some "snapshot" of cultural practices. Rather, family life educators will need to become sensitive and responsive to the needs of all families, regardless of their culture, as these families are in the process of change. Responding to the cultural diversity of families will require an understanding not only of the diverse cultures but of the process of change itself.

RELIGION

Cunningham and Scanzoni explore the connections between religion and families in Chapter 8. They identify three basic domains central to this connection (family studies, religion/theology, and education) and focus their attention on the integrated areas of study and practice that emerge from the overlap among these domains: family life education, religious education, and the study of families and religion. They see the relationships between and among these integrated areas as reciprocal and systemic rather than linear or causal.

The authors point out that theological perspectives cannot be ignored in family life education because these perspectives form a part of the general philosophical approach or worldview of both program educators and program participants. Thus these perspectives have a significant influence on the assumptions with which educators and participants alike approach and discuss various family life education topics. According to Cunningham and Scanzoni, this influence is often unexamined and calls for serious attention on the part of family life education. For example, they suggest that, because the family paradigms of at least some participants will be constructed with religious beliefs and values, the religious dimension of family life needs to be incorporated into family life education curricula.

Major attention in Chapter 8 is directed toward both the religious dimensions of family life education and family life education in religious institutions. As discussed in this chapter, the religious dimensions of family life education include overlapping goals and common concepts (e.g., helping people develop toward human wholeness, respect and consideration of others), the contributions of religion to families (e.g., the beneficial influence of religious beliefs and practices), religion-related problem areas in family life education (e.g., issues related to religion and values), and religious teachings that are in conflict with family life education (e.g., teachings that may contribute to poor self-concept, dysfunctional relationships, or self-destructive behaviors). As the authors note, family life education and religion are inextricably linked. Sometimes these areas appear to work together cooperatively and at other times they appear to be at cross-purposes. This dual nature of the connection between religion and family life education presents many challenges for family life education.

Family life education in religious institutions includes both explicit and intentional programs and more subtle and implicit socialization. Cunningham and Scanzoni identify several ways in which this family life education occurs: through life-cycle ceremonies related to forming, enlarging, expanding, extending, and reforming the family; through formal family life education programs in areas such as marriage enrichment, parent education, divorce recovery, and sexual and domestic violence; through religious education programs; and through doctrinal statements, sacred writings, and ritual liturgy. They further indicate that family life education may occur through religious education endeavors such as radio and television programming and religious books and magazines, through religious groups as communities of care, and through social action and social justice programs undertaken as one aspect of ministry.

Many challenges emerge from the discussion of the intersection between religion and family life education presented by Cunningham and Scanzoni. Among other things, it appears timely for family life education not only to acknowledge the importance of religion in family life but also to incorporate it specifically into family life education. How might family life education build upon and support the positive influences of religion on families, and how might it help to counteract those instances where the influence may not be positive for families or for individual family members? How will attention to the religious dimension of family life education influence the pedagogy of family life education? What political issues might arise from the inclusion of religion in family life education, and how might family life educators best be prepared to deal with these issues?

SUMMARY

The preceding summary and discussion indicate that it is time to become more serious and systematic about scholarly issues and questions in family life education and that a major scholarly agenda lies ahead in family life education. Some of this agenda is empirical and some of it is conceptual. Regardless of the specific questions to be answered, one of the conclusions that emerges from the preceding is the need to incorporate into family life education the use of additional forms of knowledge generation (e.g., formative research, qualitative methods, analytical methods) and to base work on *contemporary* thought from related disciplines. It is time to challenge outdated knowledge and/or the unquestioned use of literature from other fields. The development of new knowledge, whether it is in family science, in education, in feminist scholarship, or wherever, must be acknowledged and used in building a solid, scholarly basis for contemporary family life education.

There also appears to be a need to direct attention to some topics or areas that have received little specific attention in family life education in the past. For example, reference was made in several of the chapters to political issues and concerns and to the importance of these for accomplishing (or not accomplishing) the purposes and goals of the field. As noted briefly in the Preface, this theme has not been included as one of the chapters in this handbook, not because the topic was unimportant but because of the absence of any substantial amount of relevant literature on which to base a chapter. As the concept of families becomes increasingly politicized and as the demands for the accountability of family life programs increase, however, the failure of family life educators to give serious attention to the political nature and context of family life education may have serious consequences for the field.

As well, several chapters have identified important issues related to social action and social justice. Because family life education programs have typically focused on the education of individual families and family members for meeting their own needs, they have tended to give little direct attention to issues and questions embedded in the broader social context. This historical "practice" may need to be reconsidered, particularly if family life education is to respond to the challenges of cultural diversity and the new feminist scholarship. Family life educators must recognize that, although programs in family life education may be important avenues for strengthening families, in some cases educational intervention may not be enough (Arcus, 1992). It is time for family life education to clarify those issues that are likely to be addressed most effectively through educational activities and to distinguish these from issues that require other actions such as policy formulation. While it may be possible, for example, to educate families to use their resources well, it requires more than education to ensure equal access for all to basic resources and services. Thus the traditional content and educational focus of family life education may need to be expanded to incorporate both social action on the part of family life educators to benefit families and the direct education of families and family members to participate more fully in shaping the broader social context in which they live.

The foregoing has obvious implications for the preparation of family life educators. The traditional content and approaches of preparation programs will need to be modified to take into account a recognition of the growth and development of knowledge in relevant disciplines, considered expansion into new areas of study, the systematic use of additional educational and empirical strategies and approaches, and preparation for roles beyond the traditional educational role. In short, the issues and challenges identified in this volume must not be taken lightly by those who design and deliver preparation programs in higher education.

In giving consideration to these issues, however, the emphasis must be placed on the *modification* of preparation programs, not a simple expansion in content. The challenge to be met is "better," not just more. Thought must be given to the priorities to be established for preparation and to the most effective means for accomplishing these priorities. Given the importance of the educator in the design and delivery of family life education programs, the response of the field to these challenges of preparation will be critical for the future of family life education.

REFERENCES

Arcus, M. E. (1992). Family life education: Toward the 21st century. *Family Relations, 41,* 390-393.

Cuban, L. (1979). Determinants of curriculum change and stability, 1870-1970. In J. Schaffarzick & G. Sykes (Eds.), *Value conflicts and curriculum issues* (pp. 141-198). Berkeley, CA: McCutchan.

Daly, B. (1973). *The promotion of family life and sex education as a norm-oriented movement.* Unpublished master's thesis, Carleton University, Ottawa, Ontario.

National Council on Family Relations. (1984). *Standards and criteria for the certification of family life educators, college/university curriculum guidelines, and content guidelines for family life education: A framework for planning programs over the life span.* Minneapolis, MN: Author.

Reamer, F. G. (1982). *Ethical dilemmas in social service.* New York: Columbia University Press.

Smelser, N. J. (1962). *Theory of collective behavior.* New York: Free Press.

Thomas, C. J. (1986). *Forces influencing home economics curriculum change in British Columbia secondary schools, 1912-1985.* Unpublished master's thesis, University of British Columbia, Vancouver.

Appendix

SINCE ITS INCEPTION, the National Council on Family Relations (NCFR) has had an ongoing interest in promoting and supporting quality family life education. Although the NCFR has been concerned with all aspects of family life education, including program development, delivery, and evaluation, special attention has been given to the preparation of family life educators. A committee that was established by the NCFR in 1968-1970 identified the major subject matter areas needed by family life educators (Committee on Educational Standards and Certification for Family Life Educators, 1970). A second committee, established in 1975, examined issues related to the certification of family life teachers (Kerckhoff & O'Connor, 1978). The work of each of these committees has been important in developing preparation for family life educators.

In 1980 the NCFR established the Committee on Standards and Criteria for the Certification of Family Life Education "to take additional steps toward addressing the many questions involved in the delivery of quality training for family life educators" (Davidson, 1989, p. 128). This committee explored the feasibility of developing and implementing certification for family life educators and eventually recommended such a program to the NCFR Board of Directors in 1984 (Davidson, 1989), which acted on the recommendations, and a certification program for family life educators was initiated in 1985. (Information regarding the details of this program may be obtained from the National Council on Family Relations.)

In addition to its recommendations regarding a certification program for family life educators, the Committee on Standards and Criteria for the Certification of Family Life Educators (1984) also made two other important contributions. First, they developed curriculum guidelines for college/university preparation programs, guidelines that not only identified the broad subject areas that should be included in these preparation programs but that also provided more detailed information regarding essential themes within each of these subject areas.

The committee also developed an overview of the major content areas in family life education. This overview is known as the Framework for Life-Span Family Life Education (Arcus, 1987) and is reproduced here in its entirety. The framework was based on the assumption that people of all ages need to learn about the many aspects of family life and was developed to help stimulate the development and expansion of quality programs in family life education. It was believed that this specification of appropriate content for life-span family life programs would meet a critical need in the field and would help to advance both the practice and the scholarship of family life education.

Several key principles guided the development of the framework (Arcus, 1987). It was intended that the framework reflect a broad conception of family life education and that it be consistent with other writings in the field. At the same time, however, the number of topics was limited to make the framework more concise. This was accomplished by combining some related topic areas that in other documents might be listed separately. For example, "Human Development and Sexuality" was listed as one topic area rather than two, and friendships, dating, and marriage were combined into the broader topic area of "Interpersonal Relationships." It was hoped that this consolidation would make the framework more manageable without losing important concepts or ideas. Three key processes (communicating, decision making, problem solving) were not listed as separate topics but were incorporated into all of the topic areas.

It was also intended that the framework include all dimensions of learning: knowledge, attitudes, and skills. Although key concepts related to these dimensions were not designated separately under each topic area, a review of the framework will indicate that all three dimensions were included.

The developers of the framework believed that readiness to learn about family life was not tied to specific ages and that it was thus more appropriate to organize the content into broad, general age categories rather than specific ones. The framework was intended to illustrate that each topic area may be addressed at each age level by varying the focus and the complexity of the key concepts. Family life educators will need to become familiar with the entire framework to satisfactorily meet the diverse developmental needs of their program participants. Because not all adolescents are alike, for example, one would need to understand the concepts listed under "Children" to respond to the needs of the early adolescent, while the concepts listed under "Adults" would be important in meeting the needs of those adolescents who are more mature and verging upon adulthood.

The framework may be used by family life educators in a number of ways. Although it was not intended to be a curriculum, family life educators might use the framework as an aid in program development, helping to determine the content appropriate for a particular program. It might also be of value in assessing the breadth of content in an existing family life program; that is, it might assist family life educators in identifying those areas that are "missing" or that might need strengthening.

Additionally, the framework could be used to assess the comprehensiveness of program offerings in an agency, an organization, or a community. Are there particular content areas that have been ignored or that have received less attention than they deserve? For those involved in the preparation of family life educators, the framework might be used as the basis for class assignments (e.g., to critique an existing program for its breadth) or as a means to assess the continuing education needs of family life educators. Family life education scholars may also find the framework of value as they develop and test theory in family life education. There are also likely to be other creative uses of the framework.

The NCFR Committee on Standards and Criteria for Certification of Family Life Educators responsible for the development of the Framework included J. Kenneth Davidson, Sr., Committee Chair; Sharon J. Alexander; Virginia Anderson; Margaret E. Arcus; Betty L. Barber; Carol A. Darling; Sally Hansen; Judith O. Hooper; Stephen R. Jorgensen; Terrance O. Olson; Marie F. Peters; Sharon Price-Bonham; and Joanne D. Wall. Over 25 other NCFR members served as consultants during the revision of the various drafts of the framework, and their names are listed in the 1983 report presented to the NCFR Board of Directors.

REFERENCES

Arcus, M. (1987). A framework for life-span family life education. *Family Relations, 36,* 5-10.

Committee on Education Standards and Certification for Family Life Educators. (1970). Family life and sex education: Proposed criteria for teacher education. *The Family Coordinator, 9,* 183-185.

Committee on Standards and Certification for Family Life Educators. (1984). *Standards and criteria for the certification of family life educators, college/university curriculum guidelines, and an overview of content in family life education: A framework for planning life span programs.* Minneapolis, MN: National Council on Family Relations.

Davidson, J. K., Sr. (1989). The certification of family life educators: A quest for professionalism. *Family Science Review, 2,* 125-136.

Kerckhoff, R., & O'Connor, T. (1978). Certification of high school family life teachers. *The Family Coordinator, 27,* 61-64.

TABLE A.1. Framework for Life-Span Family Life Education*

*Topic Areas and Key Concepts***

Age Levels	Human Development and Sexuality	Interpersonal Relationships
Children	• Physical, emotional, social, and sexual development • Similarities and differences in individual development • Perceptions about older people (adolescents, adults, elderly) • Understanding people with special needs • Uniqueness of each person • Responsibility for keeping healthy (nutrition, personal hygiene) • Social and environmental conditions affecting growth and development • Aspects of human reproduction (prenatal development, birth, puberty) • Body privacy and protection against sexual abuse	• Building self-esteem • Identifying and enhancing personal strengths • Respecting self and others • Dealing with emotions • Communicating with others • Sharing feelings constructively • Learning from and teaching others • Making, keeping, and ending friendships • Sharing time, friends, and possessions • Handling problems with others • Acting with consideration for self and others

Adolescents
- Types of development: physical, cognitive, emotional, personality, moral, social, and sexual
- Patterns of development over the life span (conception to death)
- Interaction among types of development (e.g., social and sexual development)
- Accepting individual differences in development
- Stereotypes and realities about adulthood and aging
- Developmental disabilities
- Social and environmental conditions affecting growth and development
- Effects of chemical substances on physical health and development
- Responsibility for personal health (nutrition, hygiene, exercise)
- Body privacy and protection against sexual abuse
- Communicating about sexuality (personal values, beliefs)
- Normality of sexual feelings and sexual responses
- Human reproduction and contraception
- Varying family and societal beliefs about sexuality
- Choices, consequences, and responsibilities of sexual behavior

- Building self-esteem and self-confidence
- Assessing and developing personal abilities and talents
- Respecting self and others
- Changing and developing one's thoughts, attitudes, and values
- Dealing with emotion
- Dealing with success and failure
- Communicating information, thoughts, and feelings
- Initiating, maintaining, and ending relationships
- Assessing compatibility in interpersonal relationships
- Understanding the effects of self-perceptions of relationships
- Understanding the needs and motivations involved in dating
- Accepting responsibility for one's actions
- Acting in one's own and others' best interests
- Understanding the bases for choosing a family life-style (values, heritage, religious beliefs)
- Factors influencing mate selection (social, cultural, personal)
- Understanding the dimensions of love and commitment
- Exploring the responsibilities of marriage

continued

TABLE A.1. (*continued*)

	Topic Areas and Key Concepts	
Age Levels	*Human Development and Sexuality*	*Interpersonal Relationships*
Adults	• Dimensions of development: physical, cognitive, affective, moral, personality, social, and sexual • Patterns of development over the life span (conception to death) • Interaction among dimensions of development (e.g., social and sexual development) • Factors influencing individual differences in development • Promoting development in self and others • Myths and realities of adulthood and aging • Dealing with disabilities • Social and environmental conditions affecting growth and development • Responsibility for personal and family health • Communicating about sexuality (personal values, beliefs, shared decision making) • Normality of sexual feelings • Human sexual response • Contraception, infertility, and genetics • Responsible sexual behavior (choices, consequences, shared decision making) • Prevention of sexual abuse • Varying societal beliefs about sexuality	• Building self-esteem and self-confidence in self and others • Establishing personal autonomy • Achieving constructive personal change • Communicating effectively • Dealing with emotions • Dealing with crises • Types of intimate relationships • Exercising initiative in relationships • Developing, maintaining, and ending relationships • Understanding the effects of self-perceptions of relationships • Varying influences on roles and relationships (ethnic, racial, social) • Recognizing factors associated with quality relationships • Taking responsibility and making commitments in relationships • Evaluating choices and alternatives in relationships • Changes in the marital relationship over time • Acting in accordance with personal beliefs with consideration for others' best interests • Creating and maintaining a family of one's own

Children
- Families as sources of protection, guidance, affection, and support
- Families as possible sources of anger and violence
- Family similarities and differences
- Individuality and importance of all family members
- Responsibilities, rights, and interdependence of all family members
- Changes in families (births, separations, deaths)
- Family members as individuals
- Getting along in the family
- Expressing feelings in families
- Family rules
- Family problems
- Impact of change on families
- Family traditions and celebrations
- Personal family history

- Taking care of possessions
- Learning about time and schedules
- Helping with family tasks
- Developing talents and abilities
- Using and saving human and nonhuman resources
- Importance of space and privacy
- Learning to choose
- Selecting and consuming (food, clothing, recreation)
- Using money
- Influences on consumer decisions (wants, costs, media, friends)

continued

TABLE A.1. (*continued*)

Topic Areas and Key Concepts

Age Levels	Family Interaction	Family Resource Management
Adolescents	• Families as sources of protection, guidance, affection, and support • Families as possible sources of anger and violence • Family differences (membership, economic level, role performance, values) • Different needs and expectations of all family members • Rights, responsibilities, and interdependence of family members • Becoming an adult within the family • Interaction between family members • Communication in families • Managing feelings in families • Family rules • Coping with internal change and stress in the family • Personal and family decision making • Intergenerational relationships • Interaction of friends and family • Influence of family background and history • Family traditions and celebrations • Changes in family composition (births, divorce, death)	• Using personal resources • Assessment of and changes in personal and family resources • Selection of resources to meet personal needs (food, clothing, recreation) • Allocating time for work, school, and leisure • Negotiating privacy and independence • Developing leisure interests • Values as bases for choices • Choosing long- and short-term goals • Responsibility for decisions • Exploring career choices • Earning, spending, and saving money • Influences on consumer decisions (personal values, costs, media, peers)

Adults
- Families as sources of protection, guidance, affection, and support
- Families as possible sources of anger and violence
- Differences in families (membership, economic level, role performance, values)
- Changing needs and expectations of all family members
- Rights, responsibilities, and interdependence of family members
- Family transitions (marriage, birth, divorce, remarriage, death)
- Individual and family roles
- Individual development in the family
- Intimate relationships in the family
- Effects of family on self-concepts of its members
- Factors affecting marital and family relationships
- Giving and receiving affection
- Power and authority in the family
- Family rules—overt and covert
- Sources of stress and coping with stress
- Intergenerational dynamics throughout the life span
- Life-style choices
- Family history, traditions, and celebrations
- Varying influences on family interaction patterns (ethnic, racial, social)

- Developing personal resources
- Resource consumption and conservation—material and nonmaterial
- Using resources to meet basic needs of family (food, clothing, shelter)
- Expendability of human energy
- Balancing family and work roles
- Developing leisure interests
- Varying needs of family members for privacy and independence
- Financial planning
- Values as bases for choices
- Establishing long- and short-term goals
- Differing views about uses of family resources
- Development of personal resources through career choices
- Influences on consumer decisions (personal values, costs, media, peers)
- Retirement planning

continued

TABLE A.1. (*continued*)

Topic Areas and Key Concepts

Age Levels	Education About Parenthood	Ethics
Children	• Responsibilities of parents • Responsibilities of children • Rewards and difficulties of parenthood • Meeting the needs of children of different ages • Different parenting styles and behavior • Safety for children • Problems of family violence, abuse, and neglect • Different types of caregivers • Sources of help for parents (family, neighborhood, community) • Parents who live away from children	• Respect for all persons • Rights of all persons • Gaining new rights and responsibilities with age • Consequences of actions for self and others • Taking responsibility for actions
Adolescents	• Understanding marital and parental roles • Meeting children's needs at different stages of development • Responding to individual differences in children • Rewards and difficulties of parenting • Child-rearing practices • Parent-child communication • Family conflict and conflict resolution • Teaching life skills to children (self-sufficiency, safety) • Problems of family violence, abuse, and neglect • Varied parenting situations (single parenting, stepparenting, adoption) • Sources of help for parents (family, neighborhood, community) • Parents living away from children • Factors to consider in deciding if and when to become a parent	• Ethical principles as one kind of values • Ethical values as guides to human social conduct • Interrelationship of rights and responsibilities • Self-responsibility and social responsibility • Complexity and difficulty of ethical choices • Ethical implications of social and technological change • Developing a personal ethical code

Adults

- Changing parental responsibilities as children become independent
- Changing parent-child relationships over the life span
- Preparation for birth and parenthood
- Demands and rewards of parenthood
- Child-rearing practices, guidance, and parenting strategies
- Importance of parental communication regarding child-rearing practices
- Parent-child communication
- Family conflict and conflict resolution
- Providing a safe environment for children
- Teaching life skills to children (self-sufficiency, decision making)
- Problems of family violence, abuse, and neglect
- Varied parenting situations (single parenting, stepparenting, adoption)
- Sources of help for parents (family, neighborhood, community)
- Factors to consider in deciding if and when to become a parent
- Influences on parenting styles (ethnic, racial, social)

- Ethical principles as one kind of values
- Ethical values as guides to human social conduct
- Acting in accordance with personal beliefs with consideration for others
- Interrelationship of rights and responsibilities
- Personal autonomy and social responsibility
- Establishing an ethical philosophy of life
- Complexity and difficulty of ethical choices and decisions
- Ethical implications of social and technological change
- Assisting in the formation of ethical concepts and behavior in others

continued

TABLE A.1. (*continued*)

Age Levels	Topic Areas and Key Concepts
	Family and Society
Children	• Understanding and respecting the law • Laws and policies affecting families • Children's legal rights • Programs that support individuals and families • Importance of families, neighborhood, and the community • Families and schools working together • Jobs, money, and the family • Differing religious beliefs and practices of families
Adolescents	• Understanding laws affecting families • Families and the justice system • Impact of laws and policies on families • Respecting the civil rights of all people • Individual and family legal protection, rights, and responsibilities • Family conflict and legal protection of family members • Support for families with special needs and problems • Importance of family to society • Individual and family responsibility in the community • Functioning in the school system • School as preparation for the future • Education throughout the life span • Reciprocal influences of technology and families • Reciprocal influences of the economy and families • The influence of religion on families • Families and the workplace • Population issues and resource allocation

Adults
- Understanding and affecting laws and policies
- Transmitting values regarding education, justice, and the law
- Protecting the civil rights of all people
- Family conflict and legal protection of family members
- The influence of religion on families
- Understanding and obtaining community support services
- Supportive networks (family, friends, religious institutions)
- Role of family in society
- Individual and family responsibility in the community
- Utilizing the educational system
- Family participation in the education of children
- Education throughout the life span
- Reciprocal influences of technology and families
- Economic fluctuations and their impact on families
- Interrelationship of families, work, and society
- Population issues and resource allocation

*A wall poster of this framework is available from the National Council on Family Relations.
**Communicating, decision making, and problem solving have not been listed as separate concepts but should be incorporated into each topic area.
SOURCE: From "A Framework for Life-Span Family Life Education" by M. Arcus, 1987. *Family Relations*, 36, pp. 5-10. Copyrighted © 1987 by the National Council on Family Relations, 3989 Central Ave. N.E., Suite #550, Minneapolis, MN 55421. Reprinted by permission.

Author Index

Abbott, D. A., 194, 201, 202
Aguirre-Hochbaum, S., 217
Akbar, N., 167
Albrecht, S. L., 198
Aldous, J., 1
Allen, A. A., 110
Allen, K. R., 151, 152, 153, 155
Alsdurf, J., 208
Alsdurf, P., 208
Ambron, S., 122
American Home Economics Association, 67
American Society of Association Executives, 63, 64, 65
Anderson, H., 205, 206, 210
Anderson-Ray, S. M., 220
Andrews, M., 43
Angelou, M., 215
Aoki, T., 108, 109, 118, 121, 123
Appleton, N., 170, 171, 172, 173, 174, 175
Arcus, M., E., 2, 7, 8, 11, 12, 13, 14, 15, 18, 19, 21, 44, 57, 58, 68, 69, 70, 76, 79, 95, 98, 99, 114, 115, 116, 119, 120, 123, 152, 202, 245
Association for Values Education and Research, 83, 96
Avery, C. E., 2, 3, 5, 7, 9, 10, 15, 16, 18
Avery, W. O., 217

Babbie, E. R., 216
Bahr, H. M., 200
Baier, K., 12, 80

Baker, L. G., 131
Baldwin, K. E., 29, 30
Balk, D. E., 196
Balswick, J., 205
Bandes, H., 215
Banks, J. A., 162, 164, 165, 171, 172, 173, 180, 181, 182, 183
Barlow, S. H., 21, 110, 111, 115, 118
Barozzi, R. L., 4, 6, 10
Bates, V. L., 204
Bedau, H., 12
Beecher, C. E., 29
Beeson, W. L., 201
Belenky, M. F., 139
Belsky, J., 145
Bem, S., 140
Ben-Peretz, M., 117
Bender, R. T., 193, 216
Bergen, A. E., 201
Berger, P., 198
Berman, P., 116, 117
Berry, M., 194, 201
Bevier, I., 30
Bird, C., 45
Black, G. H., 169
Bloom, B. S., 111
Blustein, J., 100, 101
Bly, R., 137
Boggs, J. W., 166, 167, 168, 169, 170
Bogot, H. I., 202
Bolen, J. S., 199
Border, B. A., 48
Borich, G. D., 121, 127

Subject Index

About the Authors

Margaret E. Arcus is Professor of Family Science and Acting Director of the School of Family and Nutritional Sciences at the University of British Columbia. She is also a Fellow of the Association for Values Education and Research. She has been active in family life education as a secondary school teacher, university teacher educator, and community consultant. Her major areas of interest include conceptual issues, ethics and values, and teacher education, and she has published articles in journals such as *Family Relations, International Journal of Sociology of the Family, Journal of Home Economics*, and the *Canadian Home Economics Journal*. She is a certified family life educator and was a member of the committee that developed the Family Life Education Certification Program for the National Council on Family Relations.

Ruth E. Brasher is Professor in the Family Science Department at Brigham Young University. She has undergraduate and graduate degrees in home economics and obtained her Ph.D. in sociology at Utah State University. She is past Chair of Home Economics Education and Past Associate Dean of the College of Family, Home, and Social Sciences at Brigham Young University. She was also an Extension Specialist for the State of Oregon and a National 4-H Fellow. She is a certified home economist and in 1992 was selected by the American Home Economics Association to give their National Commemorative Lecture. She served as Guest Editor (with J. Joel Moss) of an issue of *Family Relations* titled "A Special Issue: Family Life Education." She has also served as President of the Utah Council on Family Relations and the Utah Home Economics Association.

Margaret M. Bubolz is Professor Emeritus of Family and Child Ecology in the College of Human Ecology at Michigan State University. Her academic work was in home economics education at the University of Minnesota, education at Cornell University, and sociology and psychology at Purdue University. She has been involved in family life education at the community level through the Cooperative Extension Service as well as at the university level. She has done research on perceptions of masculinity and femininity, factors influencing the quality of family life, and family stress. She is currently cowriting a book based on a longitudinal study of families on small-scale farms. She has made extensive contributions to the development of human ecology theory, with special application to the family. She is the coauthor of a chapter, "Human Ecology Theory," in a recent book on family theories and methods. Her article, "The Family Ecosystem: Macro and Micro Interdependence," was recently published in *Human Ecology Strategies for the Future*. She was awarded the Michigan State University Distinguished Faculty Award in 1983 and was elected a Fellow of the Institute for Human Ecology in 1990.

Jo Lynn Cunningham is Professor of Child and Family Studies at The University of Tennessee, Knoxville. Most of her work has been interdisciplinary and has focused on the application of developmental concepts in the interactions of individuals, families, and other social systems, particularly in relation to education, religion, and public policy. The foundation for her ecumenical orientation was established when she began playing the organ for several churches when she was in the fifth grade. She continues to be active in the United Methodist church and has held a variety of leadership positions at the local, district, and conference levels. For the past several years, she has been involved in the mental health field through both professional and volunteer activities and currently is providing leadership in establishing an Interfaith Collaboration for Mental Health to address the needs of the unserved and underserved in the community.

Mary Jo Czaplewski is Executive Director of the National Council on Family Relations. Previously, she was Associate Dean of the College of Professional Studies and Head of the School of Home Economics at the University of Wisconsin, Stevens Point. She is coeditor of Volumes 13, 16, and 17 of the *Inventory of Marriage and Family Literature*. She is a certified family life educator and member of the American Society of Association Executives, the World Futures Society, and the American

Home Economics Association. She has bachelor's and master's degrees in secondary education. Her Ph.D. was earned at the University of Minnesota in educational administration and higher education.

LeRoi B. Daniels is Professor in the Department of Social and Educational Studies in the Faculty of Education at the University of British Columbia. He has also had experience as a teacher and administrator in the public schools. His research areas include moral education, philosophy of mind and action, curricular integration, and critical thinking. He is a Fellow of the Association for Values Education and Research and is coauthor of their series on value reasoning. He has published numerous articles on curriculum and education in journals such as the *Journal of Curriculum Studies* and the *Alberta Journal of Educational Research*. He has also published a number of chapters in edited books, including *Culture and Ethics: Dilemmas in Educational Change, Forms of Curriculum Inquiry,* and *Teaching, Schools, and Society.*

Stephen F. Duncan obtained his Ph.D. in family science from Purdue University and is a Family Life Education and Enrichment Specialist for the Extension Services of the State of Nevada. He was previously on the faculty at Auburn University.

Gladys J. Hildreth is Visiting Professor of Family Sciences at Texas Women's University and Professor Emeritus of Human Ecology at Louisiana State University. She received her undergraduate education at Southern University (Baton Rouge), her M.S. degree from the University of Wisconsin, and her Ph.D. in human ecology from Michigan State University. She has published articles related to human development from a lifespan perspective in journals such as *Family Relations, Educational Gerontology, Journal of Home Economics,* and *Journal of Aging and Human Development.* She is currently teaching courses in multicultural counseling at Texas Women's University.

Stephen R. Jorgensen is Associate Dean in the College of Human Sciences at Texas Tech University. He is also Professor of Human Development and Family Studies at Texas Tech. His research interests and publications focus on marital structure and process, fertility regulation and family planning for high-risk groups, and adolescent sexuality, contraception, and pregnancy. He currently is conducting an evaluation study of an abstinence-based sexuality education program for early adolescents that is funded by the U.S. Office of Adolescent Pregnancy Programs. He has served on a number of ad hoc research study sections for the National Institute of Health, reviewing proposals for adolescent pregnancy risk research, and for the National Institute on Drug Abuse. He served for 8 years on the NCFR Task Force for Family Life Education Certification and chaired the Certification Review Committee. From 1987-1993 he served as Editor of the *Home Economics Research Journal.* He holds a bachelor's degree in sociology and Spanish (Hamline University, St. Paul, Minnesota, 1971) and a Ph.D. in family sociology (University of Minnesota, 1976).

Maxine Lewis-Rowley (Ph.D., C.H.E.) is Associate Professor in the Family Sciences Department at Brigham Young University. She has degrees in education administration, home economics, clothing and textiles, and journalism. She has been an editor of Kellog's award-winning publications, a technical writer for the Extension Service, a promotional writer for television, and a member of the publication board for the *Journal of Home Economics* and the editorial board for *Family Perspective.* As a teacher educator, she is a consultant for numerous state departments of education and national corporations. She was honored by the editors of *Family Circle Magazine* and the American Home Economics Association as National Teacher of the Year in 1977 and received the AHEA's National Leadership Award in 1993.

Patrick C. McKenry is Professor of Family Relations and Human Development and Adjunct Professor of Black Studies at the Ohio State University. He received his Ph.D. in child and family studies from the University of Tennessee and served as a postdoctoral fellow in Child and Family Development at the University of Georgia. He has served as Visiting Professor at the University of British Columbia and the University of North Carolina, Chapel Hill. He has published in the major journals in family science, including *Journal of Marriage and the Family, Journal of Family Issues,* and *Family Relations,* and he has published two family texts. His major interests in family life education are in gender roles, family structural variations, and stress and coping.

J. Joel Moss received his Ph.D. in sociology from the University of North Carolina and is Professor Emeritus of the Family Science Department of Brigham Young University. He has published many articles on family life education and served as Guest Editor (with Ruth Brasher) of "A Special Issue: Family Life Education" for *Family Relations.* Other editorial responsibilities include Associate Editor for the *Journal of Marriage and the Family,* Associate Editor of *Family Perspective,* Managing Editor of *Family Science Review,* and external referee for the *Journal of Home Economics.* He has served as a consultant to Project Head Start. Currently, he is teaching English at a university in the People's Republic of China.

Letha Dawson Scanzoni resides in Norfolk, Virginia, where she works as an independent scholar and professional writer and speaker, specializing in the social sciences and religion. Her major areas of interest include gender roles, friendship, marriage and family living, parenting, human diversity, feminism, aging and caregiving, sexuality, family violence, and other contemporary issues. She also serves as Adjunct Associate Professor of Religious Studies at St. Andrews Presbyterian College in Laurinburg, North Carolina. She is author of *Sexuality* (1984) and *Sex Is a Parent Affair* (1973; revised edition, 1982) and coauthor of *All We're Meant to Be* (1974; revised edition, 1986; 3rd edition, revised and expanded, 1992), *Is the Homosexual My Neighbor?* (1978; revised and expanded edition, 1994), and a college textbook, *Men, Women, and Change: A Sociology of Marriage and Family* (1976, 1981, 1988). She has written for a wide range of publications and is a frequent lecturer for conferences, universities, and theological seminaries.

Jay D. Schvaneveldt is Professor in and Head of the Department of Family and Human Development at Utah State University. He obtained his Ph.D. from Florida State University and completed a postdoctorate at the University of Minnesota. He has published in family, child, adolescent, human development, and biological journals dealing with such topics as family relations, marriage, parent-child interaction, social change, and family life education. He is coauthor of *Understanding Research Methods* and author or coauthor of several chapters in various handbooks on marriage and the family and theory. He was a Fulbright Scholar in sociology and anthropology to the nation of Thailand, Khon Kaen University.

Randall J. Stiles is a Child Development Specialist with the Nevada State Division of Child and Family Services. He obtained his Ph.D. in developmental psychology from the University of Michigan. He serves as a parent educator with the Clark County Juvenile Court Parenting Project and is a part-time Instructor in the Psychology Department of the University of Nevada, Las Vegas. He also trains child welfare social workers on the effects of abuse and neglect on child development. He has served as Clinical Director and Child Development Specialist for the Oklahoma State Child Guidance Service. Areas of interest include family life education with families involved in child abuse/neglect, juvenile delinquency, and divorce.

Alan I. Sugawara is Professor of Human Development and Family Studies at Oregon State University. He received his undergraduate education at the University of Hawaii, Manoa, and his graduate degrees at the Chicago Theological Seminary (University of Chicago), Michigan State University, and Oregon State University. He formerly served as professor-in-charge of graduate programs in human development and family studies. He has published articles on gender role socialization and teacher preparation in journals such as *Sex Roles, Journal of Educational Research, Child Development, Developmental Psychology*, and *Journal of Social Psychology*. He is currently involved in research on children with special needs and multicultural education.

Jane Thomas is a curriculum consultant with the Vancouver School Board, Vancouver, B.C. She completed her Ed.D. in the Faculty of Education at the University of British Columbia and has been a sessional instructor at that university for the School of Family and Nutritional Sciences and for the Faculty of Education. She has had experience as a family life education teacher in the secondary schools and as a teacher educator at the university level and has been involved in both local and provincial family life education curriculum development. She is a certified family life educator and is currently the Provincial Coordinator for the CLFE program in British Columbia. She has completed two qualitative studies of family life education and is currently coinvestigator on a national survey of family life education in Canada.

Margaret H. Young graduated from the Holy Cross Hospital School of Nursing and received her M.S. and Ph.D. in Family and Human Development at Utah State University. She has taught college-level courses in infant development, middle childhood, marriage and family relationships, and death education. She has also served as guest lecturer and instructor at the community level, addressing topics such as prenatal development and childbirth, transition into parenthood, parent-child relationships, family relationships, and death education. She has co-written articles on children's understanding of AIDS and new horizons in family life education and is coauthor of the chapter on historical methodology in the *Sourcebook of Family Theories and Methodologies*.